SOCIAL DOCTRINE IN ACTION

A Personal History

John A. Ryan

SOCIAL DOCTRINE
in ACTION

A Personal History

by

Rt. Rev. Msgr. John A. Ryan, D.D., LL.D., Litt.D.

*Director, Social Action Department, National Catholic Welfare
Conference*

HARPER & BROTHERS PUBLISHERS

NEW YORK AND LONDON

1941

Nihil obstat
>   ARTHUR J. SCANLAN, S.T.D.
>   CENSOR LIBRORUM

Imprimatur
>   ✠FRANCIS J. SPELLMAN, D.D.
>   ARCHBISHOP, NEW YORK
New York, Dec. 8, 1940.

Contents

CONTENTS

PREFACE

THIS book is an autobiography only in a restricted sense, for it is almost entirely concerned with my social and economic beliefs and activities. Hence, the title.

I am hoping that it will prove helpful not only to teachers and students of the social sciences and participants in social movements, but to labor leaders, social workers, clergymen and other groups that are interested in social problems. The long quotations from the writings of men who contributed to my early social education are worthwhile in themselves and have a certain historical value. The numerous extracts from my own earlier productions show, I trust, the continuity and consistency of my social beliefs. Taken as a whole, the volume presents a fairly comprehensive account of my opinions and teaching on economic problems, relations and institutions.

My thanks are due to my brother, Rev. Lawrence F. Ryan, for his careful reading of the manuscript and his many valuable suggestions; to Miss Edith Duncan and Miss Margaret Coyne for their efficient reading of the proof; and to The Macmillan Company, A. C. McClurg and Company and G. P. Putnam's Sons for permission to reprint extracts from books of which they are the publishers.

JOHN A. RYAN

Washington
February 11, 1941.

SOCIAL DOCTRINE IN ACTION

A Personal History

CHAPTER I

PARENTAGE AND BOYHOOD

IN THE year 1868 my father bought a farm in the township
of Vermillion, Dakota County, about twenty miles south
of St. Paul, Minnesota. There I was born on May 25, 1869.
My father belonged to one of the very numerous families of
Ryans in county Tipperary, Ireland; my mother's family name
was Luby and she also was born in Tipperary. She met and
married my father in Minneapolis, Minnesota. No long or
ancient traditions came down to us through either of my
parents. The only important events in their families about
which I ever heard anything occurred less than thirty years
before my birth. More than once I heard the story of an evic-
tion in which my paternal grandfather and all the members
of his family were turned out of their home because some
other man coveted the farm which they were renting and
cultivating. It was winter and one of a pair of newborn twins
perished on the roadside. A similar but not so harsh story of
landlord oppression was current in my mother's family. Her
parents, with their family of young children, including her-
self and her brothers, were driven from their holding by a
notorious landlord named Scully. Soon afterwards they emigrated to the United States, settling in Holyoke, Massachusetts, for a few years and then migrating to Minnesota. My
father left Ireland in the early fifties, lived two years in
Great Barrington, Massachusetts, and then went to Minnesota.

Both my parents could read and write but their formal

I

education was probably the equivalent of not more than that which is now obtained by pupils of the fourth or fifth grade in our elementary schools. However, they possessed in a high degree religion, virtue, and a capacity for hard work. The first-mentioned quality is well illustrated by their practice of journeying eight or ten miles to attend Mass three of every four Sundays. And the conveyance was not an automobile but a "lumber wagon" and later a "platform wagon," the motive power being provided by work horses. On the fourth Sunday they went to their own parish church, which was about three-quarters of a mile distant. When bad weather or some other very unfavorable circumstance prevented us from attending Mass at one of the neighboring churches, on a Sunday when no services were held in our own church, we assembled in "the other room" at half past ten in the morning and recited the Rosary. Every Sunday each of the children was required to read a chapter of *The Life of Jesus Christ*. My father and mother frequently extended their own reading of this book beyond one chapter per week.

My father's strict adherence to moral principles was shown when he paid the full amount of a bond which he had signed jointly with two neighbors as security for a bank loan to a fourth neighbor. When the borrower failed to meet his obligation the other two of the three signers of the bond transferred their property to their wives in order to escape payment of their shares of the joint note. Refusing to have recourse to this subterfuge, my father was compelled to fulfill not only his own part of the engagement but also that of the cosigners. In this case, however, virtue was its own reward; for some ten years later, a brother of the man on whose behalf the bond was signed, willed to my father an amount of property that was sufficient to cover both the principal and interest of the amount which he had expended in this transaction.

His capacity for work was vividly evident to his children

at all times, and his conviction that they too should abstain from idleness and loafing was consistently enforced. Although he had no economic reason for working after he had moved from the farm to the city at the age of sixty-five, he continued to do so until the moment of his death. This occurred when he was past eighty and while he was hoeing in his son's garden. Literally, he "died with his boots on."

My mother was even more devout than my father and she worked equally hard. For some dozen years—until her eldest daughter became old enough to help—she performed all the housework (and many other tasks) and took care of her ten children, without assistance, except during such short and very busy periods as that of harvesting and threshing. Despite her large family and her incessant activity, she lived to be eighty-four years of age.

During the greater part of our growing years we children thought that both of our parents gave us somewhat too good an example of industry and hard work, but as I look back upon those years and experiences, I believe that the example was beneficial; it was good discipline and good training. It was better for our formation and as a preparation for our later years than the easier conditions that surround the present generation.

My mother bore eleven children, one of whom died a few days after birth. Another passed away at the age of thirty-eight. Thirty-three of her thirty-nine grandchildren are living and there are thirty-six great-grandchildren. Of the children, two became nuns, two, priests, and six married. In view of the large proportion of the family who are celibates, the fact that the other six produced thirty-nine children is a striking refutation of the assertion still made occasionally that religious celibacy diminishes or has diminished the birth rate. The longevity of my mother in her not-too-easy economic conditions disproves another argument of birth-control advocates.

Some fifteen years ago, the late Norman Hapgood and I engaged in a radio debate in which he defended while I opposed this pestilential practice. Each was permitted a reply to the main address delivered by the other. In the course of his principal talk, Mr. Hapgood drew a rather pathetic picture of an imaginary "Mrs. Maloney" who was so poor that she had to eke out a livelihood by taking in washing. If my recollection serves me correctly her husband had either passed away or was in a continuous state of inebriation. She had produced eleven children, seven of whom were already dead. Mr. Hapgood thought that "Mrs. Maloney" should have practiced birth control. During my talk in rebuttal, I maintained that Mr. Hapgood's friend, "Mrs. Maloney," was not typical of the majority of women who have large families, and I took delight in pointing out that my own mother had given birth to as many children as had "Mrs. Maloney," of whom nine were then (and are still) living, and that she had probably worked just as hard, although she was not compelled to act as laundress for persons outside of her own family. Continuing, I said, "my mother is now almost eighty years of age, she toiled incessantly until she was well past sixty but next week she is going to take a trip across the continent with me to California."

To be sure, my mother was no more typical of married women than was "Mrs. Maloney." In the United States the majority of wives have never had eleven children nor lived to be eighty-four years of age. Nevertheless, they could, with safety and advantage, have on the average half a dozen each, even today. This is certainly true of our rural population. In our great cities, inadequate dwelling space and other deficiencies and difficulties in the environment probably make this high average practically impossible. The obvious remedy is to provide all families with sufficient house room and facilities for recreation. This goal is entirely possible of achievement in a country as rich as ours. I shall have more to say on this subject later on.

The members of the farm community where I was born and reared were all Irish immigrants and all Catholics. In the district school which I attended there was at no time in my experience even one non-Catholic pupil. The adjoining community to the south was composed entirely of Germans, likewise all Catholic. With them the people of our Irish settlement got along very well. There were no quarrels, enmities or friction between the two groups, although we Irish regarded our German neighbors as somewhat inferior. As a matter of fact, they were superior to us in some respects. In those days, however, we shut our eyes to these qualities and kept our attention only on the characteristics we thought marked us as a superior race.

The statement that our community was all Irish and Catholic is subject to one conspicuous exception. That was provided by an English family named Bottomley. For probably more than twenty years Mrs. Bottomley assisted at the birth of every child that came into the world in our neighborhood. No family there enjoyed the services of an obstetrician. Probably none of the mothers, or the fathers either, would have known what the term meant. And yet not one mother or child died in childbirth in all the forty or more families to which Mrs. Bottomley ministered. The total number of children that she helped into the light of day was probably at least three hundred. To be sure, she performed those services in rural conditions; in a city she probably would not have made such a satisfactory record. I have had many arguments on this general subject with social workers, but I have never been persuaded that the ancient and honorable profession of midwifery has become antiquated or completely inadequate to our complex civilization.

The standard of living which our family enjoyed when I

was a boy was not high but it was sufficient for health and efficiency. It took care of the three fundamental needs of food, clothing, and shelter. Although the food was plain, it exhibited the variety that is easily obtainable on a farm. Our apparel for Sunday and holiday occasions was not elaborate nor characterized by multiplicity of garments, but it met fairly well the rural standard of that day. Until the youngest of the eleven children was eight years of age, our house contained only five rooms: a large kitchen and dining room, a living room, and three bedrooms. The two bedrooms upstairs took care of, respectively, the male and female children. Although we thought we were pretty crowded at times, we had sufficient accommodations for sleep, health, and decency.

Had the economic conditions of our family been better, we probably would not have worked so hard. When I was nine years of age my father bought a second farm about four miles from the one upon which we lived. Until long after I went to college, that is, until about the year 1896, both farms were encumbered by mortgages. For about twenty years, the rate of interest on one of the two mortgages was 12 per cent annually; on the other the rate was 10 per cent for about twelve years. In the early nineties, the rate on both was reduced to 6 per cent. Although loanable money was much scarcer in those years than it is today, neither of these exorbitant rates was economically necessary. At that time there was no Federal Farm Loan law. Nevertheless, the economic situation presented no good reason for the absence of such legislation. To be sure, any attempt to enact it would have been stigmatized as "socialistic," "revolutionary," "anarchistic"—or something worse. The dominant economic opinion and policies of the United States in those days were still those of *laissez-faire*.

So much for our economic conditions in my boyhood and the provision for the satisfaction of our material wants. What about the means available for cultural satisfactions? Until my seventeenth year, any formal education was confined to that afforded by our ungraded district school. It probably did not exceed the equivalent of the sixth grade in a city school. With what was for them in those days considerable sacrifice, my parents enabled me to spend a few months (1886–1887) at the Christian Brothers' School in St. Paul. There I followed courses which were approximately those of the first or possibly second year of high school. I was graduated in June, 1887, at the age of eighteen. Whether I should have become a priest if I had passed from our country school to a city public school, I do not know; what I do know is that the idea of pursuing that vocation came to me while I was a pupil in the institution conducted by the Christian Brothers.

The following September, I entered St. Thomas Seminary, St. Paul, which was, in effect, a high school, a junior college, and an ecclesiastical seminary. For four or five years my expenses for board and tuition were defrayed by my grandfather. Although the annual amount was only two hundred dollars, it was beyond the financial ability of my parents. Few of our neighbors were in a more favorable position, and few of their children went to college before the beginning of the present century.

What were our opportunities for culture in the form of books, magazines, and newspapers? Our home contained no library; until I was about fifteen years of age it had only a few books, the principal ones being the Bible, the *Life of Christ,* a *Life of the Blessed Virgin, The Lectures and Sermons of the Reverend Thomas N. Burke,* the great Irish Dominican orator and lecturer, *The History of Dakota County,* and a small volume entitled *Ireland As She Is, As She Has Been, and As She Ought To Be,* the author of which was, as I recall, named Clancy. Nevertheless, these few volumes were probably as helpful to us as if they had been competing for our attention with a great number of printed productions of more or less indifferent quality. At any rate, they were read diligently and attentively. Father Burke's lectures and the little volume on Ireland gave me a fair acquaintance with the glories and the sorrows of the land of my ancestors, and inspired me with a keen and persistent desire for its independence and freedom. In the matter of periodicals we had no daily paper but we did receive one small monthly publication of a religious character, one Catholic weekly, and the *Irish World*. Then, as now, this journal was widely read and very influential in its advocacy of Irish nationality. It began coming into our house when I was eleven years of age, about a year after it was established. Week by week it maintained and reinforced the interest in the cause of Ireland which I had derived from Father Burke's lectures and Clancy's little book. The full title of the *Irish World* was *The Irish World and American Industrial Liberator*. Although the second part may seem a bit pretentious, it has been fairly well justified by the course which this journal has always pursued when dealing with the condition and interests of labor in the United States. At that time and for more than a third of a century longer, the Irish struggle for liberation was almost, if not quite, as much economic as political. The Irish people strove to abolish or to mitigate greatly the exactions of landlordism. One could not read the *Irish World* week after week without acquiring an interest in and a love of economic justice, as well as political justice. And a great deal of the material which appeared in its pages on the former subject had specific reference to American conditions.

CHAPTER II

EARLY SOCIAL EDUCATION (1882–1892)

IN THE preceding chapter, I credited the *Irish World* as the earliest factor in directing my thoughts to the agrarian situation in Ireland and industrial problems in the United States. Not long after I had begun to read this journal, I came across a paper-bound edition of *Progress and Poverty*. As nearly as I can recall, this happened in 1882 or 1883. I mention the binding of the volume (price 20 cents) because it indicates that some three years after publication the book had already become popularized and obtained a wide circulation. However, I have no definite recollection of the impression that it made upon me and I doubt that I read very much of it, as the copy that fell into my hands was borrowed from a neighboring farmer. As he handed it to me he declared that its main thesis, namely, that the land belonged to all the people, was in accord with Catholic doctrine. I did not then know whether this judgment was or was not correct, nor do I recall that I had any opinion on the subject when I returned the volume to its owner. Nevertheless, I feel certain that I did get something out of my cursory and partial reading of Henry George's greatest work; undoubtedly, it helped to promote my interest in social questions and to stimulate my sympathy with the weaker economic classes.

THE BLAINE-CLEVELAND CONTEST

The first political campaign which attracted my sustained attention was that of 1884. Grover Cleveland, James G.

Blaine, and General Benjamin F. Butler had been nominated for the Presidency by the Democratic, Republican and Green-back-Labor parties, respectively. Eight years previously, being then a few months past seven years of age (conventionally the age of reason) I had taken my stand (such as it was) on the side of Tilden and Hendricks as against Hayes and Wheeler, presumably because my father was a Democrat. In 1880, I favored the Democratic Hancock rather than the Republican Garfield. In 1884, I hoped for the election of James G. Blaine. At this time my father cast his first Republican vote in a national contest. He turned against the Democratic candidate mainly, I think, because of the arguments he had read in the *Irish World*. For several weeks before the Democratic convention assembled, this weekly had been printing in very conspicuous headlines "Butler or Blaine!" If the Democrats did not nominate the former as their candidate for the Presidency, the *Irish World* would support the latter. Apparently it wanted General Butler for the same reasons that moved many labor leaders to support him, namely, his advocacy of the eight-hour day, "soft" money, the suppression of contract prison labor, and the exclusion of the Chinese. When the Democrats failed to nominate Butler, the *Irish World* carried out its threat of transferring its support to the Republican candidate. The latter had two qualities that pleased the *Irish World:* he favored a high protective tariff and he was against England.

When my father voted for Blaine instead of Cleveland, he had plenty of company among his fellow Irishmen and fellow Catholics. Indeed, no such large proportion of these groups had ever previously voted the Republican ticket in the United States. Despite Blaine's shortcomings, I have always thought that these Irish and Irish-American Catholics were justified in temporarily abandoning the Democratic party in the national election of 1884. Apparently a considerable number of what might now be called "economic royalists" shifted their party allegiance in the opposite direction. The notorious "Millionaires' Dinner" at Delmonico's, attended by Blaine, was pronounced years later by Senator Stephen B. Elkins "a failure from a financial point of view; campaign contributions from the millionaires being much less generous than had been expected." According to J. S. Clarkson of Iowa, who had a very prominent part in directing the Republican campaign of 1884, "it was Republican businessmen voting against their party who defeated it in New York, Connecticut and New Jersey."[1]

At no time since 1884 have I regretted the attitude that I then took toward Grover Cleveland. While I had always thought of him as an honest man, and while I liked his views on civil service reform and on the tariff, I could never see that he supported the cause of labor, the farmer, the small businessman, or the distressed classes. He refused government relief to the victims of a drought in Texas. In the historic contest over silver, bimetalism, and the currency, he was on the wrong side. He had no adequate conception of the fundamental economic factors and issues in American life. He never grasped the significance of the struggle between plutocracy and the masses. He never understood the concept of social justice nor accepted either it or its implications.[2] Before he left the White House, however, his social and political deficiencies were completely exposed, and he himself was discredited as a Democratic leader. In the national convention in Chicago in 1896, he and his policies were dramatically repudiated by the same Democratic party which only four years earlier had overwhelmingly nominated him for the

[1] *The Politicos*, by Matthew Josephson, Harcourt, Brace and Company, New York, 1938, p. 37.

[2] "You may think Cleveland's administration was Democratic. It was not. Cleveland was a conservative Republican." . . . Woodrow Wilson, quoted in *The Politicos*, p. 392.

great office of the Presidency. No tears came to my eyes over that reversal of the attitude of the party.

IGNATIUS DONNELLY

Not long after the Blaine-Cleveland contest occurred another political event which with its consequences and implications, exercised more influence upon my political and economic thinking than any other factor of those early years. In 1886, Ignatius Donnelly was elected as an Independent to the lower house of the Minnesota legislature. During the campaign I had become much interested in the proposals for economic reform advocated by Donnelly, the Farmers' Alliance, and the Knights of Labor. When, following his success at the polls, Donnelly took his seat in the legislature, I attended its sessions almost daily. I was then a student at the Christian Brothers' School in St. Paul. Owing to this assiduous attendance, I got from my schoolmates the nickname "Senator."

Ignatius Donnelly was a very remarkable man. He was statesman, politician, agitator, social reformer, and author. In the latter capacity, he wrote several novels, some more or less scientific volumes, and the *Great Cryptogram*. In the last-mentioned work, a very large volume, he strove to prove that the works attributed to William Shakespeare were written by Sir Francis Bacon, who had put into the plays a cipher by which his authorship was disclosed and established. Donnelly came to Minnesota from Philadelphia in 1856 at the age of twenty-five years and settled in a place called Nininger, about seventeen miles southeast of St. Paul. His home was only nine miles from the place in the same county (Dakota) where I was born and reared. During the period, 1886–1896, I met him a few times and heard him make many speeches. I have listened to most of the political orators of America who achieved fame, at one time or another since

1892. As a political stump speaker, Donnelly was the most entertaining and effective of them all. He did not have a resonant voice like Bryan's, nor the power of word painting possessed by Robert G. Ingersoll or John J. Ingalls, nor the Ciceronian style of Charles A. Towne or Bourke Cockran, but he excelled them all in quick thinking, wit, repartee, and a kind of sarcasm that was always effective and rarely biting or bitter.

At the age of twenty-eight, the "Sage of Nininger" as he afterward came to be called, was elected lieutenant governor of the state, a position which he filled for four years. At the end of his term as lieutenant governor, in 1863, he became the youngest member of the national House of Representatives, where he remained for six years. He was elected to these offices as a Republican; having joined the party principally on the issue of slavery. By 1868, however, the plutocratic elements had assumed control of the party in Minnesota as in many other states, and they were able to prevent Donnelly from getting the nomination for a fourth term in Congress. Indeed, it seems clear that the only humanitarian movement, the only efforts on behalf of the poor and the weak against the rich and the powerful, that were ever conspicuous in the Republican party, had to do exclusively with the problem of Negro slavery. The summary statement by Professor Benjamin B. Kendrick seems to err only slightly on the side of severity: "The new Republican Party which came into power in 1860 was an alliance between the eastern business interests with their satellites—the eastern truck farmers—and the western grain growers."[3] Shortly after the Civil War, the party ceased to give favorable or fair consideration to the grain growers and the cattle growers of the West. To continue from Professor Kendrick's article, "business interests entered upon a period of almost unchallenged control of the

[3] *Encyclopaedia of the Social Sciences*, Vol. I, p. 510.

federal government and most of the state governments. Far from being hindered by government regulation, they received at the hands of the central and local governments every favor they desired."[4]

By 1870, Donnelly realized that the old issues were dead, that henceforth the struggle was to be between the advocates of rights of property on one side and the rights of man on the other; between those who had and those who had not.

It is for the people of the United States to determine, [he said,] whether the Republican party shall "renew its youth like the eagle" and shall be the party of liberality, justice and popular right, or whether, forgetting its glorious record in behalf of freedom and humanity, it shall become the base instrument of cliques and rings, of aristocracies and monopolies, of capital against labor, of the few against the many.[5]

During the seventies, Donnelly organized the Anti-Monopoly party, founded and edited a weekly paper called the *Anti-Monopolist* and served five years in the state senate. It will be recalled that a disastrous panic occurred in 1873 and that the depression continued five years longer. At this time Donnelly's main remedies for the economic sufferings of the farmers were: regulation of railroad rates, cooperative buying, cheap water transportation, restoration of specie payments, and direct taxation in place of the protective tariff. These proposals do not sound very radical today.

While his speeches in the legislature during this period gave more attention to the farmers than to the wage earners, he insisted then as always that both classes were victims of the same oppressive forces. In both cases the contest was between the few who exercised great economic power oppressively and the many who were too weak or too unskillful to use their great numerical power effectively.

Somewhat less than two decades later, on July 4, 1892,

[4] *Loc. cit.*
[5] Hicks' "Political Career of Ignatius Donnelly," *Mississippi Valley Historical Review*, Vol. 8, 1921–1922, p. 88.

Donnelly presented the resolutions of the Platform Committee to the national convention of the Peoples' party held at Omaha. This party had been organized at Cincinnati a little more than a year earlier, mainly by members of the Farmers' Alliance and the Knights of Labor. The Preamble to the platform was written by Donnelly and reads as follows:

The conditions which surround us justify our cooperation. We meet in the midst of a nation brought to the verge of moral, political and material ruin. Corruption dominates the ballot box, the Legislatures, the Congress, and touches even the ermine of the Bench. The people are demoralized. Many of the states have been compelled to isolate the voters at the polling places in order to prevent universal intimidation or bribery. The newspapers are subsidized or muzzled, public opinion silenced, business prostrated, our homes covered with mortgages, labor impoverished, and the land concentrating in the hands of capitalists. The urban workmen are denied the right of organization for self-protection; imported pauperized labor beats down their wages, a hireling standing army, unrecognized by our laws, is established to shoot them down, and they are rapidly degenerating to European conditions. The fruits of the toil of millions are boldly stolen to build up colossal fortunes, unprecedented in the history of mankind and the possessors of these in turn despise the republic and endanger liberty. From the same prolific womb of governmental injustice we breed the two classes —tramps and millionaires. The national power to create money is appropriated to enrich bondholders; silver, which has been accepted as coin since the dawn of history, has been demonetized to add to the purchasing power of gold by decreasing the value of all forms of property as well as human labor; and the supply of currency is purposely abridged to fatten usurers, bankrupt enterprise, and enslave industry. A vast conspiracy against mankind has been organized on two continents, and is taking possession of the world. If not met and overthrown it forbodes terrible social convulsions, the destruction of civilization, or the establishment of an absolute despotism. In this crisis of human affairs the intelligent working people and producers of the United States have come together, in the name of peace, order and society to defend liberty, property and justice. We desire our union and independence. We assert our purpose to vote with the political organization which represents our principles.

This declaration contains some echoes of a novel which Donnelly had written about three years previously entitled *Caesar's Column*. It prophesied an utterly devastating revolution to occur one hundred years later. This upheaval would destroy civilization on both sides of the Atlantic unless in the meantime the economic system were drastically reformed. One-half of that time of grace or of preparation for the revolution, has already gone by. While some present-day observers think that something like the catastrophe described by Donnelly may come long before the end of the remaining fifty years, their reasons for fearing it are not entirely identical with those set down in *Caesar's Column*. The existing grounds for pessimism and foreboding are only in part economic, and only in part based upon economic oppression. National rivalries, political and racial theories, and the personal ambitions of a few barbarous political leaders have a very large place in these fears and forecasts. To be sure, if the catastrophe envisaged today should follow from the triumph of Communism in the land of Hitler as well as in the land of Stalin, the parallel with Donnelly's forecast would be almost exact.

One obvious comment on the Preamble is that it contains a good deal of exaggeration. In this respect, however, it does not greatly exceed the platform declarations of one of the older parties out of office "viewing with alarm" the disastrous record and performances of the party which is presently in control of the government. Moreover, a considerable part of the exaggeration in the Preamble is merely rhetorical. Other writers of political platforms had more than one occasion to envy the superb skill displayed in this field by Ignatius Donnelly. In any case, his descendants and admirers can find in the Preamble more reasons for satisfaction and approval than for chagrin and apology. Every one of its indictments had some basis in fact, even though several of them were overstatements. Many of the evils noted have since been abolished or greatly diminished; for example, the importation of foreign labor by contract, the denial of organization to labor, corruption at the ballot box, and the deflation of prices and values through manipulation of the currency. Some of the evils remain with little if any mitigation; for example, mortgaged homes, a subsidized and plutocratic press, and the concentration of wealth and economic power. On the last-mentioned evil the language of Pope Pius XI is stronger, more specific, and more comprehensive than Donnelly's references to "colossal fortunes" and "concentrating land in the hands of the capitalists." Here is what the late Holy Father said in *Quadragesimo Anno*:

> In the first place, then, it is patent that in our days not alone is wealth accumulated, but immense power and despotic economic domination is concentrated in the hands of a few, and that those few are frequently not the owners, but only the trustees and directors of invested funds, who administer them at their good pleasure.

> This power becomes particularly irresistible when exercised by those who, because they hold and control money, are able also to govern credit and determine its allotment, for that reason supplying, so to speak, the life-blood to the entire economic body, and grasping, as it were, in their hands the very soul of production, so that no one dare breathe against their will.

In the body of the platform, the principal demands were for a graduated income tax, direct election of senators, expansion of the currency, an eight-hour day, postal savings banks, abolition of the present contract labor system and restriction of immigration, prohibition of speculative ownership and alien ownership of land, and government ownership of railroads and other public utilities. The first six of these are now among the settled policies of the country, while the seventh has lost most of its practical importance and the eighth has made some headway and is no longer regarded as "socialistic" or ultraradical by any realistic and impartial person.[6]

Most of the proposals and demands of the Populists at the beginning of the last decade of the nineteenth century are now regarded as relatively mild by all persons except hopeless reactionaries. At that time, however, those well-intentioned persons who fondly hugged to their bosoms the title of "conservatives" looked upon the holders of these views as "radicals" and "extremists," or as good people misled by "agitators." My first vote in a presidential election was cast in 1892, and it went to James B. Weaver, the candidate of the Peoples' party. Many of my friends deplored this choice as an indication of eccentricity or at least misguided sympathy. They wondered why I could not follow the safe and sane leadership of one of the two older political parties. However, for many years now the essential accuracy of the analysis of the economic situation in the early nineties made by the Populists and the soundness of most of their proposals have been fully recognized by competent students and historians. If election day of 1892 were somehow to return tomorrow and I were to go into the polling booth with the added knowledge and experience that I now possess, I should again and with greater confidence vote the Populist ticket.[7]

JAMES CARDINAL GIBBONS

One of the first and also one of the most enduring contributions to my social education was provided by James Cardinal Gibbons. In 1886, at the request of the bishops of Canada, the Holy See forbade the Catholics of that country to become members of the powerful organization known as the Knights of Labor. The prohibition was based upon the

[6] See Frank L. McVey, Ph.D., *The Populist Movement*, American Economic Association, Economic Studies, August, 1896, pp. 156, 157.

[7] For the history of the Peoples' party, see *The Populist Revolt*, by J. D. Hicks, University of Minnesota Press, 1931.

element of secrecy in the order and its alleged revolutionary character. Early in 1887, Cardinal Gibbons presented a long memorial to the Roman Congregation of the Propaganda, pleading against the extension of the condemnation to the United States. In his account of the events preceding his appeal to the Roman authorities, the Cardinal notes that, while many bishops

were alarmed at what they considered the revolutionary tendencies [of certain recently formed workingmen's associations], many other bishops, including Cardinal Manning and myself, were equally alarmed at the prospect of the Church being presented before our age as the friend of the powerful rich and the enemy of the helpless poor; for not only would such an alliance, or even apparent alliance, have done the Church untold harm, but it would have been the *bouleversement* of our whole history. Moreover, to us it seemed that such a thing could never take place. The one body in the world which had been the protector of the poor and the weak for nearly 1800 years, could not possibly desert these same classes in their hour of need.

The Cardinal then describes the discussion of the Knights of Labor situation which took place at a meeting of the Archbishops of the United States, and continues:

Only two out of the twelve Archbishops were for condemnation; the rest agreed with me that we must do all in our power to prevent any such condemnation of the Knights of Labor in our own country as would drive them into the camp of revolution.

Accordingly when I sailed for Europe in 1887 to receive the Cardinal's Hat it was part of my mission to present the plea of organized labor, which I did by presenting the following document to the Cardinal Prefect of Propaganda. I cannot say that the task which I had imposed upon myself was an easy one, but I am thankful to say that it proved not an impossible one, and that the Knights of Labor in the United States were not condemned.

The long Memorial which Cardinal Gibbons gave to Cardinal Simeoni, Prefect of Propaganda, urging that the Knights of Labor be not condemned in the United States stated: "Out of the seventy-five Archbishops and Bishops of the United States there are about five who desire the condemnation of the Knights of Labor such as they are in our own country; so that our Hierarchy are almost unanimous in protesting against such condemnation." At the end of the Memorial he presents in a summary of eight short paragraphs the reasons why the condemnation should not be issued. Five of these reasons seem appropriate for reproduction here:

It does not seem to be prudent, because of the reality of the grievances complained of by the working classes, and their acknowledgment by the American people.

It would be dangerous for the reputation of the Church in our democratic country, and might even lead to persecution.

It would probably be inefficacious, owing to the general conviction that it would be unjust.

It would turn into suspicion and hostility the singular devotedness of our Catholic people towards the Holy See.

It would be regarded as a cruel blow to the authority of Bishops in the United States, who, it is well known, protest against such a condemnation.[8]

The Cardinal's success in this delicate and most important mission gave me great satisfaction, not only on account of my interest in organized labor but because it vindicated the vigilance and social vision of Cardinal Gibbons and the American Hierarchy. In passing, it will be recalled that the excommunication of Dr. McGlynn occurred in this same year which saw the vindication of the Knights of Labor. How different were the effects of these two events!

The last time that I met Cardinal Gibbons, at Trinity College about a year before his death, he described at some length to the late Monsignor Kerby and myself his efforts in Rome to prevent the condemnation. How near to his heart

[8] The foregoing quotations are taken from the Section on "Knights of Labor," Vol. I, pp. 186–209, in the Cardinal's autobiography, entitled *Retrospect of Fifty Years*, published by John Murphy Co., Baltimore.

had been these efforts and this enterprise was strikingly evinced in the intensity of feeling which he displayed that day, more than thirty years after this experience.

He was a truly great man, was Cardinal Gibbons, and no small part of his greatness was due to his social vision.

ARCHBISHOP IRELAND

From boyhood until my middle forties, I was greatly influenced in many ways by John Ireland, Archbishop of St. Paul. From him I received the Sacraments of Confirmation (1880) and Holy Orders (1898). My college and seminary courses were made in his institutions, and to a considerable extent under his supervision. Immediately after my ordination, he sent me to the Catholic University of America, at Washington, for a postgraduate course which lasted four years. For the next thirteen years I was, by his appointment, professor of moral theology and economics in the St. Paul Seminary. He consented to my transfer from that position to the staff of the Catholic University in 1915. Therefore, I had exceptional opportunities to know him and to become acquainted with his opinions.

Some of those who followed his career will wonder why I mention him in the present connection. He was not an economic reformer, as was Ignatius Donnelly. In fact, he regarded the "Sage of Nininger" whom he knew very well and who for more than forty years was almost his neighbor in Minnesota, as something of a demagogue. All this is true, and more. The Archbishop's associations were with the pillars of the contemporary economic order, men like James J. Hill, president of the Great Northern Railway and William McKinley, President of the United States, rather than with such critics of the order as Ignatius Donnelly and William J. Bryan. Nevertheless, he was at heart, liberal and progressive in his attitude toward economic institutions, and their proper functions. He differed with the reformers not so much with regard to desirable objectives as in his evaluation of economic facts and tendencies.

At any rate, I did receive from him considerable inspiration in the period covered by this chapter (1882–1892), and much more in subsequent years. The first production of his that came to my attention was his discourse on "The Catholic Church and Civil Society," delivered at the beginning of the Third Plenary Council of Baltimore, November 10, 1884. It included practically no reference to economic questions, but had much to say concerning lawful government, liberty, democracy, and the compatibility of Catholic doctrine and institutions with a republican form of government. He boldly avowed his preference for that form, particularly as exemplified in the United States of America.

To be sure, political democracy is not the same as economic democracy or social justice. One can prefer a republic to a monarchy and yet favor economic domination of the many by the few. A man can think that he is loyal to the principles of popular government and yet rejoice in the possession and exercise of that economic domination which was pointedly, even dramatically, condemned by Pope Pius XI.[9] Nevertheless, there is an inherent contradiction between the spirit of the one and the spirit of the other; between political democracy and industrial autocracy. The struggle for economic freedom and social justice in the United States derives much of its encouragement and power from the perception, conscious or subconscious, of this fundamental and insoluble contradiction. Therefore, the ideas and the love of political democracy which I learned from this and similar addresses by the great Archbishop of St. Paul in the eighties supplemented and reinforced the things that I was learning about

[9] *Supra*, p. 17.

economic freedom and economic reform from men like Ignatius Donnelly.

John Ireland was an unrivaled, sincere, and genuine American patriot. Out of gratitude to his memory, I insert here the eloquent peroration to the discourse which I have been discussing:

> Republic of America, receive from me the tribute of my love and of my loyalty. With my whole soul I do thee homage. I pray from my heart that thy glory be never dimmed—*Esto perpetua*. Thou bearest in thy hands the hopes of the human race. Thy mission from God is to show to nations that men are capable of highest civil and political liberty. Be thou ever free and prosperous. Through thee may liberty triumph over the earth from the rising to the setting sun!—*Esto perpetua*. Remember that religion and morality can alone give life to liberty and preserve it in never-fading youth. Believe me, thy surest hope is from the Church which false friends would have thee fear. Believe me, no hearts love thee more ardently than Catholic hearts, no tongues speak more honestly thy praises than Catholic tongues, and no hands will be lifted up stronger and more willing to defend, in war and in peace, thy laws and thy institutions than Catholic hands. *Esto perpetua*.[10]

At the celebration, in Baltimore, November 10, 1889, of the one hundredth anniversary of the establishment of the Catholic Hierarchy in the United States, Archbishop Ireland delivered an address on the "Mission of Catholics in America." That mission in the new century then beginning for the Hierarchy was twofold, he said: "To make America Catholic, and to solve for the Church the universal, the all-absorbing, problems with which the Church is confronted in the present age." In approaching the discussion of the second topic, the Archbishop made some general observations which are still in part true, but, in part, alas! are no longer in accord with the facts: "The strength of the Church today in all countries, particularly in America, is the people.

[10] *The Church and Modern Society*, by Archbishop John Ireland, D. H. McBride and Co., Chicago, 1897, Vol. I, pp. 46–47.

Ours is essentially the age of democracy. The days of princes and of feudal lords are gone." He did not realize that the disappearance of "princes and feudal lords" would not necessarily mean the universal triumph of democracy. He did not foresee the rise of a political system which would be more despotic than the regime of "princes and feudal lords," namely, totalitarianism. What he had to say about the social question and economic injustice is, however, still true and apposite:

The care of the masses implies an abiding and active interest in the social questions that torment humanity at the present time. Our chieftain, Leo XIII, who knows his age, and whose heart-beatings are in sympathy with it, has told Catholics their duties on this point. About two years ago he recommended that social questions be made part of the special curriculum of studies which are to fit priests for their ministerial labors. Whatever be the cause, there exist dreadful social injustices. Men, made in the image of the Creator, are viewed as pieces of machinery or beasts of burden. The moral instincts are ground out of them. Until their material condition is improved, it is futile to speak to them of supernatural life and duties. Men who suffer are conscious of their wrongs, and will hold as their friends those who aid them. Irreligion makes promises to them, and irreligion is winning them. They who should be the first and the last in promise and in deed are silent. It is deplorable that Catholics grow timid, take refuge in sanctuary and cloister, and leave the bustling, throbbing world with its miseries and sins to the wiles of false friends and cunning practitioners. Leo XIII speaks fearlessly to the world of the rights of labor; Cardinal Lavigerie pleads for the African slave; Cardinal Manning interposes his hand between the plutocratic merchant and the workingman of the docks; Count de Mun and his band of noble-minded friends devote time and talent to the interests of French laborers. But as a body, Catholics are quietness itself. They say their prayers, they preach, they listen to sermons on the love of God and on resignation in suffering; or, if they venture at all into the arena, it is at the eleventh hour, when others have long preceded them, and public opinion has already been formed. Strange, indeed, is all this! Christ made the social question the basis of His ministry. The evidence of His divinity which He gave to the disciples of John was: "The blind see, the lame walk, the lepers are cleansed, and the poor have the Gospel preached to them."* Through-out her whole history the Church grappled with every social problem that came in her way and solved it. The Church liberated the Roman slave, raised up woman, civilized the barbarian, humanized medieval warfare, and gave civic rights to the child of serfdom. What has come over us that we shun the work which is essentially ours to do? These are days of action, days of warfare. It is not the age of the timid and fugitive virtue of the Thebaid. Into the arena, priest and layman! Seek out social evils, and lead in movements that tend to rectify them. Speak of vested rights, for this is necessary; but speak, too, of vested wrongs, and strive, by word and example, by the enactment and enforcement of good laws, to correct them.[11]

Be it remembered that these sentences were spoken a full eighteen months before the appearance of the great encyclical of Pope Leo XIII, "On the Condition of Labor." Indeed, Ireland's statement: "Until their [the cruelly oppressed members of the wage-earning class] material condition is improved, it is futile to speak to them of supernatural life and duties," anticipated by more than forty-one years the declaration of Pope Pius XI in *Quadragesimo Anno:* "It may be said with all truth that nowadays the conditions of social and economic life are such that vast multitudes of men can only with great difficulty pay attention to that one thing necessary, namely, their eternal salvation."

Certain statements, acts, and attitudes of the Archbishop which occurred several years after the period of time covered by this chapter will be noted briefly here, in order to complete the description of his position on economic problems.

On Labor Day, 1903, he spoke to the labor unions of St. Paul on "Labor and Capital." Here are a few sentences from that address:

Labor is not a piece of mechanism, a mere tool or instrument; it is the living activity of a member of the great human family. The laborer is a man, entitled to the honor and reverence due to a child of the

*Matt. xi:4.
[11] *Op. cit.*, pp. 77–79.

supreme God of all men. He must be allowed to respect and guard his dignity; he must be allowed to live a life worthy of man, and receive as the price of his labor the means to live such a life. Capital deserves the severest condemnation when in its dealings with the toiler it has for its aim only to secure his labor at the lowest possible price, so as to increase its own emoluments as rapidly as possible, and when it sees in the laborer only an instrument of toil, without care for him or interest in him outside the range of his activity as a toiler. Nor are the needs of the laborer and his family for which the workman must provide to be restricted to those of the moment; consideration must be given to the needs which come with sickness and old age, and for which the labor of the present day should make provision. Capital, indeed, cannot be forgetful of its own reward: but let it ever remember the laborer, and give to him, so far as circumstances permit, that generous treatment that will enable him to live not only in present comfort, but also in the assured hope that years to come hold in reserve for him no terrors of penury and suffering.[12]

Concerning the right of labor to organize, the Archbishop had the following to say in the same address:

History is witness that great benefits have accrued from unions both to labor itself and to society at large. During the Middle Ages unions or guilds brought together the members of the different trades, protecting the weak, encouraging the timorous, obtaining for all substantial justice and social recognition. Then came the French Revolution, with its wild worship of individual rights: the guilds were broken up, and every man stood alone in the battle of life. The economic doctrines of the so-called Lancastrian School authorized capital to see in the laborer only his output of labor, and to purchase that output at the lowest market price. Then it was that the operators of the "black fields" of England reduced their miners to the level of beasts of burden, and as, even at that level, men seemed still to cost too much, put women in their stead, and later, for a similar reason, substituted children for women. How very different is the condition of labor today? The change is due very largely to an improved public opinion, and an enlarged Christian humanitarianism in the whole social body; but it is due very largely, also, as facts could easily be adduced to prove, to the intelligent self-assertiveness of labor itself, and to the new strength

[12] *Op. cit.*, Vol. II, pp. 359–360.

coming to it from the aggregation of its scattered units into well organized societies. Labor unions have a noble mission, and are entitled to the sympathy and support of all intelligent men.[13]

These passages exemplify the liberal outlook of the Archbishop to which I referred above. On the other hand, the following sentences exhibit his defective evaluation of certain facts and trends which existed even earlier than 1903: "I have no fear of capital. I have no fear of vast fortunes in the hands of individuals, nor of vast aggregations of capital in the hands of companies."[14]

While the evils resulting from "vast aggregations of capital," have been more thoroughly and authentically exposed since the Archbishop spoke, they were pretty evident to students of the subject even as early as 1903. John Ireland did not credit these exposures; indeed, he probably read very few of them. He could not believe that the great industrialists whose personal friendship he possessed, and who seemed to be "good men" in all their relations with him and with their neighbors, could stoop to economic oppression of the laborer, the farmer, or the consumer. His judgment was mistaken because he was not in possession of the relevant facts.

Soon after my first book, *A Living Wage,* was published (1906), Archbishop Ireland informed me that he had not only seen the volume but had read it all. "I assure you," he said, "I do not examine many books so thoroughly. I disagree with some of the positions that you take but not with many of them." Inasmuch as *A Living Wage* was not then regarded as excessively conservative, the Archbishop's evaluation was very significant; it reflected his fundamental liberalism and progressivism.

One more indication of this attitude and I shall pass on from my notice of this genuine American, fundamental

[13] *Op. cit.*, pp. 363–364.
[14] *Op. cit.*, p. 357.

humanitarian, and sincere Christian gentleman. For thirteen years (1902–1915) I taught moral theology and economics in his ecclesiastical seminary. The addition of economics to the course which he had assigned to me was my own doing; but he was entirely sympathetic with the innovation. Once, and sometimes twice, a year he took part in the semiannual examinations of the young men who were preparing for the priesthood at the St. Paul Seminary. In my courses I always endeavored to apply the principles of morality to all important economic transactions, to those involved in interest, profits, monopolies, wages, labor unions, etc. What I taught there and then on these subjects was what I have always taught, not only in the classroom, but in books, magazines, sermons, and public addresses. The Archbishop always took an active and obviously intelligent part in questioning the students on these as well as all the other topics that were comprised in the examinations. He understood "what it was all about." Nevertheless, he did not even once declare or intimate that my teaching was unorthodox, or "too radical," putting dangerous ideas into the heads of the young men who within two or three years would be elevated to the priesthood and empowered to preach my doctrines (in reality the traditional doctrines of the Catholic Church) from their pulpits.

BISHOP SPALDING

The valedictory which I gave on the occasion of my graduation from St. Thomas Seminary in 1892, was entitled, "High Ideals in Education." The inspiration for it and, probably most of the thoughts in it, came from a little volume by John Lancaster Spalding, Bishop of Peoria. The title of the book was *Education and the Higher Life* (1890). Bishop Spalding was undoubtedly the greatest literary artist in the entire history of the American Hierarchy. Most of his productions dealt with education, but he wrote a great deal that fell under the general head of literary criticism and a not inconsiderable amount on social questions.

For many years he exercised a greater influence upon my general philosophy of life, my ideals, my sense of comparative values than any other contemporary writer. Following are a few excerpts from *Education and the Higher Life:*

Is the material progress of the nineteenth century a cradle or a grave? Are we to continue to dig and delve and peer into matter until God and the soul fade from our view and we become like the things we work in? To put such questions to the multitude were idle. There is here no affair of votes and majorities. Human nature has not changed, and now, as in the past, crowds follow leaders. What the best minds and the most energetic characters believe and teach and put in practice, the millions will come to accept. The doubt is whether the leaders will be worthy—the real permanent leaders, for the noisy apparent leaders can never be so.[15]

If democracy is the best government, it follows that it is the kind of government which is most favorable to virtue, intelligence, and religion. It is faint praise to say that in America there is more enterprise, more wealth, than elsewhere. What we should strive to make ourselves able to say, is, that there is here a more truly human life, more public and private honesty, purity, sympathy, and helpfulness; more love of knowledge, more perfect openness to light, greater desire to learn, and greater willingness to accept truth than is to be found elsewhere. It should be our endeavor to create a world of which it may be said, there life is more pleasant, beauty more highly prized, goodness held in greater reverence, the sense of honor finer, the recognition of talent and worth completer than elsewhere.[16]

Culture, then, is necessary. We need it as a corrective of the tendency to seek the good of life in what is external, as a means of helping us to overcome our vulgar self-complacency, our satisfaction with low aims and cheap accomplishments, our belief in the sovereign potency of machines and measures. We need it to make our lives less unlovely, less hard, less material; to help us to understand the idolatry of the worship of steam and electricity, the utter insufficiency of the ideals of industrialism. But if culture is to become a mighty transforming influence it

[15] *Op. cit.*, p. 28.
[16] *Op. cit.*, p. 155.

must be wedded to religious faith, without which, while it widens the intellectual view, it weakens the will to act. To take us out of ourselves and to urge us on to labor with God that we may leave the world better because we have lived, religion alone has power. It gives new vigor to the cultivated mind; it takes away the exclusive and fastidious temper which a purely intellectual habit tends to produce; it enlarges sympathy; it teaches reverence; it nourishes faith, inspires hope, exalts the imagination, and keeps alive the fire of love.[17]

Who will understand that to be is better than to have, and that in truth a man is worth only what he is? Who will believe that the kingdom of this world, not less than the kingdom of Heaven, lies within? Who, even in thinking of the worth of a pious and righteous life, is not swayed by some sort of honesty-best-policy principle? We love knowledge because we think it is power; and virtue, because we are told as a rule it succeeds. Ah! do you love knowledge for itself?—for it is good, it is godlike to know. Do you love virtue for its own sake? —for it is eternally and absolutely right to be virtuous. Instead of giving your thoughts and desires to wealth and position, learn to know how little of such things a true and wise man needs; for the secret of a happy life does not lie in the means and opportunities of indulging our weaknesses, but in knowing how to be content with what is reasonable, that time and strength may remain for the cultivation of our nobler nature. Ask God to inspire you with some great thought, some abiding love of what is excellent, which may fill you with gladness and courage, and in the midst of the labors, the trials, and the disappointments of life, keep you still strong and serene.[18]

These passages will give some idea of the lofty suggestions and inspirations which came to me from this little volume in the years 1891 and 1892. Most of the declarations by the Bishop of Peoria on social and political questions appeared in later books, principally, *Opportunity and Other Essays* (1900) and *Socialism and Labor and Other Arguments* (1902). The former includes an address delivered in Chicago, April 30, 1899, entitled "Empire or Republic," in which Bishop Spalding denounced American imperialism (which was then

[17] *Op. cit.*, pp. 22–23.
[18] *Op. cit.*, pp. 142–143.

EARLY SOCIAL EDUCATION (1882–1892) 31

fashionable among our jingoes and greedy exploiters) and opposed our retention of the Philippines. His words were not heeded, but it is pretty generally acknowledged now that his position was sound and patriotic. In the second of the two volumes just now cited will be found "An Orator and Lover of Justice," being the address which Bishop Spalding gave at the memorial meeting held in Chicago, April 29, 1902, one month after the death of John Peter Altgeld. This is a surpassingly eloquent production. Better than that, it is keen, discriminating, and realistic. It shows that the Bishop had not been misled by the cruel propaganda which stigmatized Altgeld "anarchist" because as governor of Illinois his sense of justice and his unswerving courage had moved him to pardon the three anarchists who had been unjustly sentenced to life imprisonment for alleged complicity in the "Haymarket Massacre." One of Bishop Spalding's commendations of Altgeld in this address could be applied to his own attitude toward the vilification of the great Governor by a plutocractic and hireling press: "He saw through shams and shows into the heart of things." Bishop Spalding's comprehensive acquaintance with the fundamental facts of our industrial practices, persons, and institutions, enabled him to see through the aura of "respectability" surrounding these and to perceive a great deal of the underlying plutocratic maneuvering and social injustice. Hence he could say of Altgeld in this memorial address:

He had a fine scorn of mere wealth, title, and position, and would have taken delight in a beggar who might have had power to make him wiser or better. He abhorred cant, pretense, hypocrisy, and lies. He would not have flattered a king for his crown, nor a plutocrat for all his gold. If a cause was just it commended itself to him all the more because it was unpopular.[19]

With all his heart he loved truth and hated lies; loved justice and

[19] *Socialism and Labor and Other Arguments*, by J. L. Spalding, p. 191.

hated iniquity. As he was capable of giving his life for what he held to be right, so had he infinite power of scorn for tricksters and spoilsmen, for palterers and beggars of the approval of men. He knew the blessedness of being hated and calumniated for fidelity to conscience. The best men are made great by the obstacles they surmount, by the enemies they withstand. Nearly all our speakers tread the paths of dalliance, hold their ears to the ground to catch the murmur of the crowd, make brave shots at safe objects, apologize if by chance they utter the naked truth; but here was one for whom right and wrong are parted by eternal laws, for whom compromise is treason, and connivance apostasy from God and the soul. Pallid, feeble in body, overworked, and over-wrought by the intensity of his own nature and too eager mind, he faced corruption and a hostile opinion begotten of the spirit of Mammonites and time-servers with the heroic courage of confessors and martyrs. He knew better than anyone that throughout America and Europe his name was associated with doctrines and practices which he abhorred, that he was a safe mark for the conscienceless fling of every hireling of the press, that to be his friend was to incur suspicion of not being respectable, but he faltered not; and though fallen on evil days and slandered by evil tongues, though overtaken by poverty and sneered at by idolaters of success, he continued to confront with dauntless courage all the fosterers of lies and corruption, all the contrivers of oppression and wrong, all the apologists of conquest and inhumanity. He had a heart as tender as a woman's; a soul as dauntless as a hero's. Whatever concerned the poor, the weak, the disinherited, had his earnest attention and sympathies. His faith in the people was profound, and he believed that democratic government may be so organized and administered as to make it a blessing to all, and first of all to those who most need protection and fair opportunity because they are the most defenseless and the most easily wronged.[20]

And the peroration:

Here, then, let me close, while I salute, with admiration, respect and reverence the memory of a genuine and heroic man—the truest servant of the people and the most disinterested politician whom Illinois has known since Lincoln died.[21]

[20] *Op. cit.*, pp. 196–198.
[21] *Op. cit.*, p. 200. All the volumes of Bishop Spalding cited above are published by . A. C. McClurg and Co., Chicago, whose kind permission for reproduction here is gratefully acknowledged.

Bishop Spalding's own opinion of this address was briefly but strikingly expressed at a reception tendered him by the faculty and students of the St. Paul Seminary in the year 1904. When one of the participants announced that his contribution would be a reading of the panegyric on Altgeld, Archbishop Ireland made an exclamation of surprise and dissent. Bishop Spalding promptly and vigorously retorted: "The best thing I ever wrote!" Seated only a few feet distant, I easily overheard this characteristic interchange.

These passages will provide some indication of my intellectual indebtedness to the Bishop of Peoria on account of his social outlook and teaching. I like to think that his intelligent sympathy with the economically weak and his understanding of the efforts made on their behalf by "radicals" like Altgeld, were the natural outcome of his ideals and his general philosophy of life and of society. The latter enabled him not only to distinguish between the genuine and the counterfeit ideas of worth prevalent in contemporary society, but also to perceive, despite "shams and shows," the true champions of social justice in contemporary America.

CANON BARRY

Right Reverend Dr. William Francis Barry was born in London on April 21, 1849, of parents who had emigrated from Ireland shortly before the Great Famine. Best known as essayist, critic, and man of letters, nevertheless, he always maintained a lively interest in the poor and lowly and in the economic causes of their condition. As he informs us in his autobiography *Memories and Opinions*, he had abundant opportunity to observe their wretchedness in London in the fifties and sixties of the nineteenth century. Before he was ten years of age he had acquired from his reading of both the Old and New Testaments the inspiration to join his father and associates in "grappling with the ills, economic and social under which we suffered. Thus the lessons of Holy Scripture took a practical and instant shape. Whatever happened to me afterwards," he continues, "I never changed from this point of view." He calls his attitude toward the economic misery that he saw all about him, "this passion for humanity," and discloses that he tried to breathe it into one of the characters in his first novel, *The New Antigone*. This character, Ivor Mardol, was, says Canon Barry, "my ideal self—the dreamer, reformer, enthusiast for the Reign of Justice among men."

The following extracts from *The New Antigone* will give a good idea of his descriptive powers, capacity for feeling, and deep sympathy with the victims of economic oppression:

She saw only a festering heap of human beings, flung on top of one another and kneaded into a pestilential mass by the iron heel of necessity. And morning after morning flowers sprang up on the black dunghill and turned their leaves hopelessly towards the sun that would not shine on them, and withered, and were trampled into the foul mass. For in this horrible world children were born by the hundred thousand —delicate children, sometimes beautiful, with their large tender eyes, always frail and in need of sustenance and of love. Every house into which Miss Desmond led her swarmed with children as a hive swarms with bees. When they were fortunate they died young. And how short was the youth of those that lived! At six years old a child in the deeps of London has seen most that can happen of foul, unclean, and heartbreaking on this planet of ours. But ere its birth it is predestined by the laws of the dark realm into which it must enter to be a devil's child and never to know the face of its Father in heaven. Its very breath and bones are made of vice. The typical child of the well-to-do classes looks beautiful, strong, happy, and innocent. The typical child, encountered again and again by Hippolyta as she moved in that short radius of which Denzil Lane was the centre—the angel of the house whom she beheld in every nook and corner of that dismal universe—was ugly, deformed, ailing, accustomed to stripes and blows, full of premature greed, a thing of rags and disease, old in sin, and steeped in impurity. No hand of redemption or blessing had ever come nigh it. And was there any production of Nature alone so complete in hideousness?[22]

[22] *The New Antigone*, by William Barry, 1887, Vol. III, pp. 11–12.

In these regions there was no such thing as solitude, privacy, or a house with closed doors. There was not room to move in, not air enough to breathe. The confusion of ages and sexes, of strong and feeble, even of good and bad, was beyond description. No slave-ship was ever more crowded than the miles of narrow streets through which Hippolyta, shuddering and sick at heart, was forced to thread her way. For those who dwelt in them Nature had no meaning; the green of the meadows, the grace of field and forest, the beauty of running water, nay, the very lights of heaven did not exist for them. All they knew was this living prison of human bodies which hemmed them round, and from the walls and roofs of which came incessantly, as in a falling shower, sounds of blasphemy, rage, cursing, pain, hunger and thirst, intoxication, insanity, and murder.[23]

The New Antigone was published in 1887. Referring to the years that immediately followed, Cannon Barry writes in his autobiography: "But now I was called upon to fulfil other duties, though always in pursuance of the resolution I had taken to help in the social uplifting of the so-called Proletariat."[24] Something more than five years after this sentence was written, Pope Pius XI declared in *Quadragesimo Anno*: "This is the aim which Our Predecessor [Pope Leo XIII] urged as the necessary object of our efforts: the uplifting of the proletariat." Less than two pages further on in the autobiography, the Canon describes his part in a conference of the Catholic Truth Society, June 30, 1896, in the town hall of Birmingham when he was the house guest of Herbert Chamberlain, brother of the famous Joseph:

I startled some of those Midland magnates by my doctrine of a fuller share due to Labour in the glorious products I saw about me than the Birmingham dwellings or amenities apparently afforded. But my resounding stroke was delivered from the platform where I read my paper, in the presence of Bishop Vaughan of Salford, and other prelates, somewhat to their consternation. I spoke on behalf of the class which was coming to be known as the "proletariat." They were not the

[23] *Idem*, pp. 13–14.
[24] *Memories and Opinions*, p. 184.

lapsed Masses, but the abandoned Masses. Were they Christians? I asked frankly, "How could they be?" Cardinal Manning said: "One half of the people never set their foot in any place of divine worship, and if they are without God and the world, it is not their fault." I drove this home with statistics, authorities, instances. The conclusion I drew was: "First civilize, then Christianize." We stood in need of a social and a lay Christianity. "To make the people Christian, they must be restored to their homes, and their homes to them." I concluded, "If I am asked how Christianity is to be brought to the Masses I reply, 'Show them how they can be saved by it, and enabled to live a true and human life, in this world, then perhaps they will believe you about the next; but until you do, they never will.'" When I had finished, amid applause and wonder, Bishop Vaughan shook hands with me. I thought it uncommonly brave of him. The tempest followed in that hall, then in the newspapers.

I was indicting a policy which everywhere in the modern world had brought forth fruits of death. Happily, Manning, in London; Gibbons and Ireland, in the United States; and more than one leading Bishop in Germany, had taken this cause to heart. The question raised in America concerning the Knights of Labour had been carried to Rome; and Leo XIII was consulting these enlightened men, who taught him their views. He was already acquainted with the economic problem, and willing to take it up. His memorable defense of the Rights of Labour created a new epoch in the Catholic Church, and frankly recognized the democratic position, both as regards government and in the matter of the living wage. I knew well that my pronouncement, however daring, was altogether right in principle and would be approved by the Holy Father. But I must say that, however uncomfortable I made some of their Lordships, the Bishops were very considerate to me, and I suffered no harm by this violent, though, as I think needful, outburst. I had said that of the social problem our Colleges, our education, knew nothing. I was uttering the thoughts that had been provoked in me by thirty years of direct experience. It was time that this isolation should come to an end.[25]

Canon Barry's declaration that the masses will not be induced to accept Christianity until they can be shown that it

[25] *Memories and Opinions*, by William Barry, pp. 186–187. Published by G. P. Putnam's Sons, New York, whose kind permission for reproduction here is gratefully acknowledged.

will enable them "to live a true and human life in this world, and then perhaps they will believe you about the next"— recalls the very similar statements quoted earlier in this chapter from Archbishop Ireland and Pope Pius XI. For myself, I have always held that acceptance of this fundamental truth as a working principle is an essential prerequisite to the Christianizing of large sections of the wage-earning classes.

So far as I can recall, I first came upon *The New Antigone* in 1890 or 1891. Naturally it made a considerable impression upon me, although not nearly so great as that which I received when I read it again in 1897. The Birmingham speech, noticed above, I never knew anything about until I read *Memories and Opinions* in 1926. After 1898, when his second novel, *The Two Standards,* was published, I read almost everything that he currently wrote, novels, biographies, histories, magazine articles on various topics, and works of criticism. Under the last-mentioned head, I would cite particularly his *Heralds of Revolt* which comprises reprints of articles that he had published in the *Dublin Review* and the *Quarterly Review.* Among the authors reviewed and evaluated are: George Eliot, Carlyle, Heine, and Nietzsche; among the essays, "The Modern French Novel," "Neo-Paganism" and "Latter Day Pagans." The book is still well worth reading. In passing, here is the author's own estimate of *The Two Standards*: "I would have this book regarded as my verdict on modern society, its finance, art, social ethics, when put under Christian observation."[26]

On September 14, 1906, *The Catholic Times* of Liverpool published a review by Canon Barry of my first book, *A Living Wage.* Noting that a recent English Trade Union Congress, had again "laid down the principle of a minimum or living wage," he went on to cite the declaration of Pope Leo XIII on the same subject and pronounced it "a challenge to base

[26] *Memories and Opinions*, p. 213.

modern capitalism, not unworthy of the successor of that
Hildebrand who wrested from feudal lords the Church's
freedom." The review closes with these sentences:

> To those who need enlightenment Professor Ryan's book will fur-
> nish it in ample measure. *The Living Wage* is a genuine cure for eco-
> nomic disorders. It lies within the reach of social effort. It makes for
> progress while escaping the perils of revolution. The Church blesses it;
> why should not law and custom put it beyond the range of monopo-
> listic assault?

In July of that same year, I spent a week as Dr. Barry's
guest at his parish house in Dorchester, a few miles from
Oxford. Needless to say, the experience was pleasant, indeed,
—at least to me—and very profitable. In 1911 and again in
1922, I was his guest at Leamington, where he had become
pastor of St. Peter's Church in 1908, and where he remained
until 1928. He was elected Canon of the Birmington Chapter
in 1907 and in 1923 was elevated by the Holy Father to the
rank of Prothonotary Apostolic. After that his adequate title
was neither "Doctor" nor "Canon" but "Monsignor." He
died on December 15, 1930.

By far the greater part of the guidance and inspiration that
I derived from Canon Barry's writings came after the period
covered by this chapter. Nevertheless, I received definite and
powerful impressions from *The New Antigone* between the
years 1890 and 1892. His subsequent writings confirmed,
amplified, and made more explicit the earlier impressions,
suggestions, and ideas. This sentence applies likewise to the
influence upon me of Bishop Spalding. Incidentally, the
writings of both Barry and Spalding not only presented
sound social doctrine but very frequently exhibited the
qualities of genuine literature.

The curriculum which I followed at St. Thomas Seminary,
from 1887 to 1892, covered three years of high school and
two years of college. In the fall of 1892, I began the six years

of seminary courses in preparation for the priesthood. My classroom work during the five years noted above included no course in economics nor in any other social science. In other words, up to 1892, I had obtained no formal training in the subjects which would have interested me most. The ideas, knowledge, and opinions which I had acquired in the field of economics had their source in such books, magazines, and newspapers as came to my attention, together with lectures and political speeches.

Aside from the events already recounted in this chapter, I can recall no experience during this period that is worth putting on paper. From 1882 until the late fall of 1886, when I entered the Christian Brothers' School in St. Paul, I had attended our ungraded district school in Dakota County for six or seven months each year, and during the remaining months worked hard on the farm. From 1886 until 1892, I spent practically every day of the summer vacations in the fields—not contemplating nature but wrestling with it. But the labor was good for me, physically and spiritually. Had I grown up in the city my entrance into high school and college might well have been at least three years earlier, and I should have been ordained at twenty-five or twenty-six instead of at twenty-nine. But I have no regrets on this score. Perchance, I might have been born in a palace, and thus compelled to confront the discouraging hazard cited by Bishop Spalding: "Hence a philosopher has said there are ten thousand chances to one that genius, talent and virtue shall issue from a farmhouse rather than from a palace."[27]

[27] *Education and the Higher Life*, p. 35.

CHAPTER III

EARLY SOCIAL EDUCATION—*Continued* (1892–1898)

MY SIX years of ecclesiastical, or seminary, training began in September, 1892, at St. Thomas Seminary, where I had pursued my five years of preparatory studies. From 1885 until 1894, St. Thomas was at once a high school, junior college, and ecclesiastical seminary. The seminarians occupied one half of the building which was the material part of St. Thomas Seminary, while the students of the high school and junior college departments studied, ate, and slept in the other half. As is customary in such institutions, the ecclesiastical or seminary branches of study were divided into two main groups, philosophical and theological. The former occupied two years, the latter four years. It will be noted, therefore, that the entire body of courses taught in the seminary normally required a period of twelve years: four of high school, two of junior college, and six of professional studies. A student who began his courses there at fourteen years of age and continued through all the departments was ordained a priest at the age of twenty-six. A few managed to complete the twelve years' work in eleven years. In passing, it might be noted that when St. Thomas Seminary was opened in 1885 there were some institutions in the United States which permitted and enabled the students to get through all the courses from high school to ordination in ten years; but the last half century has witnessed such an improvement in the academic studies of both the preparatory and professional branches of priestly training that the required period now is almost universally twelve years.

The two years that I spent in my philosophical studies comprehended, so far as I can recall, only three events which had any special significance. The first was the rehabilitation of the Reverend Dr. Edward McGlynn. In December, 1886, he had been "suspended," i.e., forbidden by his ecclesiastical superior, Archbishop Corrigan of New York, to exercise his sacerdotal functions. The reason for this censure was his continued and persistent advocacy, at public meetings and elsewhere, of the single-tax doctrine, taught by Henry George. For disregarding a summons to Rome to explain and defend his opinions and teachings on this subject, Dr. McGlynn was excommunicated by the Holy See July 3, 1887. On that day, the College of the Propaganda directed the Archbishop of New York to promulgate the decree of excommunication. This order was carried out by Archbishop Corrigan through a letter published in the churches of the Archdiocese of New York, July 10, 1887. On December 23, 1892, the decree of excommunication was revoked and Dr. McGlynn was authorized to resume the exercise of his priestly functions by the Papal Ablegate, Archbishop Francis Satolli.

The McGlynn case and its issues did not make a great impression on me during the six years that elapsed between his suspension and his restoration. When the latter event came to my attention, it did not cause me to spend much time in the study or discussion of the questions involved. In subsequent years, I devoted a great deal of time to the single-tax theory and learned all that I could about the career of Dr. McGlynn. About one year before his death, which took place in 1901, I heard him preach in St. Stephen's Church in Washington, but was not greatly impressed. By that time his days as an orator had passed.[1]

[1] A biographical sketch of Dr. McGlynn which I prepared for the *Dictionary of American Biography* appears in that work. A fairly adequate biography by Stephen Bell, *Rebel, Priest and Prophet*, was published in 1937, by Devin-Adair Co., New York. For a critical account of Henry George's theory, see my *Distributive Justice*, Chapter III.

The second event of those years deserving notice here was the delivery of an address by my own Archbishop. On October 18, 1893, at the celebration of Cardinal Gibbons' twenty-fifth anniversary as a bishop, Archbishop Ireland preached a sermon on "The Church and the Age." From this discourse I select two paragraphs:

The great theologians of the Church lay the foundations of political democracy which today attains its perfect form. They prove that all political power comes from God through the people, that kings and princes are the people's delegates, and that when rulers become tyrants the inalienable right of revolution belongs to the people. The Church is at home under all forms of government. The one condition of the legitimacy of a form of government, in the eyes of the Church, is that it be accepted by the people. The Church has never said that she prefers one form of government above another. But, so far as I may from my own thoughts interpret the principles of the Church, I say that the government of the people, by the people, and for the people, is, more than any other, the polity under which the Catholic Church, the church of the people, breathes air most congenial to her mind and heart.

It is an age of battlings for social justice to all men, for the right of all men to live in the frugal comfort becoming rational creatures. Very well! Is it not Catholic doctrine that birth into the world is man's title to a sufficiency of the things of the world? Is not the plea for social justice and social well-being the loud outburst of the cry which has ever been going up from the bosom of the Church since the words were spoken by her Founder: "Seek first the kingdom of God and His justice and all these things shall be added unto you"? It is not sufficiently understood that the principles which underlie the social movement of the times in its legitimate demands are constantly taught in schools of Catholic theology; as, for instance, the principle which, to the surprise of his fellow-countrymen, Cardinal Manning proclaimed: that in case of extreme necessity, one may use, as far as it is needed to save life, the property of others. We have, of late, been so accustomed to lock up our teachings in seminary and sanctuary that when they appear in active evolution in the broad arena of life they are not recognized by Catholics; nay, are even feared and disowned by them.[2]

[2] *The Church and Modern Society*, Vol. I, pp. 99–101.

In these extracts the Archbishop repeats the sentiments that he had expressed in 1884 and 1889 and anticipates some that he uttered later, in 1903. One noteworthy fact in the second of the paragraphs cited above is the Archbishop's use of the term "social justice." Not in 1893 nor for many years thereafter, was this phrase in common use by American priests or bishops. Writing in the year 1931, the Reverend Othmar Nell-Bruening declared:

In theological treatises the concepts of "social justice" and "social charity" have been as yet only slightly studied and investigated. To be sure, the concepts are neither new nor strange, even though the terms have come into use quite recently. . . . An important task confronts theological science to build up and deepen the teaching on both social justice and social charity.[3]

Since Pope Pius XI stressed and defined social justice in his encyclicals on "Reconstructing the Social Order," and "Atheistic Communism," the term has become current coin in Catholic discussions of economic subjects. For example, it occurs eight times in the letter of the American bishops on the "Church and Social Order," published in February, 1940.

Inasmuch as the sermon containing the foregoing excerpts was delivered by the Archbishop who was the founder, superior, and constant overseer of St. Thomas Seminary, it was brought adequately to the attention of the students. From it I know that I derived information, inspiration, and encouragement.

The third event alluded to above occurred in the last six months of my course in philosophy, January or February, 1894. One of our professors assigned to his class in postgraduate English the task of writing an essay on the encyclical of Pope Leo XIII entitled "On the Condition of Labor." As the encyclical had been published May 15, 1891, it was then

[3] *Die Soziale Enzyklika*, Rev. Othmar Nell-Bruening, S.J., p. 170. Cf. English translation, *Reorganization of Social Economy*, by Bernard W. Dempsey, S.J., Bruce Publishing Company, Milwaukee, 1936, p. 251.

almost three years old; nevertheless, this was the first occasion when it was brought formally to the attention of the students of St. Thomas Seminary. Unfortunately, this oversight was typical of the treatment accorded to the encyclical by the Catholics of the United States for several years after it was issued.

I recollect very clearly the portion of the encyclical to which my own essay devoted most time and emphasis. It was not the teaching on a living wage, nor on labor unions, nor on the right of property, nor on Socialism. It was Leo's discussion of the state and the very large scope that he assigned to legislation as an instrument of social reform. To American Catholics, who, like their fellow Americans had been indoctrinated with theories of nonintervention which were not far removed from *laissez-faire*, the declarations of Pope Leo on the regulatory functions of the state over industry were new and, indeed, startling. For example, the Holy Father declared:

Whenever the general interest or any particular class suffers, or is threatened with evils, which can in no other way be met, the public authority must step in to meet them. . . .

The richer population have many ways of protecting themselves, and stand less in need of help from the state; those who are badly off have no resources of their own to fall back upon, and must chiefly rely upon the assistance of the state.

Inasmuch as I had for almost a decade been listening sympathetically to the proposals made by the Farmers' Alliance and the Populists for state regulation of industry, I found Pope Leo's pronouncements on this subject not only pleasing but reassuring. The doctrine of state intervention which I had come to accept and which was sometimes denounced as "socialistic" in those benighted days, I now read in a Papal encyclical. Only those who know the condition of American

Catholic social thought before 1890, can understand how and why Leo's teaching on the state seemed almost revolutionary.

In September, 1894, occurred the opening of the St. Paul Seminary. From that date on, the study of philosophy and theology was pursued there instead of in St. Thomas Seminary. Thenceforth, the latter became known as the College of St. Thomas. Although the St. Paul Seminary had been built and endowed by James J. Hill, president of the Great Northern Railway, he never, so far as I know, attempted to interfere with the instruction given within its walls. My own economic views differed very considerably from those of a railroad president; nevertheless, I taught them for thirteen years in the seminary that Mr. Hill founded, without any objection from him or in his name. Possibly some of the sting was taken out of my "radical" doctrines by the moderate language in which I awlays tried to express them. At any rate, I have known more than one writer whose opinions were no more "advanced" than mine, but who gave offense by their lack of restraint in presentation.

The teaching staff which Archbishop Ireland assembled for his new institution was well above the average of American ecclesiastical seminaries in the year 1894. Most of the faculty members had been trained with special reference to the chairs which they were respectively to occupy. Almost without exception they were comparatively young men, but only one of them is now living. Of my instructors in St. Thomas Seminary, only one survives.

Although the courses given at the St. Paul Seminary were as good as those presented in any other training school for priests in the United States, and probably somewhat better than the majority, the curriculum in the nineties did not include the study of economics or sociology or social problems. Whatever of this character the students learned in the classroom was given to them in connection with the treatises on "contracts" and on "justice and right" in the courses of moral theology. Then, as now, those treatises dealt with buying and selling, hiring and renting, employer and employee relations, just prices, monopoly, usury and interest, and contracts of association. Of course, the instructor expanded the text in the classroom, for example, to discuss the teaching of Leo XIII on wages and labor unions. The treatise on "justice and right" included, of course, the right of property, and the instructor usually supplemented the textbook presentation of this subject with a discussion of the doctrines taught by Leo XIII on ownership and Socialism. Obviously, the treatment of these subjects enabled the students to learn something about many important economic institutions and practices. However, the courses did not provide even an elementary treatment of economics as such.

My own interest in social and economic subjects was kept up and extended during those four years (1894–1898) at the St. Paul Seminary through reading such pertinent articles in newspapers, magazines, and books as came into my hands, and through the political speeches which I heard, particularly those delivered during the Bryan-McKinley campaign of 1896. In the summer vacation of 1894, I read for the first time a manual of economics. This was an English translation of a work written in Italian by the Rev. Matteo Liberatore, S.J. The English version was entitled *Principles of Political Economy* and was published in 1891. With the exception of a small and inadequate volume by Charles A. Devas, *Groundwork of Economics* (1883), the translation of Liberatore's work was the first economic text by a Catholic to appear in the English language. The following year, however, 1892, Mr. Devas published his *Political Economy*, which is an excellent production, and has gone through many editions, and has had a wide circulation.

Recently, I looked into Liberatore's work for the first time in more than thirty years and was glad to find that on the whole it is as useful as many other elementary economic texts that have come to my attention. It is superior to the majority of the manuals because it includes moral evaluation of economic actions and institutions. Its pronouncements on just wages are entirely sound, but those on labor unions and rent leave something to be desired. However, I do not recall that I judged these pronouncements very critically in 1894. What I got from Liberatore at that time was a fair idea of the ground covered by the science of economics, insofar as it is a science.

MR. WILLIAM SAMUEL LILLY

Among the writers who influenced me considerably during this period, in addition to those mentioned in the immediately preceding chapter, I shall present only two: W. S. Lilly and Richard T. Ely. The former was an English Catholic publicist endowed with great ability, a keen and logical mind, and a forceful style. While he probably would have resented the appellation "radical," his writings on economic subjects were radical in the true sense, for he tried to go to the roots of every matter that he handled, and his method and habits of thought were fundamental and philosophical. Although by temper and associations something of an aristocrat, he scorned the pseudo-aristocracy that has its foundations in the possession of money or in the acquisitive achievements of trade and industry. For him, the supreme values of life were ethical, and he tested all social institutions by that standard. He wrote an enormous number of magazine articles and upwards of a score of books. Of the latter, those that influenced me most in my seminary years were: *A Century of Revolution, On Shibboleths,* and *On Right and Wrong.* Here are a few summary paragraphs from the "Ethics of Property" which is chapter eight of the last-mentioned work:

Is it possible to maintain that the existing distribution of wealth is reasonable? A division which "instead of being proportioned to the labour and abstinence of the individual, is almost in an inverse ratio to it." . . .

Unrestricted competition is unjust: the necessity of the seller does not render it right to underpay him: to give him less than a *justum pretium* is to rob him. Moreover to constitute freedom of contract there must be parity of condition. . . .

As a matter of fact, to much of the wealth of the rich classes in modern Europe the saying *La propriété c'est le vol*, is strictly applicable. . . .

But even if a man's property has been justly acquired, to render his possession of it valid according to the moral law, there lies upon him the obligation of employing it in a proper manner for himself and others. He has not a right to do what he likes, but only what he ought, with his own, which after all is his own only in a qualified sense. The community is his overlord: and the very constitution of civilized life gives rise to the duty that ownership must be made a common good to the community. . . .

So much is involved in "the order of reason" regarding property. The task before the world is the reorganization of industry in accordance with these dictates of the moral law.

On Right and Wrong was published in 1890; hence the foregoing sentences were written about two years before the appearance of *Rerum Novarum* and some forty-two years earlier than *Quadragesimo Anno*; yet they agree perfectly with the subsequent pronouncements on property by Leo XIII and Pius XI. For example, Pope Leo said: "It is one thing to have a right to the possession of money, and another to have a right to use money as one pleases." And Pius XI declared: "It follows from the twofold character of ownership, which we have termed individual and social, that men must take into account in this matter not only their own advantage but also the common good. To define in detail these duties, when the need occurs and when the natural law does not do so, is the function of the government."

Mr. Lilly died in 1920. Twenty years later his writings are rarely cited, even in Great Britain. Nevertheless, they exercised a very considerable influence upon his contemporaries, non-Catholic as well as Catholic, and many of his books are still well worth reading. The benefit that I derived from them between 1892 and 1898, and, indeed, for several years afterwards, was, I am sure, much greater than I could now recount in specific language.

Dr. Richard Theodore Ely

Much better known to Americans than W. S. Lilly, is Dr. Richard T. Ely. His professional career began when he became head of the Department of Political Economy at Johns Hopkins University, in 1881. Eleven years later, he accepted the chair of political economy at the University of Wisconsin, retaining that position until 1925, when he was appointed research professor of economics at Northwestern University. In recent years he has been director of research in the Ely Economic Foundation. When the manuscript for my first book, *A Living Wage,* was completed, he read it carefully and then undertook to find a publisher. He also wrote an appreciative and discriminating Introduction to the volume which aided mightily in gaining recognition for it. Although he is past eighty-six years of age, he is still vigorous and active.

In the development of American economic thought, Dr. Ely played a very large and very creditable part. He was one of the most prominent and active founders of the American Economic Association, of which he was secretary during its first seven years. Most of the doctrines, or dogmas, prevalent in American economic teaching previous to 1885, reflected the theory of *laissez-faire*; but Dr. Ely put the following sentences into the "Prospectus" which he drew up for the guidance of the new society:

We regard the state as an educational and ethical agency whose positive aid is an indispensable condition of human progress. While we recognize the necessity of individual initiative in industrial life, we hold that the doctrine of *laissez-faire* is unsafe in politics and unsound in morals; and that it suggests an inadequate explanation of the relations between the state and the citizens.[4]

These sentences did not get into the "Statement of Principles" drawn up for the Association by an authorized committee, because it was feared that some of the members would be unable to accept such a "strong condemnation of the *laissez-faire* doctrine." However, the first sentence in the "Statement" declares: "We regard the State as an agency whose positive assistance is one of the indispensable conditions of human progress."[5]

Some four years after the founding of the Association, Dr. Ely included a chapter on "Ethics and Economics" in his little volume entitled *Social Aspects of Christianity* (1889). From that chapter I take the following extracts:

It is well to describe somewhat more in detail the ethical ideal which animates the new political economy. It is the most perfect development of all human faculties in each individual, which can be attained. There are powers in every human being capable of cultivation; and each person, it may be said, accomplishes his end when these powers have attained the largest growth which is possible to them. This means anything rather than equality. It means the richest diversity, for differentiation accompanies development. It is simply the Christian doctrine of talents committed to men, all to be improved, whether the individual gift be one talent, two, five, or ten talents. The categorical imperative of duty enforces upon each rational being perfection "after his kind." Now, the economic life is the basis of this growth of all the higher faculties—faculties of love, of knowledge, of aesthetic perception, and the like, as exhibited in religion, art, language, literature, science, social and political life. What the political economist desires, then, is such a

---

[4] *Ground Under Our Feet*, by Richard T. Ely, The Macmillan Company, New York, 1938, p. 136.
[5] *Idem*, p. 140.

production and such a distribution of economic goods as must in the highest practicable degree subserve the end and purpose of human existence for all members of society. . . .

The adherents of the ethical school apply ethical principles to economic facts and economic institutions, and test their value by that standard. Political economy is thus brought into harmony with the great religious, political, and social movements which characterize this age; for the essence of them all is the belief that there ought to be no contradiction between our actual economic life and the postulates of ethics, and a determination that there shall be an abolition of such things as will not stand the tests of this rule. If industrial society as it exists at present does not answer this requirement, then industrial society stands condemned; or, in so far as it fails to meet this requirement in so far is it condemned. It is not that it is hoped to reach a perfect ideal at one bound, but that the ideal is a goal for which men must strive. The new conception of the state is thus secondary, in the opinion of the adherents of the ethical school, to the new conception of social ethics. Doubtless there is a new conception of the state; for in this cooperative institution is discovered one of the means to be used to accomplish the end of human society, the ethical ideal. Perhaps still more important is the departure of economists from the individualistic philosophy which characterized the era of the French Revolution, and which has gained such a stronghold in America, because our republic happened to be founded at a time when this view of individual sovereignty was in the ascendant.[6]

It is interesting to compare the first of these two paragraphs with the following passage in the encyclical *Quadragesimo Anno,* which appeared some forty-two years later:

For then only will the economic and social organism be soundly established and attain its end, when it secures for all and each those goods which the wealth and resources of nature, technical achievement, and the social organization of economic affairs can give. These goods should be sufficient to supply all needs and an honest livelihood, and to uplift men to that higher level of prosperity and culture which, provided it be used with prudence, is not only no hindrance but is of singular help to virtue.

[6] *Social Aspects of Christianity*, by Richard T. Ely. Thomas Y. Crowell and Co., New York, 1889, pp. 123–124, 128–129.

Unfortunately, the "ethical school," described by Dr. Ely in the foregoing excerpt, has not been able to convert or greatly influence the great body of economists in the United States. While the majority of economic texts and of articles in economic magazines have gone beyond mere descriptions of economic phenomena, and beyond the discussion of economic theory and so-called economic laws, their attitude toward practical matters and what "ought to be," is expressed in terms of social or political or managerial policy, rather than in propositions concerning what is ethically right or ethically wrong. For example, very few economic treatises explicitly define or deal with the moral rights of the wage earner. A similar statement may truthfully be made concerning the discussion of interest, profits, monopolies, and several other practices and institutions.

Naturally, my own college and seminary training had predisposed me to welcome the ethical element in economic discussion by such a prominent economist as Dr. Ely. I rejoiced, too, in his insistence upon the obligation of Christian teachers and believers to bring their religious principles into their economic practices and relations. These pronouncements occur frequently in *Social Aspects of Christianity* but they are not absent from Dr. Ely's *Socialism and Social Reform.* For example: "If one out of ten persons who call themselves Christian should actually guide his conduct by the precepts of Christianity, all reforms of a social nature which can now be suggested would be speedily accomplished." I found this volume even more satisfactory and helpful than *Social Aspects of Christianity*. It came into my hands shortly after it was published, in 1894. Its chapters on the nature, the strength, and the weakness of Socialism, are still pertinent, useful, and persuasive. Part IV of the volume, "The Golden Mean and Practical Social Reform," proved the most helpful section of the book because it presented the first systematic program of social reform that had come to my attention up to that time. Among the measures of reform there recommended were: government ownership and operation of natural monopolies, such as railroads, street railways, telegraph, telephone, lighting systems, coal mines, and forests; higher taxes on unused land held for speculative purposes, and a policy of leasing rather than selling publicly-owned lands; labor legislation and the eight-hour day, accident compensation, safety and sanitation in factories, abolition of sweatshops, legal requirement of one-day rest in seven, abolition of child labor, prohibition of night work to women and minors under eighteen, provision of government credits, and flexibility in the supply of money.

In the chapter on development of the social side of property, this volume calls for greater public regulation of the use of land and a progressive tax on inheritances. The social aspect of private ownership is developed in several paragraphs. Calling attention to the Christian doctrine that ownership is stewardship, the author declares that the presentation of the doctrine is ordinarily "so vague that it does not lead to a great amount of positive action," and that "an attempt on the part of the Church to make real the doctrine of stewardship would increase greatly the advantages of private property. . . ." These statements recall the pronouncements of Pope Pius XI in *Quadragesimo Anno* some thirty-seven years later:

It follows from the two-fold character of ownership, which We have termed individual and social, that men must take into account in this matter not only their own advantage but also the common good. To define in detail these duties, when the need occurs and when the natural law does not do so, is the function of the government. . . .

However, when civil authority adjusts ownership to meet the needs of the public good it acts not as an enemy, but as the friend of private owners; for thus it effectively prevents the possession of private property, intended by nature's Author in His wisdom for the sustaining of human life, from creating intolerable burdens and so rushing to its own destruction. It does not therefore abolish, but protects private ownership, and, far from weakening the right of private property, it gives it new strength.

Many of the reforms advocated by Dr. Ely in *Socialism and Social Reform,* for example, progressive taxation of inheritances and the various 'orms of social insurance, have since been enacted into law, and government ownership of public utilities has made some progress. When Dr. Ely published this book all his reform proposals were relatively new, had received very little attention from American economists, and to the average middle-class person still seemed "radical." Inasmuch as I accepted all of them and have never ceased to believe in any of them, at least in principle, the contribution which Dr. Ely made to my social education was very large, indeed.

THE DEMOCRATIC NATIONAL CONVENTION

The year 1896 brought a series of events which helped greatly to clarify and strengthen the views which I had gradually been adopting on economic questions, particularly on the relations between economics and politics. I allude to the Democratic National Convention of 1896, its platform, and the ensuing political campaign. The depression which had begun in 1893 was still extensive and intensive when the Democrats met at Chicago to name candidates for the Presidency and Vice-Presidency. And Grover Cleveland was in the White House.

In all the critical situations that he was compelled to face in his second administration (1893–1897), President Cleveland showed a remarkable capacity for doing the wrong thing. Only two of these blunders need be noticed here. He antagonized labor and mortally offended Governor Altgeld by sending federal troops into Chicago during the Pullman strike, disregarding the strong protest of the Governor, who insisted that the state militia of Illinois was fully competent to preserve order. In the second place, Cleveland permitted the banking interests of New York to dictate unfair terms for the purchase of federal bonds in order to replenish the dwindling supply of gold in the Treasury of the United States. Instead of yielding to this dictation, he should have tried to bring about the suspension of specie payments, the coinage of silver, and the provision of sufficient paper money to meet the country's commercial and financial needs. The latter course would have exemplified the policy of a "managed currency" which has since become fairly orthodox and which contained no serious element of danger even in 1895.

Through these and other blunders, by the middle of 1895, Cleveland had become widely discredited among his fellow Democrats. At the Chicago convention, a resolution commending "the honesty, economy, courage and fidelity of the present Democratic National Administration" was defeated by a vote of 564 to 357.

The platform adopted at the convention called for the "free and unlimited coinage of both silver and gold at the ratio of sixteen to one without waiting for the aid or consent of any other nation." Other important planks in the platform were: "opposition to the issuing of interest-bearing bonds of the United States in time of peace"; a tariff for revenue only; denunciation of the decision of the Supreme Court which declared the federal income tax unconstitutional; federal legislation providing for the arbitration of difficulties between employers and employees; enlargement of the powers of the Interstate Commerce Commission over the railroads; and abolition of government by injunction, as carried on by federal judges "in contempt of the laws of the states and the rights of citizens."

I recall clearly and almost vividly the proceedings of the

convention, including its domination by Governor Altgeld who there was avenged for his humiliation at the hands of Cleveland during the Pullman strike only two years previously; also, Bryan's famous "Crown of Thorns and Cross of Gold" speech which stampeded the convention into nominating him as its candidate for the Presidency. I fervently desired the triumph of Bryan and the other candidates who had accepted the Chicago platform because they defended the poor, the weak, and the oppressed; because they were opposing plutocracy and fighting for some measure of social justice. While I did not regard the money question as the most important issue between the two parties, I believed that the free coinage of silver would give the country a badly needed increase in basic money and halt the progressive enslavement of the farmers and of debtors through inadequate currency and continually decreasing prices. Recall that no central banking system then existed, nor any such thing as a flexible currency. Recall, moreover, that the theory of the silver advocates was vindicated substantially by the prosperity which presently followed the great increase in the supply of basic money resulting from the opening of the Rand gold fields in South Africa and the discovery of the cyanide process for treating low-grade ores. My main reason for desiring a Democratic victory was provided by the other planks of the platform enumerated above, and by the general fact that under the leadership of Bryan the Democratic party was battling for the common man against the unjust economic domination exercised by a few. The majority of Bryan's supporters were more concerned with this aspect of the contest than with the money question in general or free silver in particular. At that time, as now, it seemed clear to me that the directing minds in the Republican party recognized and were mainly concerned with this general issue and alignment. As Paxton Hibben wrote in *The Peerless Leader*:

The "gold standard" was, after all, largely a curtain behind which were concealed all the gigantic vested interests, built up with such appalling rapidity under benign Republican rule since the war between the states. It was not the Democratic platform that frightened the successful of the land out of their wits, but that Populist programme drawn up by the Hon. Lyman Trumbull and including such revolutionary items as a graduated income tax and the declaration that "the government should own and operate the railroads in the interests of the people."[7]

Since the campaign of 1896, I have never been seriously tempted to support the Republican party, for the simple reason that in the main its policies have been opposed to social justice. It has been the party of plutocracy rather than of the masses. In 1904, I did not vote the Democratic ticket because I realized that the party had temporarily become reactionary, but neither did I vote the Republican ticket. Theodore Roosevelt had not yet demonstrated the degree of progressiveness which he displayed later and which Paxton Hibben thus describes:

In Bryan's promise to support the measures of a Republican President there was no inconsistency. The truth was that Roosevelt was cleverly adopting and promoting measures originally blazoned on Bryan banners. Roosevelt was taking the road along which Bryan had, for twelve years, been trying to guide the Democratic party. Political observers knew it. Sydney Brooks pointed out that "Bryan's words and Roosevelt's deeds bear comparison." And the *New York Sun* asked querulously whether Mr. Bryan had flopped to Mr. Roosevelt or Mr. Roosevelt to Mr. Bryan.[8]

But Theodore Roosevelt's successors in the Republican party have not carried on his policies. Individuals have been conspicuous as progressives but they have always constituted a minority too weak to determine party courses of action. To be sure, there have been and are still too many reactionaries

[7] *The Peerless Leader, William Jennings Bryan,* by Paxton Hibben. Farrar and Rinehart, New York, 1929, p. 190.
[8] *Idem,* p. 260.

in the Democratic party, but with the exception of the years 1904 and 1924 they have not shaped its platforms or policies.

To the possible objection that the immediately preceding paragraphs describe not my social education but my political education, I would reply that the events and issues under consideration were basically economic. They involved the function of the state in relation to industry, and that is still one of our most important and difficult public questions. Whether one thinks of it as mainly political or mainly economic is not a matter of great importance.

My academic life at the St. Paul Seminary (1894–1898) was devoid of events or experiences that could be accounted either exceptional or noteworthy. I did not find any of the courses in the theological curriculum tedious or uninteresting, although I naturally had preferences among them. For example, I devoted an exceptional amount of time to the various theories then current on the inspiration of Scripture and to the different opinions concerning the effects of original sin. In passing, I would emphasize the fact that the student of theology is allowed a much greater freedom of opinion than the average person assumes. The official Catholic doctrines of faith and morals are, of course, binding upon all Catholics, lay and clerical, but there are a great number of related questions concerning which even the authoritative specialists are not in full agreement. In this broad field of theological opinion there are very few views for which a student cannot invoke the authority of a distinguished theologian, and frequently an entire "school" of theologians. Indeed, the student is occasionally tempted to wish that the area of disputed and free questions was not quite so comprehensive, and that the area of obligatory doctrine and theological unanimity was somewhat wider.

My deepest and most sustained interest, however, was not in questions of dogma or Scripture or church history, but in those treatises of moral theology which dealt with the morality of economic transactions; namely, those on justice and right and contracts. In this field my collateral reading took in not only the standard works of moral theology but also a fair amount of books and magazines which fell under the head of sociology and economics.

With each succeeding year of my theological studies, my desire and determination increased to devote as much time and labor to the study of economic conditions, institutions, and problems as would be possible and permitted after my ordination. I wanted to examine economic life in the light of Christian principles, with a view to making them operative in the realm of industry. It seemed to me that the salvation of millions of souls depended largely upon the economic opportunity to live decently, to live as human beings made in the image and likeness of God. That this is proper work for a priest, seemed clear to me from the teachings of ethics and moral theology: the moral law governs economic transactions, as well as every other sphere of conduct. In addition to this general truth, I had before me the specific exhortation and command of Pope Leo XIII. Near the close of his encyclical, "On the Condition of Labor," he declares: "At this moment the condition of the working population is the question of the hour; and nothing can be of higher interest to all classes of the State than that it should be rightly and reasonably decided." Having pointed out the parts to be taken in this task by the wage earners, by the employers, and by the state, he outlines the contribution to be made by the Church. "Every minister of Holy Religion," he says, "must throw into the conflict all the energy of his mind, and all the strength of his endurance. . . ." No man could have desired clearer or more authoritative encouragement than this.

At the time of my ordination to the priesthood at the St. Paul Seminary, June 4, 1898, I had just passed my twenty-ninth birthday anniversary. Therefore, I was some three years above the age at which the majority of students began their priestly careers. Had the authorities of St. Thomas Seminary and the St. Paul Seminary accepted the recommendations of my professors, I could have received Holy Orders when I was twenty-seven; for these professors believed that I could acquire by private study under their direction an adequate knowledge of the subjects presented in the classroom during one of my two years of college work and one of my four years as a student of theology. At that time, I strongly felt that the judgment of these professors was correct and that I ought to have been permitted to shorten my course of study and anticipate ordination by these two years. However, it is now many years since the matter has seemed of as much importance to me as it appeared when I was refused that opportunity. Possibly two additional years in the ministry would have been marked by solid achievement; possibly the preparatory work that actually occupied the years in question has enabled me to do more and better work in the long run. In any case, observation has persuaded me that a delay of one or two years in a man's entrance upon the work of his profession does not seem to him in later life nearly as detrimental as he regarded it when he was compelled to acquiesce in the postponement. Hindsight is better than foresight.

Immediately after ordination, Archbishop Ireland put me in charge of a small country parish for about three months. These were among the happiest weeks that I have ever known, not only because they introduced me to the life and the functions of the priesthood but also because the people to whom I ministered were simple, genuine, unsophisticated, and unspoiled. Nevertheless, I did not request, or even desire the opportunity to continue in parish work, for I had been notified before ordination that I was to take up a course of postgraduate study the following October at the Catholic University of America. I had also been informed that when my course at the University was completed, I should be appointed professor at the St. Paul Seminary. Both parts of the program coincided with my own preferences.

Chapter IV

AT THE CATHOLIC UNIVERSITY OF AMERICA
(1898–1902)

UNTIL I left home for the Catholic University, the latter part of September, 1898, I had never seen as large a city as Chicago. The two or three days that I spent in that metropolis on my way to Washington were extremely interesting. I still recall the powerful impression made upon me by the elevated railroads, the tall buildings, the lake front, the crowds and the noise, hurry, and bustle. At that time, no other large city offered a greater contrast with Chicago than was provided by Washington. Of course, neither city contained automobiles, but Washington lacked large apartment houses, masses of pedestrians, and real congestion. The leisurely manner in which the inhabitants and the visitors moved about the city was different from the street life of the big city on Lake Michigan. Indeed, the street life of Washington then differed greatly from its own street life in 1941. The pedestrians of that earlier day seemed to have all the time that existed.

Archbishop Ireland directed me to pursue the courses in moral theology at the University, but left me free with regard to other studies. In the School of Theology, at that time, candidates for degrees were obliged to study two and only two subjects. My preference for the second course was economics, but I found that arrangement impossible because the rules required that both the courses be taken in the School of Theology. For the second, or minor, subject, I chose canon law. However, students of theology were permitted to attend lectures in other schools in the University as auditors. Economics, sociology, and English were my selections for the optional courses, but economics received by far the greater amount of my time and attention. My instructor in economics was Dr. Charles P. Neill, later United States Commissioner of Labor; in sociology, Rev. Dr. William J. Kerby, founder of the National Conference of Catholic Charities; in English, the distinguished literateur, Maurice Francis Egan, subsequently appointed United States Minister to Denmark by President Theodore Roosevelt.

The most fortunate experience in my student life at the University was association with the Very Rev. Dr. Thomas Joseph Bouquillon, professor of moral theology from 1889 until his death in 1902. He was the most erudite man that I have ever known. He was also one of the most conscientious and most scientific in the best sense of the term. He never came into the classroom without scrupulous preparation of the material upon which he was to lecture. He had a passion for exactness, for accuracy, and for thoroughness, and he constantly emphasized the importance of these qualities. His lectures and seminars were especially helpful to me because they gave comprehensive attention to social problems. Whenever he had to apply a moral rule or principle to economic or social conditions, he set forth in specific terms the pertinent economic or social transaction or institution. In other words, he took adequate account and gave an adequate description of the economics or the sociology as well as the ethics of the problem. He was not satisfied with merely general knowledge of the nonethical factors. My indebtedness to him because of his devotion to and exemplification of this method is much greater than I can describe.

Two other men who greatly helped and influenced me during those student years at the University differed entirely from my professors and from each other. They were both English-men: W. J. Ashley, later Sir William Ashley, and John A. Hobson. Ashley's great work *English Economic History*, gave me a fair introduction to the medieval economic system of the guilds, to the teaching of the medieval canonists and theo-logians on the morality of economic practices and institutions, and to the principles and spirit of the Catholic social tradition. The comfort which I derived from reading those volumes is still vivid in my memory. Ashley died in 1927 at the age of sixty-five.

John A. Hobson was born at Derby, England, in 1858 and died in London, in March, 1940. He was the author of up-wards of a score of books and many score of magazine arti-cles, the great majority in both categories dealing with eco-nomic subjects. The book of his that first fell into my hands was the *Evolution of Modern Capitalism*, published in 1894. It seemed to me that this volume described and explained the structure and development of the modern economic system in a way comparable with the treatment of the precapitalist systems by Ashley, Cunningham, Levasseur, and other eco-nomic historians. Some years later, I found in his work, *The Industrial System* (1909), the most satisfactory analysis that I had ever seen of the way in which the system works, and the most persuasive exposure of its principal defects. His *Eco-nomics of Distribution* which I read soon after it appeared in 1900, struck me as the most intelligible and suggestive work that had come to my attention in this department of eco-nomic theory.

More than twenty-five years ago, I drafted a dedication which I thought of using (but ultimately did not use) for my book, *Distributive Justice*. It reads as follows: "To John A. Hobson, whose illuminating analysis of the economics of pro-duction and distribution has greatly facilitated the author's attempt to determine the morality of these processes."

The part of Mr. Hobson's economic doctrine which interested me most when I was a student at the University, is also the part to which I have given most attention ever since, and for which my indebtedness to him is greatest. I allude to his theory that underconsumption and oversaving are the main causes of industrial slumps and depressions. It was first set forth by Mr. Hobson in a book which he produced jointly with a businessman named A. F. Mummery. This volume was entitled *The Physiology of Industry* and was published in 1889. Subsequently, Hobson restated, amplified, and defended the theory in many other productions, chiefly *The Evolution of Modern Capitalism, The Problem of the Unemployed* (1896), and *Economics of Unemployment* (1922). However, the theory of underconsumption and oversaving was not invented by either Hobson or Mummery, for it had been expounded and defended, at least in substance, by the Earl of Lauderdale, Malthus, and Chalmers, in Great Britain, by Sismondi in Switzerland, and by Von Kirchmann and Father Franz Hitze in Germany. The first four of these wrote in the first quarter of the nineteenth century, the fifth about 1830 and the last in 1880. Under the influence of J. B. Say, John Stuart Mill, and David Ricardo, however, the classical economists completely rejected this theory, mainly by ignoring it. They held that no matter how much of the national income was saved and converted into instruments of production, the resulting product would always find buyers, somehow, somewhere. Commenting on their failure to deal formally with the underconsumption theory, John Maynard Keynes remarks: "Their method was to dismiss the problem from the *corpus* of economics not by solving it but by not mentioning it."[1]

[1] *The General Theory of Unemployment, Interest, and Money*, p. 364. It should be noted that among American economists there was at least one exception to this generalization. In his work, *Economics*, published in 1896, Professor A. T. Hadley said (p. 147): "The modern civilized world is in perpetual danger of under-consumption. Too many of its members use their supplies of products, not to purchase the consumable products of others, but to duplicate machinery and other permanent investments."

When I first met Hobson, at the Liberal Club in London, in 1922, I asked him whether the great destruction of capital during the then recent war had not weakened his theory of oversaving. He replied in the negative, and added that he was about to publish a restatement of the theory which would take adequate account of the new situation, without surrendering anything essential. Those who have read his *Economics of Unemployment* realize how well he carried out that purpose. Indeed, the task was not difficult, for the wartime destruction of capital did not abolish the disproportion between saving and spending. The masses were still without sufficient income to enable them to buy all the products of even the shrunken volume of capital and the reduced volume of savings and investment. The great problem was still that of properly dividing the national product and the national income between savers and consumers. So far as employment and prosperity were concerned, the relation between the total amount of capital in existence after and before the war was, in most of the countries of Europe, of only secondary importance.

In the decade of 1920–1930, I met Mr. Hobson several times in Washington, where he was delivering a course of lectures at the Brookings Institution. At that time I heard him surprise a very prominent fellow Englishman by declaring that it might have been better for the world if the United States had not participated in the Great War; for in that case, said Mr. Hobson, "we might have got a negotiated peace, instead of the peace that we did get." Other pleasant recollections of him derive from visits at his home in Hampstead in 1932 and 1938.

For more than three decades, Hobson's exposition and defense of the theory which we are considering was as widely ignored by contemporary economists as had been the writings of the earlier protagonists of the theory by Ricardo, John Stuart Mill, and the other great authorities of the Classical

School. Soon after the beginning of the 1929–1933 depression, however, many economists began to notice the theory; subsequently a few accepted it with modifications. Probably the most distinguished names in the latter category are J. M. Keynes in England and Alvin H. Hansen in the United States. The new attitude is significantly indicated in the following extract from a short article in the July, 1940, issue of the *Journal of Social Philosophy,* by Professor John Maurice Clark:

Today, the central idea of Hobson's original heresy has been adopted in altered form and with a shifted emphasis by economists of unquestioned standing and around it centers also perhaps the most active and frontier economic thinking. Serious investigation of this former heresy has become unqualifiedly respectable.[2]

Soon after I had become acquainted with Hobson's writings, I realized that this theory of underconsumption and oversaving was the most satisfying explanation that I had yet seen of industrial depressions and unemployment. From his statement of it in *The Problem of the Unemployed* I selected four pages (pp. 169–172) for insertion in my first book, *A Living Wage.* In a footnote to the quoted paragraphs I wrote:

Professor Smart observes that this theory has not met with the attention that it deserves. Anyone who will carefully examine it cannot fail to be impressed with its superior value as an explanation of the phenomena that constitute an industrial depression.[3]

[2] Heresy in religion is unwarranted and irrational because it opposes infallible pronouncements; heresy in economics may be and sometimes is in accord with truth, because the exponents of the "orthodox" doctrine do not enjoy the prerogative of infallibility. Some economic doctrines are "orthodox" merely because their recognized protagonists are too conventionally minded, too timid, too slothful, too uncritical or too unprogressive. In more than one instance I have professed heresies in economics and politics because they seemed to me to reflect more comprehensive investigation and deeper thinking. To prevailing or dominant opinions I have always been willing to concede some degree of presumption but no necessary certainty.

[3] When I congratulated Mr. Hobson, in 1932, on the improved attitude of the economists toward his underconsumption theory, he replied, with a wistful smile: "Yes, but it has taken almost fifty years of constant argument to win this small measure of assent." Even so, he was more successful than many other champions of unpopular and unprofessional doctrines.

Although I have read carefully most of the criticisms of the theory by both economists and businessmen, I have not been tempted to abandon it. Most of the attacks are indirect, partial, unfair, or supercilious. In many cases, they rest upon a naive faith that somehow, somewhere, new industrial inventions will be forthcoming to absorb the excessive savings and to lure money from the pockets of those who cannot or will not spend it for the commodities that are currently produced; or the criticisms are based upon an empty hope that the mysterious and intangible thing called "confidence" will somehow obtain sufficient potency to induce men to convert savings into new investments, even though they have no solid ground for expecting that the products thereof will find buyers. Most owners of capital and most receivers of profits reject Hobson's theory as the basis of a remedy for unemployment because they realize that as a consequence they would receive a smaller share, while labor and the farmers would get a larger share, of the national income.

For more than fifteen years, I have steadily and consistently defended the theory of underconsumption and oversaving, in books, articles, and speeches. Following is a fairly recent statement of my views on the subject:

What do I mean by "bad distribution"? Simply that the actual division of the product of industry among our industrial groups prevents our industrial plant from operating continuously. The actual distribution gives to one group of income receivers more than they can spend for goods of any sort, and to two other groups less than they could and would spend if they had the money. The first group does not want to spend more for consumption goods and cannot spend all its savings for capital goods, that is, in the form of business investments. The second and third groups would like to buy more consumption goods but cannot do so because they have not the requisite purchasing power. The first group is composed of those who receive interest, rent and profits; the second and third groups comprise, respectively, wage earners and farmers. Speaking generally but not quite accurately, we may say that capital receives too much purchasing power and labor too little.[4]

One of the prerequisites to the degree of Licentiate in Theology, which I received from the Catholic University in June, 1900, was the production of a dissertation or essay within the candidate's major branch of study. My effort was entitled, "Moral Aspects of Speculation on the Exchanges." Some of the conclusions which I put into this production ran counter to the economic defenses of speculation then prevailing. Thirty-three years later, these conclusions received a considerable measure of support in the Securities and Exchange Acts. The final paragraph of the dissertation reads as follows:

The question—"Is speculation wrong?"—cannot, therefore, be answered categorically. The phenomena with which it deals are too complex. But, with the help of the distinctions above drawn, an answer may be obtained that is fairly definite. To resume, then: speculation as an institution is *economically* of doubtful utility; *socially,* it is productive of great and widespread evils; and *morally,* it is vitiated by a very considerable amount of dishonest "deals" and practices.[5]

In the fall of 1900, I became the beneficiary of a fortunate combination of circumstances. According to Archbishop Ireland's intention, I was to spend only two years as a postgraduate student at the Catholic University. At the end of that period I was to be given a teaching position in St. Paul. However, the Archbishop had not made the appointment, nor even mentioned the matter to me, before he departed for Europe in the late summer of 1900. When the end of September arrived, leaving me still without any official assignment, I faced the necessity of deciding whether I should stay in St. Paul until the Archbishop's return from Europe or assume that he was now willing to grant me a longer period of study at the University. Giving myself the benefit of the doubt, I went back to Washington in time for the opening

[4] "Can Unemployment Be Ended?" April 8, 1940.
[5] *The Church and Socialism and Other Essays,* 1919, p. 179.

of the scholastic year. Shortly after his return to St. Paul, sometime in November, the Archbishop wrote me to the effect that his failure to give me a teaching assignment before he had left the country was due to inadvertence, but that since I was back at the University, I might remain there for the rest of the year. As a matter of fact, he permitted me to remain for two years longer.

Had I been compelled to terminate my studies at the University in 1900, my subsequent activities in economic and social fields would probably have been considerably handicapped and restricted, inasmuch as my teaching assignment would not have included any of the social sciences. In the second place, and more important, I should have been deprived of the opportunity to continue my ethical and social studies under favorable conditions. Moreover, I could not have produced the doctoral dissertation into which I put the greater part of my social doctrine and which for many years was the principal source of whatever influence I exerted upon social and economic thought and practice.

November, 1900, saw the appearance of my first magazine article. It received first place in that issue of the *Catholic World* and was entitled "A Country Without Strikes," being a review of the book with the same title, by Henry Demarest Lloyd. My article presented the main provisions of the compulsory arbitration law which New Zealand had enacted in 1894; noted its successful operation up to 1900, when Lloyd's book was published; described the specific benefits which the new legislation brought to women workers and the fairness of its administration; defended its morality as against freedom of contract; pointed out the superiority of compulsory arbitration over strikes, as an instrument of impartial justice; emphasized the lack of equal bargaining power between employer and employee; praised the enforcement of the minimum-wage principle in the administration of the law and the decisions of the arbitration courts, and pronounced the enactment a "splendid success."

Three matters in this article deserve brief comment in view of positions that I have taken subsequently. The first is the defense of state interference with freedom of contract. On this topic, I said:

> The right to contract freely is therefore, like every other right, limited. . . . Suppose that the state finds that one of the parties is insisting upon an unreasonable freedom of contract, upon a conception of his individual liberty that encroaches upon the individual liberty and rights of others, and suppose that the party whose rights are being violated by such insistence is the public, the state itself—is the state powerless to defend its own rights? Certainly it is not. For instance, if the community is put to great inconvenience by a strike, the state has surely the right to interfere, and even compel the disputants to accept the decision of a disinterested arbiter. This interference will, indeed, be a limitation of the right of free contract; it will prevent both sides, perhaps, from entering the precise contract desired by each—but the right of free contract is, as a matter of fact, a limited right. Neither employer nor employees live unto themselves; they have obligations to the community. And the community has a right to insist on the fulfillment of these obligations. . . .
>
> The whole argument for an unlimited right of free contract is based on a false assumption, the assumption that in all agreements between labor and capital the contract is really free. As a matter of fact whenever an employer, relying on an overstocked labor market, forces his men to accede to his terms, the name free contract is a misnomer. There can be no freedom of contract between laborers who must work today or starve and a capitalist who may pay the wages demanded or wait until hunger compels the men to submit. And, as the labor market is overstocked the greater part of the time, the employer's plea for noninterference and freedom of contract is in reality a demand that he be allowed to use his economic advantage to force his men into a contract that on their side is not free in any adequate sense of that word. I use the words "economic advantage" advisedly, for most political economists, I think, agree that the capitalist does possess an advantage over the laborer in the economic struggle.

Secondly, I wish to present the statements that I made on minimum wages for labor and fair profits for the employer:

The fixing of wages by compulsory arbitration includes, as a matter of course, the fixing of a minimum wage. Such has been the invariable rule of the New Zealand Court of Arbitration. This recognition of the minimum wage by public law is in itself a great advance toward the reign of justice in the world of industry. It means that the state pronounces unlimited competition immoral; for it fixes a limit below which the laborer's wage may not be forced. This policy is indeed contrary to the principles of that antiquated political economy of which I spoke above, but it is in agreement with the principles of sound morality. . . .

The New Zealand law does more than recognize the right of the laborer to a minimum wage. It authorizes the court to award fair profits to the employer, thus assuming that there is such a thing as excessive profits. Indeed, the whole difficulty that is expressed in the phrases, "the labor question" and "the social question," may be summed up in one sentence: "Capital gets too large a share of the wealth that it helps to create." The history of the New Zealand Court of Arbitration shows that in most of the disputes it has acknowledged this complaint to be true. Hence it has not hesitated to lower profits and raise wages where the conditions seemed to justify this course.

Finally, I have to note my gradual abandonment, in later years, of the central position taken in this article and my adoption of the view that compulsory arbitration is not generally feasible or desirable. In the *Dearborn Independent,* April 29, 1922, I criticized the industrial court of Kansas, which had powers of compulsory arbitration, on the ground that this tribunal was not provided with legal standards or principles to guide it in making its decisions. In other words, it lacked an industrial code. The only guidance which the court had from the enabling act was the requirement that it should "award fair and reasonable wages to labor and a fair return to capital." It left the interpretation and application of these concepts to the ethical intuitions of the court.

As I look at the situation now, I believe that even if equipped with a comprehensive and fair industrial code, such, for example, as that recommended for the coal industry by Senator Kenyon almost twenty years ago, no arbitration board or court should have the final power of legally compelling the disputants to accept its findings. Organized labor unanimously rejects the proposal and probably the great majority of employers take the same attitude. This is an objection which, in the United States at any rate, renders compulsory arbitration impracticable.

Moreover, it is unnecessary. No major strike has occurred . on our railroads since the enactment of the Railroad Mediation Act about fifteen years ago, for the simple reason that the law provides so many preliminary and intermediate processes that before a strike or lockout becomes really imminent, the decision of the mediating board is accepted by both parties. The provisions of this Act are practically far superior to complete compulsory arbitration.

During the first three decades of the University's existence, a candidate for the degree of Doctor of Theology was required to spend four years "in residence." That is, he was obliged to follow lectures in his major subject for that length of time. The second prerequisite was submission to an oral examination which lasted six hours and covered the whole field of the sacred sciences. The third and most exacting condition was the production of an original work of scientific merit and respectable length.

In October, 1900, I selected with the approval of my academic superiors as the subject of my doctoral dissertation "A Living Wage: Its Ethical and Economic Aspects." The suggestion of this subject came to me from the encyclical of Pope Leo XIII "On the Condition of Labor," particularly from that famous passage which reads as follows:

Let it be granted, then, that, as a rule, workman and employer should make free agreements, and in particular should freely agree as to wages;

nevertheless, there is a dictate of nature more imperious and more ancient than any bargain between man and man, that the remuneration must be enough to support the wage earner in reasonable and frugal comfort. If through necessity or fear of a worse evil, the workman accepts harder conditions because an employer or contractor will give him no better, he is the victim of force and injustice.

As the explanatory part of the title implies, the dissertation involved a great deal of economic study and investigation. When the work was finished I had a much wider knowledge of economic theory and practice than I had possessed at its inception. As an illustration of the purely economic study which went into the making of the volume, I cite the contentious topic of "value." On that subject, I must have read more than five thousand printed pages in the productions of economists of every school. I spent such a great amount of time and thought on this topic because I assumed for a time that economic value had an essential relation to ethical value or just price. As a matter of fact, the two concepts differ completely from each other and rest upon entirely different foundations. The economic value of a commodity, or its exchange value, may sometimes be identical with its ethical value or just price. But the manner in which the former is determined throws no light upon the problem of determining the latter. This statement applies likewise to the relation between the market value and the ethical value or just price of labor. Theories of economic value do not enable us to know the ethical value of labor in terms of price; nor do they give us adequate information concerning the moral responsibility of the employer, the consumer, or the state for unjustly low wages; nor do they tell us how to bring about a regime of just wages. A theory of value, whether it be cost of production, marginal utility, or any other, is merely an attempt to explain why a commodity has its present value in an economic system ruled by competition. It is merely a description of the factors, economic, psychological, and other, which cause present economic values to be what they are. It is an attempt to account for what *is,* not a declaration of what *ought to be.*

Therefore, I derived no direct help in the task of writing the dissertation from my study of the various theories of value. As I recall, my final disillusionment on this score occurred when I read these words of Boehm-Bawerk: "The law of price may be correctly though less expressly and less unambiguously formulated in terms of supply and demand." Since price, at least market price, is merely the monetary expression of economic value, the words just quoted apply to the latter as well as to the former. I found that when dealing with the unjustly low wages which were due to competition, the economic conditions of the problem could be stated much more clearly and conveniently in terms of supply and demand than in terms of any theory of value. So far as the relevant ethical judgments depend upon economic factors, they involve mainly the problem of changing the existing relations between supply and demand through labor unions, concerted action by employers, or the intervention of the state. To the formulation of such ethical judgments and conclusions, theories of value are entirely irrelevant.

Sterile as I found theories of value for the purposes of the dissertation, the time that I spent upon them was not entirely wasted. It provided a means of mental discipline and an introduction to the method, spirit, and limitations of economic theory in general. As mental discipline, the study of theories of economic value is at least as useful as the legendary researches and discussions of medieval philosophers concerning the number of angels who could simultaneously and comfortably stand on the point of a needle.

Some idea of the ground covered and the method followed in writing the dissertation may be obtained from the titles of the four sections into which the work was divided. Each section was subdivided into several chapters: Section I, "Introductory and Historical"; Section II, "The Basis, Nature, and Content of the Right to a Living Wage"; Section III, "Economic Facts by Which the Right is Conditioned"; Section IV, "The Obligations Corresponding to the Right."

On the basis of length of residence I was entitled to receive the doctor's degree in June, 1902, but I could not then fulfill the other two conditions. I was not prepared to pass the final examination nor had I put the finishing touches upon the dissertation. When I requested from my Archbishop permission to spend a fifth year at the university in order to supply these deficiencies, he demurred, expressing the opinion that it was time for me to "come home and go to work." While I was considerably disappointed over this decision, I realized that it was reasonable. Later on I had occasion to look back upon it with feelings of positive complacency.

When I bade final farewell to the Catholic University as a student in June, 1902, I took with me nothing but pleasant recollections. Intellectually and scholastically, I had obtained greater benefits from the years that I spent under the roof of Caldwell Hall than I had thought possible. The advantages of access to the Library of Congress and of hearing the debates in Congress, were great and evident. One speech that I heard in the Senate is still clear in my memory. It was delivered by Charles A. Towne, who for a few months was a senator from my own state. In this address, Senator Towne opposed the ratification of the peace treaty ending the Spanish-American War, because he was not in favor of American acquisition of the Philippine Islands. Although he read his speech and took three hours in its delivery, all but a half a dozen of the occupants of the Senate gallery, several of them standing, remained in their places until he had finished. It was a great triumph for an oration that was constructed on the classical rather than on the modern model.

At that time, senators were chosen by the state legislatures instead of by the popular vote, but I do not think that the general average of the body was any higher than it is now, either in ability or patriotism, and it was much lower in its comprehension of economic issues and its views on social justice.

Chapter V

EARLY YEARS AS PROFESSOR: PUBLICATION OF
A LIVING WAGE

WHEN I began to teach in St. Paul Seminary in September, 1902, I found myself again favored by fortune. Two years earlier, I had been enabled to return to the Catholic University as a student instead of becoming an instructor in subjects outside the field of my predilection. Happily, my teaching assignment in 1902 was within that field. In the St. Paul Seminary at that time, moral theology was divided into two main sections, each of which covered a period of two years. The instruction given in the second of these periods dealt with the sacraments, while that of the first two years comprehended the treatises on the fundamental principles of right conduct, the norm of morality, human acts, laws, conscience, virtues and vices, justice and right, and contracts. The professor who had been teaching these courses greatly desired to continue in that division of the Department of Moral Theology, but Archbishop Ireland insisted upon his transfer to the division which dealt with the sacraments, because he was considerably older than I and presumably better fitted to handle such subjects as matrimony and penance. Naturally, I rejoiced in the relative youth and immaturity which were responsible for assigning to me the subjects which I preferred above all others. In an earlier paragraph I have mentioned the fact that I added to the traditional branches of instruction elementary courses in economics and sociology. This, I believe, was the first time that these sub-

78

jects were taught in any ecclesiastical seminary in the United States.

At this time I was hoping to begin almost immediately the task of revising and completing my doctoral dissertation. It seemed to me not impossible that I should find time to do this and also to equip myself to pass the final examination at the Catholic University by the end of the scholastic year 1902–1903. As a matter of fact, all my time and energy during that and the following year were required for the preparation of my lectures for the classroom. Hence I was unable to turn my attention to the unfinished work connected with my pursuit of the doctorate until the beginning of my third year of teaching, when the cycle of courses was completed and I could utilize the lectures already written. When I took up the task of what I expected to be merely that of revision, I realized that such moderate changes in the dissertation would be entirely inadequate. I found that it had to be completely rewritten. This work, together with that of preparing for the examination, occupied most of my spare time during my third and fourth years as professor in the St. Paul Seminary.

On May 31, 1906, at the Catholic University, I successfully defended seventy-five theses, twenty of which were taken from the dissertation, while the other fifty-five represented all branches of the sacred sciences, apologetics, sacred Scripture, dogmatic theology, moral theology, canon law, and church history. On June 6, I received the degree S.T.D., that is, Doctor of Sacred Theology. One of my examiners was Rev. Dr. Richard L. Burtsell, who had been Dr. McGlynn's canon lawyer during his years of trouble.

Thus, eight years had elapsed from the time my postgraduate studies were begun until they were crowned by the highest academic honor bestowed by the Catholic University. Nevertheless, I never regretted that long interval. Had I received the doctor's degree at the end of my fourth year at the

University, or even at the end of a fifth if I had been permitted to spend it there, I know that the dissertation would have been much poorer in quality. Although I was thirty-seven years of age when I published the dissertation, I did not then feel nor have I ever felt since that life was too short to have spent so much of it in the task of preparation.

The only important thing that I published during these first four years as professor in the St. Paul Seminary was an article entitled "The Small Family and National Decadence." It appeared in the *American Ecclesiastical Review,* February, 1904. At the beginning of this production, I called attention to the "abnormal" decline in the birth rate of families where the parents were native-born; identified as the main cause of the decline the immoral practice of birth control; and declared that the resulting small family system "tends inevitably to the degeneracy and extinction of the human race." Fully four-fifths of the article was an elaboration of the proposition that the small family system is both cause and effect, principally cause, of "enervating self-indulgence," which is bringing about "a decline not merely in the number but in the quality of our people." The damaging effects of deliberately arranged small families were described in considerable detail as regards the parents, the children, and the nation.

In the years that have since passed, I have produced scores of articles and speeches against birth control. In some of them, I have emphasized phases of the subject that I scarcely touched in the 1904 production, but in none of them did I deal quite so thoroughly or so effectively with the physically and morally degenerative effects of this pestilential practice.

When my very good friend, Dr. Richard T. Ely, undertook to find a publisher for my dissertation in the latter part of the year 1905, he encountered some difficulty. Two of the largest publishers in the United States were unwilling to undertake the venture. Both were of the opinion that the sales would not be sufficiently numerous to make it profitable. Dr. Ely was greatly disappointed with this decision and remarked in a letter to me, "I was enthusiastic about the book and said all I could in its favor." He then suggested to these two firms that I might be willing to pay for manufacturing the plates. In a letter announcing the agreement of both publishers to that proposal, Dr. Ely said: "For my part, I am more hopeful than either one of the publishers concerning the sale of your book, but, of course, I must acknowledge that they have had far larger experience." I readily agreed to this arrangement and the work was published by The Macmillan Company, in April, 1906.

Concerning the volume of sales achieved by the book, Dr. Ely was right and the publishers were wrong. It attained a circulation which was considerably larger than that of the majority of works of its character outside the field of textbooks. One non-Catholic reviewer described it as, "probably the most thorough discussion and defense of the laborer's right to a decent livelihood that has appeared in any language." A Catholic professor said: "The field he has chosen is practically unbroken ground. . . . But in spite of these difficulties, Dr. Ryan has attacked the problem with the true spirit of a pioneer, handling them with a courage and frankness which are admirable." A few, a very few, Catholic reviewers rejected some of the ethical propositions in the book, but these critics have since been refuted and discredited by much higher authorities. For example, one Catholic professor objected to the principle that in the distribution of the produce the employer-capitalist has no right to any interest until all his employees have received living wages. In *The Church and Social Order,* however, the Archbishops and Bishops of the Administrative Board of the National Catholic Welfare Conference lay down this proposition: "The first claim of labor, which takes priority over any claim of the owners to

profits, respects the right to a living wage." (Paragraph 40.)
Two or three other Catholics denied that the claim to a living
wage is one of strict justice. Nevertheless, in the encyclical on
"Atheistic Communism," Pope Pius XI refers to "the salary
due in strict justice to the worker for himself and his family."
(Paragraph 31.)

The few reviewers who based their dissents upon economic
theory were all Englishmen. For example, one London journal objected to the proposal "to graft the living wage on to
the existing system which . . . is in reality indestructible in
its main features, based as it is on certain cardinal and eternal
principles of human nature. . . . Economics having no relation with ethics, ethical economics cannot be scientific." If
the man who wrote those sentences in August, 1906, is still
living, he probably finds his faith considerably shaken in the
"indestructibility" of the existing system, whatever he may
think about the relation between ethics and economics.

Although this was the first book in the English language to
advocate a legally established, compulsory minimum wage
sufficient for the decent maintenance of the worker's family
as well as of himself, no Catholic reviewer and few non-
Catholics dissented. No American reviewer and only one
Englishman rejected the estimate of six hundred dollars a year
for a family as too high.

In 1909, *A Living Wage* appeared in a Spanish translation
and a French version was published in 1910. The latter included a Preface of some forty pages by Lucien Brocard. One
paragraph of M. Brocard's contribution is well worth insertion here.

Dr. Ryan is not among those who would return to the social traditions of the Middle Ages. The American people are too deliberately
turned toward the future, they have too clearly broken with European
traditions for one to find even among the most traditionally minded of
them the least predilection for the institutions of the past. Dr. Ryan

also separates himself very frankly from some social Catholics of socialistic tendency; he does not even cooperate with them; at least, one does not find in his book any aspiration toward a socialistic state from which the capitalist system of enterprise would be banned. Nevertheless, he separates himself no less frankly from some social Catholics whose tendency is toward conservatism. His reformist spirit is not exactly timid, inasmuch as he attacks a problem which in Europe, at least, the legislator has not yet dared to confront. Dr. Ryan places himself then among the social Catholics who adhere with the greatest firmness to a program sufficiently variable, following the exponents and the methods of state intervention. In a word, we have here a moralist who does not abandon moral principles and who desires at all costs that the essential moral principles should not remain a dead letter. Having shown through the experience of many centuries that the method of persuasion serves only to cause the precepts to be forgotten instead of assuring their application, he devotes himself to the task of restoring the precepts to a place of honor and insuring their observance, by coercion. His endeavor to reach some practical solutions and to utilize all the benefits of human experience has made of him a very competent economist who proves by his example that political economy and ethics can, as someone has said, manage well together and have a supreme interest in joining hands.[1]

Following is the summary of the main propositions of the book which appeared in its concluding chapter. In subsequent writings, I have elaborated and expanded many of these propositions, but I have abandoned none of them nor have I modified any of them substantially:

The main argument of this volume may be summarized as follows: the laborer's right to a Living Wage is the specific form of his generic right to obtain on reasonable conditions sufficient of the earth's products to afford him a decent livelihood. The latter right is, like all other moral rights, based on his intrinsic worth as a person, and on the sacredness of those needs that are essential to the reasonable development of personality. Among the things to which these needs point there is included a certain amount of material goods. A man's right to this indispensable minimum of the bounty of nature is as valid as his right to

[1] *Salaire et Droit a L'Existence*, Paris, 1910, pp. XLI, XLII.

life: the difference is merely in degree of importance. Now when the man whose social and economic function is that of a wage earner has expended all his working time and energy in the performance of some useful task, he has fulfilled the only condition that in his case can be regarded as a reasonable prerequisite to the actual enjoyment of his right to a decent livelihood. The *obligation* of providing him with the material means of living decently rests in a general way upon all his fellow men. That is to say, they are all under moral restraint not to do anything that would be an unreasonable interference with his access to these means. However, it is only those persons who are in control of the goods and opportunities of living that are practicably within his reach, who can effectively hinder or promote his enjoyment of the right in question. When they prevent him from peaceably getting possession of the requisite amount of goods, they are morally responsible for his failure to obtain a decent livelihood. Their action is as unjust as that of the majority of the first occupants of a No-man's Land who should force the minority to work for a bare subsistence. This specific obligation of the class of persons that we are considering falls primarily upon the employer; for his economic position as direct beneficiary of the laborer's exertion and as payer of wages, renders this the only practicable outcome of any reasonable division of the community's opportunities of living and of the corresponding responsibilities. Nor can the employer escape this duty of paying a Living Wage by taking refuge behind the terms of a so-called free contract. The fact is that the underpaid laborer does not *willingly* sell his labor for less than the equivalent of a decent livelihood, any more than the wayfarer willingly gives up his purse to the highwayman. It is the superior *economic force* (which consists essentially in the ability to wait, while the laborer must go to work today or starve) possessed by the employer that enables him to hire labor for less than a Living Wage. And the employer who can afford to pay a Living Wage is no more justified in using his superior economic strength in this way than he would be justified in using superior physical strength to prevent the laborer from taking possession of a sack of flour or a suit of clothes that the latter had bought and paid for. In both cases the laborer is deprived by superior strength of something to which he has the right. As a determinant of rights, economic force has no more validity or sacredness than physical force. The other economic classes in the community, the landowner, the loan-capitalist, the consumer and the man of wealth, share the responsibility of providing the laborer with a decent livelihood in a secondary degree, and in accordance with the nature and possibilities of their several economic positions. Finally, the State is morally bound to compel employers to pay a Living Wage whenever and wherever it can, with a moderate degree of success, put into effect the appropriate legislation.[2]

[2] *A Living Wage,* 1906, pp. 324-326. Reprinted through the courtesy of The Macmillan Company.

CHAPTER VI

IN THE FIELD OF ORGANIZED CHARITY

SOON after *A Living Wage* was published, I began to take considerable interest in charitable activities and particularly in the theory and practice of organized charity. This interest grew naturally out of my concern with living wages and with industrial reform generally. A minimum just wage, the alleviation of poverty, and relief for needy individuals, are interrelated concepts; the actions and policies which they involve all aim at the uplifting of ill-fed, ill-clothed, and ill-housed men, women, and children to a level of existence worthy of creatures made in the image and likeness of God. The motive of charity does, indeed, differ from that of justice: in the former case, it is brotherly love; in the latter it is personal dignity, equality, and independence. Charity contemplates the human needs as those of a brother, while justice regards them as affecting an independent person endowed with rights; but the needs in both situations are or can be identical.

To be sure, charity is not an adequate substitute for justice. In his encyclical *Quadragesimo Anno,* Pius XI declares: "Charity cannot take the place of justice unfairly withheld."[1] On an earlier page of the same document, Pope Pius had written:

Towards the close of the nineteenth century the new economic methods and the new development of industry had sprung into being in almost all civilized nations, and had made such headway that human society appeared more and more divided into two classes. The first,

[1] N.C.W.C. edition, p. 44.

small in numbers, enjoyed practically all the comforts so plentifully supplied by modern invention. The second class, comprising the immense multitude of workingmen, was made up of those who, oppressed by dire poverty, struggled in vain to escape from the straits which encompassed them.

This state of things was quite satisfactory to the wealthy, who looked upon it as the consequence of inevitable and natural economic laws, and who, therefore, were content to abandon to charity alone the full care of relieving the unfortunate, as though it were the task of charity to make amends for the open violation of justice, a violation not merely tolerated, but sanctioned at times by legislators.[2]

The assumption that the "full care of relieving the unfor-   ˇ tunate" belongs to charity and charitable agencies alone, was for a long time "tolerated" and "sanctioned" not only by legislators but by the leaders of organized charity. Both in Great Britain and in the United States, these men ignored or were ignorant of the relation between social distress and economic injustice. They endeavored to remove the causes, as they saw them, of individual dependency and individual distress, but they gave very little attention to the social and economic causes. They regarded the indigence which they sought to relieve as due mainly to individual fault and individual misfortune. By 1906, however, this attitude had un-ˇ dergone a considerable change. Many of the ablest leaders in the field of charity or social work had come to recognize the inadequateness, indeed, the essential falsity of the traditional assumptions about the causes of poverty. Discussing English conditions and attitudes in 1908, a historian of English philanthropy, B. Kirkman Gray, mentioned the formerly prevailing "notion that poverty and the diseases now known to be consequent on poverty, were usually the result of personal misdemeanor on the part of the sufferer." Continuing, he noted:

It is now generally recognized that in addition to such want as results to the ill-doer from his own ill-doing there is a vast amount of

[2] *Idem*, p. 4.

suffering which comes from general social causes; and for which the sufferer is responsible either remotely or not at all.[3]

In the United States, the most striking expression of the new attitude came from Dr. Edward T. Devine, in his presidential address at the Thirty-third Annual Session of the National Conference of Charities and Correction in Philadelphia, in 1906:

If I have rightly conceived the dominant idea of the modern philanthropy it is embodied in a determination to *seek out and to strike effectively at those organized forces of evil, at those particular causes of dependence and intolerable living conditions which are beyond the control of the individuals whom they injure and whom they too often destroy.*

Other tasks for other ages. This be the glory of ours, that the social causes of dependence shall be destroyed.[4]

Although I had not read the foregoing sentences when I delivered a short address before the National Conference at its meeting in Minneapolis the following year, I had adopted substantially the same view. My subject was "The Standard of Living and the Problem of Dependency." The following extract from the first paragraph expresses the main thought of the address:

Intelligent students and workers in the field of charitable effort no longer impute all pauperism and poverty to deficiencies in the individual. They realize that a considerable proportion of dependency occurs despite the utmost efforts of the individual, despite the absence of unusual sickness, accidents or other misfortunes, despite the presence of individual capacities that are fully up to the average. The true cause of such dependency is to be sought in insufficient incomes and insufficient standards of living.[5]

⅃ In the succeeding paragraphs, I described the minimum normal standard of living for a family, in terms of both goods

---

[3] *Philanthropy and the State*, by B. Kirkman Gray, P. S. King and Son, London, 1908, pp. 1–2.

[4] *Proceedings of the National Conference of Charities and Correction*, 1906, p. 3.

[5] *Op. cit.*, 1907, p. 342.

and money, and noted the very large proportion of American families who were unable to maintain this standard owing to insufficient incomes, which in the case of wage earners meant insufficient wages—less than living wages. Finally, I urged the members of the Conference to ascertain what is a minimum normal standard of living and how many families are below this standard because of inadequate wages. Continuing, I said:

Possessing this knowledge, the members of charity organizations, and all who speak or write on the problem of dependency, can accomplish a splendid work of education. They can bring home to well-meaning but thoughtless employers some idea of the amount of poverty that is due to their failure to pay living wages; they can help very materially to bring upon employers who are not well-meaning the condemnation of public opinion; they can contribute to the enactment of laws which directly or indirectly will enforce an adequate standard of compensation and of living; they can educate the whole public into a more accurate conception of the proportion of poverty that is due to social causes, and out of the complacent notion, which is still all too common, that the poverty stricken have only themselves to blame.[6]

The foregoing extract sets forth two distinct but closely related propositions: first, a very large proportion of destitution is caused by economic factors; second, these factors cannot be removed without a large measure of intervention by the state. The latter proposition I had already defended in *A Living Wage*. In the succeeding years, my conviction on this point has grown stronger rather than weaker. I have never ceased to regard the economic causes of social distress as providing a pertinent application of the profound principle laid down by Pope Leo XIII in the encyclical *Rerum Novarum*:

Whenever the general interest, *or any particular class* [italics mine] suffers or is threatened with mischief which can in no other way be met or averted, it is the duty of public authority to intervene.

Early in the year 1908, I wrote an article of some fifteen

[6] *Op. cit.*, 1907, p. 346.

thousand words on "Charity and Charities" for the Catholic Encyclopedia.[7] The introductory section described the nature and obligations of the virtue of charity as taught by the Catholic Church and gave brief accounts of the charitable achievements of the non-Catholic religions, particularly Judaism. The concluding paragraphs discussed the place of Catholic charity in present society. Fully four-fifths of the article was devoted to the history of charity in the Catholic Church from the Apostolic age to our own time. The historical section concludes with the following sentences:

. . . Surveying the whole historical field of Catholic charity, we are justified in saying that, in proportion to her resources, the Church met the various forms of distress of every age more adequately than any other agency or system; that her shortcomings in charitable activity were due to the nature of the peoples and civilizations, and to the political, social, economic, and religious conditions in which she worked; that the instances of heroic charity which stand to her credit surpass by an immeasurable distance all instances of that class outside her fold; that the individual gifts to charity which she has inspired are likewise supereminent; and that, had she been permitted to reorganize and develop her charities without the interference of the Reformation, the amount of social distress, and of social injustice as well, would be much smaller than it is today.

In March, 1910, I addressed the annual meeting of the National Consumers League at Milwaukee on "A Minimum Wage by Legislation." This paper, with some amplification, I presented again in May of the same year before the Division on Occupational Standards at the Thirty-seventh Annual Session of the National Conference of Charities and Correction in St. Louis.[8] In this addresss, I stated that considerably more than one-half of the male, adult wage earners of the country were receiving less than $700 annually. This amount, I said, was the minimum that would suffice for the decent mainte-

[7] Vol. II, pp. 592–604.
[8] *Proceedings of the National Conference of Charities and Correction*, 1910, pp. 457–475.

nance of a family in the smaller cities. For the larger urban centers I put the required sum at $800 and for New York City at $900. These estimates I based upon the findings of a volume published in 1909 by Professor Robert Coit Chapin and entitled *The Standard of Living Among Workingmen's Families in New York City*. It will be observed that these estimates are some 15 to 20 per cent higher than those which I had embodied in *A Living Wage*, but the difference is readily explained. In the first place, Dr. Chapin had made a much more extensive investigation of the cost of living than was possible for me in 1905; in the second place, his computations were made some four years later than mine, and during that period there had occurred a not inconsiderable rise in prices and in the cost of living. In passing, I note that Dr. Chapin's book was the first of a long series of carefully prepared and well-balanced studies on the minimum cost of living of the working class in the United States.

Returning to the address under consideration, I observe that after reciting at some length the manifold evil results, so-cial, industrial, moral, intellectual, and physical of the low-wage situation, I declared that the only measure holding out any hope as a remedy was "the establishment by law of mini-mum rates of wages that will equal or approximate the nor-mal standards of living for the different groups of workers." Finally, I endeavored to meet and refute the principal objec-tions confronting this proposal: it was novel; it would re-strict freedom of contract; it was contrary to the "due process" clause of the Constitution; it was not enforceable; the resulting increase in wages would bring about higher prices, lessened demand for goods, and greater unemployment. In this year of 1941, the first of these objections has become antiquated; the second has lost most of its appeal, whether popular or technical; the third has been effectively refuted by a decision of the United States Supreme Court;[9] the fourth and fifth have been in large measure discredited respectively by the administration of the Federal Fair Labor Standards Act and by general experience. No additional objection possessing any great degree of cogency has been brought forward in the thirty-one years that have gone by since I delivered that address.

These two addresses were probably the first important public utterances made in the United States in advocacy of minimum-wage legislation. They hastened and promoted the introduction of bills for this purpose in more than one state legislature.

Later on, in the same year of 1910, I took part in the discussion of a paper on "The Problem of Dependency" read by Robert Biggs at the first annual meeting of the National Conference of Catholic Charities held in Washington. My contribution was very short and dealt with only one aspect of the subject, namely, "Insufficient Housing." Several other papers and discussions at this meeting showed that the new Catholic organization was quite as much concerned with the social causes of poverty as was the older and larger association.

As already noted, my address at the St. Louis Conference of Charities and Correction was given before the Division on Occupational Standards. This division of the Conference had been set up one year previously for the specific purpose of formulating a set of employment and living standards which would describe the minimum conditions sufficient to place the worker beyond the need of charitable assistance. In other words, the members of the Conference wanted to ascertain as accurately as possible the quantity of goods and the quality of living which would enable wage earners to do without the ministrations of the social worker. Since the committee for this division was not ready to make a final report in 1910, its

---

[9] *West Coast Hotel Company v. Parrish*, 1937.

existence was continued, but under a new title, "Standards of Living and Labor." I was a member of the committee from its inception in 1909 and was elected chairman for the year 1913.

At the Thirty-ninth Annual Conference held in Cleveland in 1912, the committee presented its report on "Standards of Living and Labor." Although the chairman of the committee, Mr. Owen R. Lovejoy, discussed and explained at considerable length the standards adopted by the committee, the formal statement of "Social Standards for Industry" was relatively brief. The first paragraph of the statement is as follows:

The welfare of society and the prosperity of the state require for each individual such food, clothing, housing conditions, and other necessaries and comforts of life as will secure and maintain physical, mental and moral health. These are essential elements in a normal standard of living, below which society cannot allow any of its members to live without injuring the public welfare. An increasing percentage of our population derives the means to maintain this normal standard through industry. Industry, therefore, must submit to such public regulation as will make it a means of life and health, not of death or inefficiency.[10]

The minimum standards were arranged under six heads: Wages, Hours, Safety and Health, Housing, Term of Working Life, and Compensation or Insurance. Under the first head, the most important paragraph demanded a living wage which should be sufficiently large to provide the worker and his family with insurance against sickness and old age. Under the second head, a demand was voiced for the eight-hour day and the six-day week. Safety and health were held to include the provision of safety appliances and sanitary conditions, the prohibition of poisons, standardized inspection and regulation of occupation according to the degree of hazard. Under housing, the committee demanded for every family a safe

[10] *Proceedings of the National Conference of Charities and Correction*, 1912, p. 388.

and sanitary home and laid down in considerable detail the specifications implied in the concept. The term of working life was described as the period between "a minimum age to protect against premature labor and a maximum age beyond which the laborer should find himself economically independent of daily labor." Translating this generality into specific requirements, the committee called for prohibition of all wage-earning occupations for children under sixteen years of age and also prohibition of employment of women in occupations where work compels standing constantly. Finally, the committee demanded compensation for industrial workers on account of accidents, trade diseases, permanent disability, old age, and unemployment.

Such were the principal but by no means all the items in the "Platform of Minimums," as this collection of standards came to be called. While a considerable number of them have been adopted through legislation or otherwise, some of the most important and most necessary still await establishment; for example, living wages and adequate housing. The task assigned to the committee by the National Conference was brilliantly and comprehensively executed. For various reasons it will be a long time before the National Conference will be required to formulate another group of "Standards of Living and Labor."[11]

For some half-dozen years before I left for Washington in September, 1915, I had served as vice-president of the Associated Charities of St. Paul. While my contribution to the effectiveness of that organization was neither great nor conspicuous, I took considerable interest in its activities, first, because they were directed to the welfare of human beings and, second, because of the discussions and differences at the meetings concerning methods and policies.

In 1912, I was chosen president of the Minnesota State

[11] *Proceedings*, 1912, pp. 376–395.

Conference of Charities and Correction. At the annual meeting that year I took as the subject of the presidential address "The State and Social Distress." At some length, I endeavored to define the principles and policies which separate the proper sphere of the state from that which properly belongs to the individual. Concerning the former, I said:

The State, and only the State, can prevent a large part, probably the larger part, of the social distress which is due primarily to environment. In the physical order it can and ought to provide suitable economic conditions, by enforcing reasonable minimum standards of labor and livelihood. Specifically, it should prohibit the employment of any worker of average capacity at less than living wages, or for a longer day than is consistent with the material and moral health of the individual and the race, or in unsafe and unsanitary work places. It should also forbid child labor, and interdict the employment of women and young persons at tasks that are harmful to health or morals. Insofar as the wage earners are unable to protect themselves against the unfavorable contingencies of life and employment by adequate savings or insurance, the State should supply the deficiency. Hence the need in many communities of workmen's compensation laws, labor exchanges, insurance against sickness, accidents, unemployment, and disability, and a system of old age pensions. In a word, the State ought to provide and enforce all those economic and industrial conditions which are necessary and sufficient for normal and reasonable human life. This will not injure individual initiative, or individual freedom, or the individual desire to excel. It will merely lift the plane of competition, and confine these qualities within reasonable and healthy limits. . . .[12]

By way of conclusion, then, we observe that the sphere of the State in dealing with social distress is by no means small. Neither is it indefinitely large. It is confined within fairly definite limits by certain clear and fundamental principles. Neither in the field of prevention nor in that of relief is it wise or right for the State to do anything that can be done as well by voluntary agencies; and wherever practicable it should subsidize, cooperate with and supplement private effort.[13]

In order to complete in this chapter the record of my

[12] *Catholic Charities Review*, January, 1920, p. 5.
[13] *Idem*, p. 8.

activities in the domain of charity or social work, I shall include a brief account of my connection with the *Catholic Charities Review,* and several paragraphs from two addresses before groups of social workers. The first issue of the *Catholic Charities Review* appeared in January, 1917. For the first four years, I was the editor and manager, writing all the editorials and finding "copy" to fill each issue. After I gave up that responsibility, I acted for several years as contributing editor. Most of my editorials and practically all my contributed articles dealt with industrial questions rather than with topics in the field of social work; nevertheless, most of my productions had some fairly obvious relevancy to the problems of social workers. I never permitted myself to forget the relation between poverty, charitable relief, and low wages.[14]

The first of the two addresses mentioned above was delivered at the commencement exercises of the New York School of Social Work in 1920. The subject was "A Practical Philosophy of Social Work." It dealt almost entirely with the differences between the two philosophies of social work held respectively by the members of secular agencies and those in Catholic organizations. I grouped the principal differences between these two theories or philosophies under these heads: Motives; Attitude Toward Religious Principles; Methods; Attitude Toward State Administration. What I said on these points in the address I still hold to be substantially correct.

[14] For some two or three years before I returned to the Catholic University, in 1915, I had occasionally considered the project of establishing and editing a weekly journal devoted to the discussion of industrial problems and reforms in the light of Catholic social doctrine. Since the best place for such a publication would evidently be New York City, I put the matter before the Cardinal Archbishop, His Eminence, John M. Farley. His reply and attitude were unfavorable. This is not surprising, for I was still regarded as "too radical" by many Bishops as well as others; moreover, very few members of the Hierarchy at that time (1914) were sufficiently interested in the social question to appreciate the need or the utility of such a publication. When the *Catholic Charities Review* was established in 1917, I welcomed the opportunity to put into its pages a few of the things that I should have got into the journal that I had been contemplating some years earlier.

The following paragraphs present the interpretation that I then gave of the Catholic philosophy on these four subjects:

The Catholic philosophy regards love of God as the highest and most fundamental motive of social service. That is to say, it holds that the needy neighbor should be assisted because of his relation to God, because he is made in the image and likeness of God, because he is the adopted child of God and the adopted brother of Christ; and also because Christ has commanded us to relieve the neighbor who is in distress, particularly as seen in the twenty-fifth chapter of St. Matthew. Catholics maintain that this is a much more effective motive than love of the neighbor for his own sake or for the sake of society; for the human being in distress assumes a much greater value when he is thought of in relation to God, and there is grave danger that assistance to the neighbor for his own sake alone will be converted into the service of society as a whole, and the ignoring of the intrinsic worth of the individual. . . .

According to the Catholic philosophy, religious principles are of supreme importance in social service. We believe that religion and religious morality should control every department of human life; and we maintain that religion and religious morality are a most important element in the life of the person to whom social service is extended. Young dependents, all delinquents and defectives, and a very large proportion of adults who are in distress require the aid of religion in order to enable them to lead normal lives. . . .

All intelligent Catholics admit that all the modern scientific methods of social service are essentially sound. Indeed, we are predisposed to this conclusion, inasmuch as these methods, in their main outlines at least, were stated and defended nearly four hundred years ago by the Spanish philosopher, Juan Luis Vives, and repeated at greater length more than three-quarters of a century ago by Frederic Ozanam, the founder of the Society of St. Vincent de Paul. The views of Vives on this subject have been so well appreciated in this institution that a translation of them into English was published by the school some three years ago. Scientific methods of social service are sometimes misused and made odious by injudicious exponents of the secular philosophy, just as they are sometimes mistrusted and condemned by incompetent Catholics. But there is no difference of principle between the two philosophies on the subject of scientific methods; the only difference that occurs is in their application. . . .

According to the Catholic view, the question whether State funds devoted to the relief of the distressed and to the care of dependents should be administered by the State, or by private agencies, is entirely one of expediency. There is no question here of principle. If a private agency can administer State funds, always under adequate State supervision, in such a way as to produce a greater amount of more beneficial service, that is the better arrangement. Moreover, there are special reasons for desiring that dependents, especially young dependents, should be cared for in Catholic, rather than in State institutions; namely, the necessity of giving them adequate training in religion and religious morality. If this can be done with the aid of State money in Catholic institutions so as to produce better social and civic results than would be obtained through the same expenditure of State money in State institutions, there can be no possible doubt that this arrangement is preferable.[15]

The second discourse was spoken before the National Conference of Social Work, in Cleveland, May 30, 1926. The subject was "The Spiritual Element in Social Work." Here are the most significant paragraphs:

. . . The spiritual element in social work is the recognition of the soul as the supreme good in a human being. It is the soul which gives to man his intrinsic worth as a person, instead of a mere means to the welfare of society. Because of his soul, his personality, his intrinsic worth, the human individual is endowed with certain rights which may not be disregarded even in the interest of social progress. After all, social progress means the progress of human beings. Apart from human beings, social progress and society itself are empty abstractions. To use any class of human beings as mere instruments to social advantage is in reality to subordinate one group of persons to another, albeit a larger, group of persons. For such a policy there can be no moral justification. The only defense available is that which may be based upon considerations of brute force.

If this conception of the human individual as having intrinsic worth seem intangible or metaphysical, the answer is that every ultimate standard of values is intangible and metaphysical. To the person who believes that weak and socially useless individuals ought to be sacrificed to social welfare, society appears as good in itself, as metaphysically

[15] *Catholic Charities Review*, October, 1920, pp. 243–244.

good. To the question, why should we further the interests of society, the answer must be in terms of metaphysics. At least the assumption must be made that society is its own justification, that there is no further end to which society might be made an instrument. . . .

Disregard the spiritual element in man and his essential sacredness, and you can set no logical or certain limit to the process of subjecting the supposedly less desirable individuals to the assumed welfare of society. If the abstraction which we call society is worth more than certain individuals, then it may be worth more than any number of individuals, however large, whom the social experts or the politicians may regard as a social liability.[16]

[16] *Proceedings, National Conference of Social Work*, 1926, pp. 62–70.

CHAPTER VII

IN THE FIELD OF SOCIAL REFORM (1907–1915)

ETYMOLOGICALLY, social reform means the reform of any condition or institution which affects a social group. Divorce, the liquor traffic, public health, and methods of poor relief, may be objects of social reform, as well as the distribution of wealth, the hours of labor, and the incomes of the laboring classes. All the six standards formulated by the National Conference of Charities and Correction as described in the immediately preceding chapter, exemplify proposals of social reform. However, there is a widespread practice of confining the term to reform of industrial or economic conditions and institutions. Apparently, the underlying idea is that these comprise the most important province of social reform. It is chiefly in this sense that the phrase will be used in the present chapter. The reform movements, activities, and writings to be described and discussed herein are mainly economic.

In November, 1907, I published an article in the *Catholic World,* under the title, "The Fallacy of Bettering One's Position." The general thesis was that the indefinite improvement of one's economic condition and the unlimited elevation of one's standard of living, are detrimental to right and reasonable life. After describing in some detail the ways in which increased income can be and usually is expended for "better" housing, food, clothing, amusement and recreation, and "social" activities, I concluded that the theory underlying this expenditure implies that "more abundant life means the multiplication of sensations, possessions and pleasurable experiences." This theory, I continued, is false, for the important thing is not the number but the kind of wants that a man satisfies. When the needs of health and moderate comfort have been supplied, "additional sense-satisfactions contribute little or nothing to the development of body, heart or mind. . . . They exert a damaging influence upon morals, mind, health and happiness."

The foregoing propositions I endeavored to establish by specific descriptions of the evil effects of excessive expenditures upon health, morals, character, religion, altruism, the control of the animal appetites, the capacity for hard work, the birth rate, and genuine happiness. In relation to happiness, I quoted a passage from Friedrich Paulsen's well-known work, *A System of Ethics*:

When we compare the self-confidence of the dying eighteenth century, with the opinion which the dying nineteenth century has of itself, we note a strong contrast. Instead of the proud consciousness of having reached a pinnacle, a feeling that we are on the decline; instead of joyful pride in the successes achieved and joyful hope of new and greater things, a feeling of disappointment and weariness, and a premonition of a coming catastrophe.[1]

In the awful events and conditions that now afflict the world, this premonition seems to be finding complete and devastating fulfillment.

In the February, 1908, issue of the *Catholic World* I discussed, in a complementary article, "The Cost of Christian Living," under each of the five most important needs: housing, food, clothing, amusement and recreation, and "social activities," and concluded that "the annual expenditure for material goods in the case of the overwhelming majority of moderately sized families, ought not to exceed $6,500.

[1] *The Church and Socialism*, by John A. Ryan, The University Press, Washington, 1919, p. 193.

Probably the range of expenditure which would afford the best conditions of Christian life for a considerable majority of all American families lies between $2,000 and $5,000 per annum."[2]

Eight years later, I returned to this subject in my book *Distributive Justice*. There I discussed it in connection with the "Duty of Distributing Superfluous Wealth."[3] Having defended the proposition that in our society men are morally obliged to distribute *all* their superfluous goods in some form of charity, philanthropy, civic or social betterment, I said that the chief obstacle in the way of this highly desirable practice was an exaggerated conception of "reasonable" needs, and an inadequate conception of superfluous goods, both arising out of a false theory of welfare. "It is commonly assumed that to be worthwhile life must include the continuous and indefinite increase of the number and variety of wants, and a corresponding growth and variation in the means of satisfying them."

My estimate of the maximum reasonable annual expenditure by a family at that time is stated in the following sentences:

Somewhere between ten and twenty thousand dollars a year lies the maximum expenditure that any family can reasonably devote to its material wants. This is independent of the outlay for education, religion, and charity, and the things of the mind generally. In the overwhelming majority of cases in which more than ten to twenty thousand dollars are expended for the satisfaction of material needs, some injury is done to the higher life. The interests of health, intellect, spirit and morals would be better promoted if the outlay for material things were kept below the specified limit.[4]

The increase which the above estimate indicates over that

[2] *Idem*, pp. 207–208.
[3] Chapter XXI.
[4] *Distributive Justice*, by John A. Ryan, The Macmillan Company, New York, 1927, p. 280.

which I made in 1907 is mainly accounted for by the intervening rise in prices, but partly by a more comprehensive acquaintance with actual living needs and standards. About ten years later, in an address before the Canadian Conference of Social Work, I cited the estimate given by Paul H. Douglas and Mrs. Douglas in their little book entitled *What Can a Man Afford?* They held that an expenditure of $20,000 per year was sufficient to cover all items of family expenses except charity, religion, and education. This figure they arrived at, not in the endeavor to find a reasonable maximum, but as incidental to their attempt to ascertain the proportion of income which should be given by the various classes of families in the United States in order to meet the required national budget of philanthropy. To the objection of the man with an income of one-half a million dollars that he should not be required to give 50 per cent of it in charity and that he ought not to be asked to live like the man with an income of $50,000, Mr. and Mrs. Douglas replied:

Our scale is indeed somewhat of a counsel of perfection if one is going to take all our present standards as normal. But the fact plain to our view is that the luxury side of current standards is not and need not be normal. . . . The social climbers of all ranks, especially the great middle groups of incomes, will be more quickly affected to sane living and reasonable generosity by the concrete example of their financial superiors than by any amount of preaching.[5]

The analysis and evaluation of the items of family expenditure which I made in 1907 and the conceptions of welfare and reasonable standards of living which I then defended, I still hold to be sound. The estimate which I made in 1916 of the maximum expenditure which any family can reasonably devote to its material wants, is likewise still adequate and valid. If all our rich and well-to-do families adopted this standard they would do more to allay class antagonism than

[5] *What Can a Man Afford?* Supplement No. 2, *American Economic Review*, December, 1921, p. 83.

is attainable by any quantity of reactionary criticism or platitudinous exhortation.

Someone might object that the recommendations made in the immediately preceding paragraphs are out of harmony with the economic theory of underconsumption which I have for a long time defended. If the full operation of our industrial plant and full employment requires that our people spend more and save less, should we not welcome large expenditures by any group of persons, regardless of the income class to which they belong? The answer is that such spending is desirable as a lesser evil than an equal amount of saving, but it is not normal nor ideal. Although the total expenditures of those families that exceed $10,000 to $20,000 a year is large, it is much smaller than would be the additional spending by the lower income groups if the rich and the well-to-do dispensed all their surplus in the form of wages, charitable giving, and philanthropy. To be sure, if these classes should reduce their living standards and expenditures for consumption goods without distributing the amount thus saved to the lower income classes, the net effect would be harmful to industrial welfare.

The situation is simply this: our economy demands a great increase in spending for consumers' goods; the bulk of this will have to come from the lower economic classes; therefore, anything which enables them to increase their total amount and proportion of consumption, whether through higher wages, lower interest rates, or wider distribution of the superfluous goods of the rich and the well-to-do, will directly make for larger employment and greater business activity. In a word, reasonable standards of living maintained by the rich and the well-to-do, combined with a better distribution of their superfluous income, would be in accord with both the Christian teaching on wealth and our national economic welfare.

In 1908, I addressed the National Catholic Educational Association on "The Study of Social Problems in the Seminary." After describing briefly the importance of the economic factor in political, civil, social, and international life, I said that the priest who does not realize this situation will accomplish considerably less than would otherwise be within his power. The priest needs to know the following facts and the reasons therefor: that the attitudes of many governments toward the Church are largely determined by economic factors; that many popular movements which seem to be political are at bottom industrial; and that the economic status of men greatly influences their notions about the morality of some of the most important activities and institutions of our time. The priest who does not discern the economic causes of the differing ethical judgments which men pass, for example, upon the trust, the trade union, profits and wages, will not command adequate authority as a teacher of morality. I quoted the following saying of Archbishop Von Ketteler, the first and probably the greatest of modern Catholic social reformers:

If we wish to know our age, we must endeavor to fathom the social question. The man who understands that knows his age. The man who does not understand it finds the present and the future an enigma.[6]

Continuing, I said that the priest "must give special attention to the condition and aspirations of the wage earners," and I pointed out that in some of the countries of Europe a large proportion of the workers had become alienated from the Church because the clergy lacked knowledge of and interest in their specific problems. While there is little danger that the Catholic clergy of America will lose sympathy with the desire of the masses for industrial freedom and industrial opportunity, there is a real danger that their sympathy will not be equaled by their knowledge:

[6] *American Ecclesiastical Review*, August, 1908, p. 115.

The great majority of our clergy in the United States have not yet begun to study systematically or take more than a superficial interest in the important social problems of their age and country. Too often their social views and impressions are derived from newspapers and periodicals which are unfriendly to the aims of the working classes, and to the cause of social reform generally. It is natural and proper that the priest should prefer those journals which are conservative, both in their methods and in their attitude toward the existing order. But it is unfortunate that these publications are, as a rule, ultra-conservative with regard to modifications or reforms in that portion of the existing order which we call economic. On the other hand, the periodicals which advocate effective and vital reforms are not infrequently radical in their views of moral, religious, and educational institutions. As a consequence of this situation, the average priest is apt to possess only a one-sided and superficial knowledge of the social question. While sympathizing in a general way with the aspiration for social betterment, he is not unlikely to misunderstand and antagonize many of the particular doctrines, aims, and methods of the actual reform movements of the time.[7]

In order that the priest of the future may be equipped to deal intelligently with the social and economic problems faced by the people, he must receive in the seminary social instruction which will be fundamental and scientific; which will be sufficiently extensive

to make him acquainted with the vital facts of current social conditions, tendencies, and doctrines; which will be sufficiently stimulating to give him a lasting interest in these phenomena; and which will be sufficiently thorough to enable him to deal intelligently, justly, and charitably with the practical situations that he will be compelled to face afterward. Here, again, we may profitably perhaps take example from the experience of some of our brethren in the Old World. It has been frequently asserted that one explanation of the failure of the clergy of France to retain their hold upon large masses of their countrymen, is to be found in their inadequate and impractical seminary training. It is not impossible that we shall one day find ourselves similarly impotent on account of our insufficient instruction in social problems. Such questions as just wages, just interest, just profits, a living wage for

[7] *Idem*, p. 117.

the worker versus normal profits and interest for the employer and the capitalist; reducing wages to maintain dividends; the responsibility of stockholders, including educational and charitable institutions, for the improper practices of corporations; stockwatering and other questionable methods of high finance; the aims and methods of monopoly; the aims and methods of the labor union; socialism, materialistic and non-materialistic—are all of vital importance to large masses of people, are the subject of endless discussion in public and in private, and involve definite and far-reaching consequences to morality and religion. Do they, or any of them, receive sufficient attention either in the manuals used or the oral instruction at present imparted in our seminaries?[8]

Finally, I pointed out that, despite the objection drawn from the already crowded seminary curriculum, I was devoting to such subjects one-fourth of my two-year period in moral theology at the St. Paul Seminary, and that the allotment of so much time to social topics had not been detrimental to the traditional courses in that branch of ecclesiastical training.

Today practically all our seminaries provide courses in economics or sociology or both. While I have reason to believe that the address which I have cited and the example set by the St. Paul Seminary helped greatly to bring about this condition, I am sure that the main impetus came from the exhortation of Pope Pius XI in *Quadragesimo Anno*. Speaking of the Social Apostolate to the workingman, he said: "No easy task is here imposed upon the clergy; wherefore all candidates for the sacred priesthood must be adequately prepared to meet it by intense study of social matters."

In July and August, 1909, I published in the *Catholic World* two articles under the head, "Program of Social Reform by Legislation." The first dealt with legislative measures in favor of wage earners, while the second proposed legislation in the interest of the consumers. Under the former head, I advo-

[8] *Idem*, pp. 118–119.

cated minimum-wage legislation, the eight-hour day, minimum working age of sixteen years for children, the creation of boards to provide for conciliation and arbitration in labor disputes, state employment agencies, municipal housing, and state insurance against unemployment, accidents, sickness, and old age.

In the second group of proposed legislative measures, I placed national and state ownership of railroads, express companies, telegraphs and telephones, and municipal ownership of gas and electric lighting, waterworks, and street railways; also state and national retention of the ownership of all mineral and forest lands that have not been alienated. As regards monopolies which are outside the field of public utilities, I recommended government control of the prices of things produced by those concerns whose exceptional efficiency suggested that they should continue to exist as monopolies. In the field of taxation, I advocated progressive imposts upon incomes and inheritances, and also partial appropriation of future increases in the value of land. Finally, I declared that the government should regulate the stock and produce exchanges in order to prevent the manifold evils of speculation.

Three years after these articles appeared, I gave an address on "Principles and Proposals of Social Reform" in a social study course conducted by the Central Verein at Fordham University. About one-third of the speech dealt with the topics that I had discussed in the *Catholic World* articles. For labor, I advocated the same legislative measures as in the earlier production. With regard to such utilities as natural monopolies, I said that they ought to be so regulated as to leave the owners only the prevailing rate of interest, computed on their actual investment. If this method should not prove effective "after a fair and sufficient trial," recourse should be had to public ownership; and I suggested a new method of preventing extortion by artificial monopolies, namely, that the state should compete with some of the obstinate and intractable trusts by manufacturing and selling their kinds of products. In the matter of taxation, I insisted even more strongly than in 1909 on heavier taxes on land, so that its average value "should not rise above the present level." My main reason for this emphasis was the rapid increase in the value of land, both rural and urban. "Between 1900 and 1910, farm land rose in value 108 per cent per acre, while great tracts in the cities have advanced with even greater rapidity." The particular changes that I suggested in the fiscal system were "a gradual transfer of some of the taxes from the necessaries of life and from improvements to land and a special tax on the increases in land value, particularly in cities."

Some of the proposals advocated in the foregoing paragraphs have already been enacted into law; all of the others I still hold to be valid, with a few modifications which are suggested by changes in economic conditions that have occurred in the last three decades. Government ownership of railroads is no longer required in order to prevent excessive charges for carrying freight and passengers and the receipt of excessive returns on railroad investments. For the great majority of the railroads, these socially undesirable advantages no longer exist. When government ownership comes, its principal cause will probably be the inability of the railroads to pay dividends and to perform their public functions adequately. The last three sentences apply likewise to street railways.

Since public regulation of most of the other utilities has shown more or less improvement in the last thirty years, the necessity for public ownership is not so acute as it was at the beginning of that period. While I still believe that the latter would be preferable to private ownership, I realize that it can come about only gradually and in piecemeal fashion.

The proposal to curb the exactions of private monopolies through government determination of prices, is less valid now than it seemed to be in 1909. When the National Emergency Economic Committee has completed its long investigation and made its recommendations for legislative policies concerning monopolies, the American people will be in a better position than ever before to find the proper solution of this baffling problem. In the meantime, one proposal which I offered in 1912 remains sound and helpful, namely, government competition with the most intractable of the monopolistic concerns. This method has proved very effective in electric power production: witness the T.V.A. So far as feasible, it should be extended throughout that industry.

The principal modification which I would now make of the proposals which I offered in 1909 and 1912 has to do with the taxation of land. While I still believe that the transfer to land of taxes on improvements and the taxation of future increases in land value are reasonable, I realize that their scope has been greatly diminished. As a matter of fact, the general increase in land values, both urban and rural, has practically ceased. More than one factor accounts for this change but the principal one is the decline in the birth rate. The recommendations which I made in 1912 concerning land taxation have practical application now to only a few cities and a small amount of other lands which are exceptionally situated.

In 1910, I wrote an article for the *Catholic Encyclopedia* on "Moral Aspects of the Labor Union."[9] Premising that the moral aspects of an institution are ascertained by examining its constitution, its end, its results and the means employed in pursuit of the end, I declared that no evidence exists to show that the constitution of the typical labor union in the United States today is immoral. With regard to the aims and

[9] Vol. 8, pp. 724-728.

results of the union, I said that the former were generally good, and that the evil results were morally outweighed by the good results, admitting, however, that there are and have been some exceptions to both these generalizations.

About three-fourths of the article dealt with the means and methods of the labor union. These are principally the strike, the boycott, the closed shop, or the union shop, and the limitation of output and of apprentices. On the whole, my statements on these topics were the same as those set down in any of the larger Catholic manuals of ethics; consequently, they need not be repeated here. Certain problems that are not usually discussed in the manuals but which are of considerable practical importance, may with advantage receive brief treatment.

1. *The strike.*—The claim that a man on strike has a right to his job, and, therefore, may use force to prevent strikebreakers from taking his place, I rejected. An employee has not the same kind of right to his job as he has to a horse or a hat; nevertheless, if he cannot find other employment without grave inconvenience, the employer who discharges him without grave reason will "sin against not merely charity but justice." And the same may be true of the worker who quits his job without serious reason and at the cost of grave injury to his employer. While admitting that the use of force to prevent a strikebreaker from co-operating with certain injustice committed by an employer against his employees who have gone on strike, might be theoretically justified, I declared that, practically, the good effects to be obtained through the use of violence are never sufficient to outweigh the evil social effects. Concerning the general strike, I said: "While we cannot be certain that it is never justified, we can safely say that there is against it an overwhelming presumption."

2. *The boycott.*—The primary boycott will be justified under the same conditions that render a strike morally lawful.

The secondary boycott, however, "is ordinarily immoral because it is an unreasonable interference with the right of an unconcerned person to pursue and possess the advantages of social or business intercourse with his fellows. . . ."

3. *The closed shop.*—This demand will be justified whenever it is really necessary in order to obtain reasonable conditions of employment. The right of the non-union man to work in the same shop with members of unions is no more valid than the right of the union man not to work beside the former. Neither alleged right is unconditionally valid.

4. *Limitation of output and of apprentices.*—Limitation by the union upon the amount of the product to be turned out by its members is reasonable if the aim is to prevent excessive speed in the pace at which the employee is required to work. It is not reasonable when the motive is indolence or the objective is to make the job last longer. The limitation of apprentices is unjustifiable if it keeps the supply of skilled workers small so that their wages become unreasonably high.

Having re-read this article recently, I found nothing in it that I should want to withdraw or modify. Some statements need to be amplified, for example, in order to deal with the "sit-down" strike, the unfortunate dissension between A.F. of L. and the C.I.O. and Communist infiltration; but no additions are necessary to the essential doctrine.

In the years between 1908 and 1915, I made many public addresses on labor unions, their economic justification, their moral aspects, and their practices; in none of them did I depart from the essentials of the article in the *Catholic Encyclopedia*. During the same period, I made a few speeches on public ownership of public utilities, and always expounded the doctrine that has been summarized earlier in this chapter. On Socialism, I spoke more frequently and more fundamentally. My usual plan was to describe three phases or meanings of Socialism: as a social philosophy; as a social movement; and as an economic program. Its philosophy, I contended, was historically false and ethically wrong; the Socialist movement was anti-religious; and the proposed reorganization of economic society was impracticable and unjust. In all the addresses on Socialism, however, I had a good deal to say about social reform.

My discussions of the social question differed from those carried on by some Catholic journals and speakers in two main respects. The latter sometimes explained and denounced Socialism without offering any constructive proposals; hence, they created the impression that existing industrial conditions stood in no need of reformation. While they based their criticism of Socialism upon Pope Leo's encyclical, *Rerum Novarum,* they not infrequently ignored the positive and reformist doctrines of that great document. Persons who listened to these men or read their productions sometimes drew the inference that Pope Leo had said nothing favorable to labor unions, and that his only reference to private property was in his denunciation of Socialism. As a matter of fact, the great "Pontiff of the Workingmen" made some of the strongest statements ever uttered on the necessity and justice of labor organization, and his proposal for the reform of the property system is one of the most fundamental and far-reaching that has been offered in modern times:

Speaking summarily, we may lay it down as a general and perpetual law, that Workmen's Associations should be so organized and governed as to furnish the best and most suitable means for attaining what is aimed at, that is to say, for helping each individual member to better his condition to the utmost, in body, mind and property.[10]

. . . The law, therefore, should favor ownership, and its policy should be to induce as many people as possible to become owners.

Many excellent results will follow from this; and first of all, property will certainly become more equitably divided. For the effect of civil change and revolution has been to divide society into two widely dif-

[10] *Rerum Novarum,* International Catholic Truth Society edition, p. 57.

ferent castes. On the one side there is the party which holds the power because it holds the wealth; which has in its grasp all labor and all trade; which manipulates for its own benefit and its own purposes all the sources of supply, and which is powerfully represented in the councils of the State itself. On the other side there is the needy and powerless multitude, sore and suffering, always ready for disturbance.[11]

The second difference between my speeches on economic questions and the pronouncements of some Catholic speakers and journals, was that mine were sometimes criticized as too "radical." When I advocated forthrightly the organization of labor and defended most of the principal methods of labor unions, I was occasionally put down as a "dangerous agitator" (the epithet "subversive" had not yet been invented). When I advocated public ownership of public utilities, or a legal minimum wage, I was sometimes stigmatized as a Socialist, or at least as "socialistic." Did not the professional labor leaders, the labor organizers, and all the other disturbers of peaceful relations between capital and labor, use much the same arguments as mine? And did not Socialism propose government ownership of public utilities and government fixing of labor compensation?

Of course, I appealed to the authoritative declarations of Pope Leo XIII; but this defense did not always silence critics whose study of Leo's great encyclical was neither extensive nor profound. Many years later, when Leo's teaching had become much better and much more widely understood, an able non-Catholic clergyman, who was also a high official of the Federal Council of Churches said to me: "You have a very great advantage over men in my position. We have to guard against offending the members of many different denominations, while you can hang your 'radical' utterances upon a Papal encyclical."

In the years of which I am now writing, however, the

11 *Idem*, p. 49.

procedure thus humorously characterized by my good Methodist friend was not always effective. While my knowledge of the traditional social teaching of the Church (I have already referred to my extensive reading of economic history at the turn of the century) as well as my intimate acquaintance with *Rerum Novarum,* assured me that I was on solid ground, I occasionally felt anxiety over the reflection that some of my prominent fellow Catholics regarded my teaching as unorthodox. However, I never permitted myself to become discouraged, nor was I ever seriously tempted to lessen my activities or to compromise or soften the principles in which I believed. At the banquet which was given in my honor on the occasion of my investiture as Domestic Prelate to His Holiness, Pope Pius XI, December 6, 1933, I said:

Many times men, both within and without the Church, have expressed admiration at what they were pleased to term my courage in enunciating and defending my opinions on industrial questions. At the risk of losing that particular halo, I will confess that whatever courage I may seem to have displayed was quite unconscious or at least inadvertent. What was there to fear? Ecclesiastical censure? But I knew that I was not departing from the teaching of the Church. Suspicions of my orthodoxy by prominent persons within the Church? Denunciations by industrialists and newspapers? The knowledge that my name was sometimes spoken without affection in the highest social circles? No normal person could be indifferent to this sort of disapproval. I do not pretend that I enjoyed it, but to withstand it did not require courage. All that was necessary was a right sense of comparative values. To have been deterred by such opposition from teaching the sound doctrine would have been to turn my back upon my plain duty, to apostatize from the truth. It would have meant not merely burying, but dishonoring what talents I had received from God.

Probably the most extreme instance of unfriendly and unfair criticism of my writings occurred at the meeting of the Federation of Catholic Societies in the summer of 1912. In the Resolutions Committee someone proposed that the

Federation express its approval of the legal minimum wage. One of the delegates objected to the proposal because, he said, "Dr. Ryan's book *A Living Wage* is about to be condemned by the Holy See." As a matter of fact, nothing of the kind happened, or so far as I could ascertain, was even considered in Rome. This delegate's objection was motivated by the fact that he was at that time in the employ of the Republican National Committee and wanted to prevent the Progressive party headed by Theodore Roosevelt from deriving the support that would undoubtedly be forthcoming from some Catholics if this resolution were adopted by the Federation of Catholic Societies. It will be recalled that the platform of the Progressive party that year contained a resolution in favor of the legal minimum wage. Since the other delegates credited the false assertion about the imminent condemnation of *A Living Wage,* they did not adopt the proposed resolution.

When I was in Rome in the summer of the year 1911, I took advantage of a dinner party given in my honor in the rectory of the English Catholic Church of San Silvestro to ascertain, if possible, whether my social teaching was liable to "get me into trouble" with the authorities of the Church. One of the dinner guests was a distinguished Irish Franciscan who had lived a long time in Rome, Canon Peter Fleming. To him I mentioned the fact that some three years earlier I had rallied Rev. Francis E. Gigot, the celebrated Scripture scholar, concerning the danger that confronted men in his field on account of the recent condemnation of Modernism. His reply was: "It is easy for you to joke about that matter but your time is coming; one of these days you will be censured for your economic doctrine." Canon Fleming's comment was entirely reassuring: "So long as your teaching avoids the stigma or implication of Socialism, you have nothing to fear. There is much more freedom of teaching in the Catholic

Church than most persons outside the Church, and many persons within it, assume." The correctness of Canon Fleming's judgment I never doubted. Complete and overwhelming and final testimony on the point was provided, twenty years later, by the encyclical of Pope Pius XI, *Quadragesimo Anno*.

In the spring of 1914 an event occurred which practically silenced accusations of me as a Socialist or even as socialistic. This was the publication in book form of the debate between Morris Hillquit and myself on the subject, "Socialism: Promise or Menace." A little less than two years previously, the late Monsignor Joseph H. McMahon, pastor of Our Lady of Lourdes Church in New York City, had invited the late Monsignor William J. Kerby to take part in such a debate, to be published serially in *Everybody's Magazine*. Dr. Kerby declined on the ground that the proposed discussion would be unsatisfactory and inconclusive. Whereupon Dr. McMahon requested me to take the part which he had offered to Dr. Kerby. The same reasons that moved the latter to decline seemed compelling to me also. Then Dr. McMahon wrote me in rather vigorous terms (those who enjoyed an intimate acquaintance with this very able and forthright clergyman will understand what I mean by "vigorous terms") pointing out that *Everybody's Magazine* was offering the Catholics of the United States an unparalleled opportunity of getting before the American people their views on Socialism and the reasons for them. This and other considerations persuaded me to accept the assignment.

The procedure of the debate, agreed upon at several meetings attended by the staff of *Everybody's Magazine,* and by Dr. McMahon, Mr. Hillquit, and myself, was briefly as follows: the debate was to comprise seven divisions: Introduction; Social Evils and Remedies; The Socialist Industrial State; The Philosophy of Socialism; Socialism and Morality; Socialism and Religion, and Summary and Conclusion. In the first, second, fourth, and seventh divisions, Mr. Hillquit took the leading and affirmative part while I assumed that position in the other three divisions. In all but the first and last divisions each debater read before publication the papers produced by his opponent. Each of these five divisions contained four productions: the affirmative paper, the reply by the opponent, a rejoinder by the affirmative participant, and a surrejoinder from the negative side. As a consequence of this arrangement, each debater had ample opportunity not only to state his case in positive terms but also to take full account of the arguments of his opponent.

The first instalment of the debate was published in *Everybody's Magazine,* October, 1913, and the last, April, 1914. In the latter month the whole series was brought out in book form by The Macmillan Company. The volume received a generous amount of attention from the newspapers and magazines. As was natural, the reviewers differed from one another in their answers to the question: "Who won the debate?" The Catholics decided in my favor and a fair number of the non-Catholic reviewers agreed with them. The Socialists declared that Mr. Hillquit had the better of the argument. Practically all the reviewers who noted the point at all had words of praise for the high level of mutual courtesy upon which the debate was conducted. At the opening of my own part in the last division of the debate I put down the following paragraphs:

Before summing up the main issues of the debate, and stating the conclusions that seem to me to have been established, I desire to call attention to a few gratifying features of the discussion which are apparently beyond the reach of controversy.

In the first place, Mr. Hillquit and I have succeeded in demonstrating that it is possible for men to differ as widely as the poles and yet carry on a protracted argument with fairness and without bitterness, and conclude it with both self-respect and mutual respect unimpaired.

Second, we have on all substantial points agreed concerning the meaning and the doctrines of Socialism. Only those readers who have some knowledge of the average controversy on this subject can realize the tremendous importance and advantage of this agreement. It has enabled us to confine the discussion to positions and principles, instead of fighting over definitions, and to make things correspondingly satisfactory to the reader.

In the third place, we have formally and deliberately covered all the important phases of Socialism. We have considered it not merely as a scheme of politico-economic reconstruction, but as a living movement, and as a system of fundamental principles. The movement has been exhibited as affecting many other departments of life and thought besides the economic sphere. The principles have been set forth as embracing a philosophy of history, of society, of life, of the universe. Owing to this fundamental and comprehensive discussion, the intelligent reader has obtained some idea of the larger aspects of Socialism, and some explanation of the hold which it takes on many of its followers. It professes to give them a complete theory of life and of reality.

In view of this thoroughgoing treatment of the subject, may we not hope to hear less frequently in the future than in the past the shallow and ignorant assertion that Socialism is merely an economic programme?

Not the least important part of my contribution to the debate was the paragraph in the second division which I devoted to social reform measures as a remedy for current economic evils. These included all the proposals that I had put into the *Catholic World* articles in 1909, together with one notable addition, which was stated in the following sentences:

That the majority of the wage earners should, in a country as rich as America, possess no income-bearing property, have no ownership in the means of production, is a gross anomaly. It is not normal, and it cannot be permanent. No nation can endure as a nation predominantly of hired men. Until the majority of the wage earners become owners, at least in part, of the tools with which they work, the system of private capital will remain, in Hilaire Belloc's phrase, "essentially unstable."

This section gave more satisfaction to progressive-minded Catholic students than perhaps any other portion of my contribution. A few of the reviewers raised the question whether these paragraphs were not somewhat in advance of the social doctrine of the Church. For example, one reviewer reported: "Some Catholics say that Ryan concedes too much." William Marion Reedy, for a long time the able editor of the *St. Louis Mirror* observed: "One feels that the Church is less solidly behind Dr. Ryan than Socialists are behind Mr. Hillquit." On the whole, however, these questioning voices were feeble and not numerous. The great majority of the Catholic reviewers approved my part in the debate as sound, discriminating, and enlightening.

Returning to the observation which I made at the beginning of these paragraphs on the Hillquit-Ryan debate, I repeat that my contribution to it had the effect of disassociating me sharply from the advocacy of anything that could properly be called Socialism. The American public that gave any attention to the matter at all, including the great majority of Catholics, realized that I did not accept the doctrines of Socialism, even though some of my economic beliefs could properly be characterized as "advanced." To me that was not the least satisfactory result of the debate. In fact this consideration had influenced considerably my decision to take part in the controversy.[12]

In the early part of the year 1911, I wrote and had introduced in the lower house of the Minnesota legislature, a bill for a minimum-wage law. The bill did not get out of the committee to which it was referred. In 1912, the legislature of Massachusetts enacted a minimum-wage law which was

[12] In the notorious volume entitled *The Red Network*, by Elizabeth Dilling, my name appears, followed by several specifications which are supposed to entitle me to be regarded as a "red." One of these specifications reads as follows: "Co-author (with Morris Hillquit, alias Hilcovicz, radical left-wing Socialist) of *Socialism—Promise or Menace*, 1914. . . ." (p. 318). Whether this extraordinary reference was due to crass ignorance or outright intellectual dishonesty, I do not know. Nor does it matter.

merely directive and not mandatory. It set up a minimum-wage commission empowered to determine minimum wages for women and minors sufficient "to supply the necessary cost of living and maintain the workers in health." However, employers who should disregard the orders of the commission were subject to no penalty beyond that of seeing their names and the fact of their refusal published in four prominent newspapers of the state. In 1913, eight additional states enacted such legislation but these laws were all mandatory; i.e., they imposed penalties of fines and imprisonment on employers who should refuse to pay the wage rates determined by the minimum-wage commissions.

In that same year I rewrote the somewhat imperfect bill which I had prepared two years earlier, brought about its introduction in both houses of the 1913 legislature, and saw it enacted into law without much difficulty before the legislature adjourned the latter part of April. In writing the bill I had considerable assistance from a student of mine in the St. Paul Seminary, a very able young man who had been a practicing attorney before he took up his studies for the priesthood. Like all the other state laws of this nature, the Minnesota statute applied only to women and minors. It resembled the majority of the others also in setting up a commission to administer the law and to determine the rates of wages necessary to comply with the standards set forth in the statutes. The Minnesota commission was composed of the Commissioner of Labor, a woman who was also to act as secretary of the commission, and an employer of women. The standard which was to guide the commission in fixing the actual wage rates was substantially the same as in the laws enacted by the other states. It reads as follows:

The commission shall determine the minimum wages sufficient for living wages, for women and minors of ordinary ability, and also the minimum wages sufficient for living wages for learners and appren-

tices. . . . The term "living wage" or "living wages" shall mean
wages sufficient to maintain the laborer in health and supply him with
the necessary comforts and conditions of reasonable life.

Most of the other statutes employed the language of the
Oregon law which provides that the wage fixed by the commission "shall be adequate to supply the necessary cost of
living to women workers of average ordinary ability and
maintain them in health; . . ." In this matter the Minnesota
statute is unique because it uses the phrase, "necessary comforts and conditions of reasonable life."

As in all the other state laws except one or two, provision
was made in the Minnesota statute for the establishment by
the commission of advisory minimum-wage boards comprising representatives in equal numbers of the employers,
employees, and the general public. Two boards were set up
under the Minnesota law: one for mercantile and office occupations, the other for factories, laundries, restaurants, and
hotels. As chairman of the former advisory board I acquired
a great deal of information about the minimum cost of living
for women workers in conformity with the standard set up
in the statute. It may seem amusing now to find that the
weekly wage rate which we recommended to the commission
was $9, but the cost of living was much lower at that time
than it is now. Five years later I acted as chairman of one of
the advisory boards established to recommend rates to the
Minimum Wage Commission of the District of Columbia.
The schedules then fixed were $15, $15.50 and $16.50 per
week. However, the cost of living had arisen at least 60 per
cent between 1914 and 1919. The rates ordered by the Minimum Wage Board of the District of Columbia after the law
was resuscitated in 1937 vary from $14.50 to $18 per week.

The first minimum-wage orders of the Minnesota commission were issued on the twenty-third of October, 1914.
Exactly one month later a district judge of Ramsey County,

in which the city of St. Paul is located, granted an injunction against the enforcement of these orders, on the ground that the law was unconstitutional:

first, because it delegates legislative power to an appointive commission; second, because it necessarily abridges the right of individuals to make contracts, interferes with the right of both employee and employer to contract for the labor to be furnished by one to the other and thus violates the provisions of the fourteenth amendment to the federal constitution. . . .

A few weeks later the attorney general of the state appealed the case to the state supreme court. The latter reversed the action of the district judge and found the law to be constitutional. Some eight years later the Supreme Court of the United States invalidated the law of the District of Columbia and with the latter fell all the other minimum-wage statutes except that of Massachusetts. But this is another story and will receive further consideration in a later chapter.[13]

From 1910 until I left for Washington in 1915, I took a fairly active part in the movements for economic and social reform which were under way in the Twin Cities. I was chairman of the State Child Labor Committee and spoke at many public meetings and before legislative committees on behalf of labor and social legislation. Twice I addressed state legislatures outside of Minnesota, advocating the enactment of minimum-wage laws, namely, in Wisconsin and Pennsylvania. At that time, the leadership in social and economic

[13] On leaving the courtroom where I had heard Judge Catlin pronounce the Minnesota law unconstitutional, I met my very good friend the late Thomas D. O'Brien who facetiously asked what I thought of myself now as a lawgiver. I replied that we would appeal from "Philip drunk to Philip sober," alluding to the highest court of the state. A few years later I listened to the arguments for and against the District of Columbia law before the Supreme Court of the United States and within three weeks heard the death sentence pronounced by that tribunal upon all the mandatory minimum-wage laws in the United States. But I refused to believe that this was the final judicial word on the subject. Fourteen years later my faith in the constitutionality of the legislation was confirmed by the decision of our highest judicial tribunal in the case of the *West Coast Hotel Company v. Parrish*. "Time moves on."

reform movements was mainly held by social workers and officials of labor unions.

In these activities, I found only a handful of Catholics who were prominent. Few were leaders. This condition I always deplored although I had some idea of the reasons for it. Intelligent and competent Catholics were willing to work for laudable objectives in a Catholic organization, but seemed to be timid or fearful about associating with non-Catholics for similar purposes. They did not realize that social reforms, particularly those which involve legislative action, cannot be effectively pursued without the comprehensive organization and sincere cooperation of all interested groups. Some Catholics were unduly fearful of such association with their fellow citizens because some of the latter were seeking undesirable and improper ends, for example, birth control; others were afraid to join or cooperate with organizations which included possibly two or three socialists, while still others regarded the aims of some of these organizations as "too radical." Today, the last-mentioned group would be small, indeed, among Catholics who are acquainted with the encyclical *Quadragesimo Anno* or with the set of basic principles on "Catholic Action and Social Action" presented to the first National Catholic Social Action Conference in Milwaukee in May, 1938, by the Most Reverend Edwin V. O'Hara.[14]

[14] Notwithstanding the more friendly attitude now taken by American Catholics toward reform organizations and civic and social movements generally, there is room for still more improvement. Undoubtedly the matter is complex and difficult, but it is not incapable of satisfactory adjustment. In the first place, any non-sectarian, or secular, organization of a civic, social or economic character, which is dominated by anti-Catholic or anti-Christian leaders, or which continually promotes evil doctrines or projects should, of course, be avoided by Catholics unless there exists a solid hope that the bad situation can be corrected by an adequate and alert Catholic membership.

On the other hand, when the organization is not under such domination and when it only occasionally, or exceptionally, or partially, supports evil principles or practices, Catholic members ought to examine the whole situation without emotion or prejudice. Obviously, they should make quite clear their opposition to the wrong doctrine or practice and should constantly and prudently strive for a change of policy. If they are unable to bring about a reformation immediately, they need not always leave the organization or refuse to cooperate with its laudable objectives.

My own association with non-Catholics in reform movements has always been pleasant and profitable. In the meetings
held under these auspices I have occasionally heard social
doctrines expounded which I rejected and opposed, but never
any attack upon the Catholic Church. My non-Catholic
fellow citizens in Minnesota gave me more than my share of
leadership and when it became known that I was to accept a
permanent appointment in Washington, some of them
wanted to go to my Archbishop and appeal to him to keep
me in St. Paul. I dissuaded them by earnestly asserting that
my transfer to Washington was in accord with my own deep-
felt desire.

Perhaps the best example of the procedures and attitudes
which I have just described was provided by my membership
in the Saturday Lunch Club of Minneapolis. This group met
every Saturday at luncheon (they called it "lunch") for the
purpose of listening to some more or less prominent speaker,
usually not a member of the Club, and for discussion. The
club included one socialist, two single taxers, and less than a
dozen Catholics. It aided greatly in bringing about the selec-
tion of more competent and more socially minded representatives in the state legislature, more effective regulation of
public utilities, and better social and labor legislation. The
few Catholics in the organization were glad of my member-

For example, the League of Women Voters, a labor union, or a charity organization, adopts a resolution in favor of birth control, while ninety-five per cent of its
activities remain not only unobjectionable but socially beneficial. In such a situation,
the Catholic members, while protesting on every appropriate occasion against its
improper policies, might well continue to participate and cooperate in the good
activities of the organization. Through this course, they not improbably would be
able to effect a reform in the attitude of the organization toward the undesirable
objectives. To quit it entirely or to refuse cooperation with its good purposes would
injure the cause of charity and social justice, and might readily provoke the charge
that Catholics are lacking in civic and social mindedness and act as though they were
aliens in the community. Moreover, the policy of aloofness, except sometimes as a
temporary expedient, is quite unlikely to bring about a reform in attitudes or activities. In the long run and in the majority of such situations, more good will be accomplished by a prudent course of participation and cooperation.

ship, while the non-Catholics were delighted but somewhat surprised, since most of the Catholics that they knew were either political and economic reactionaries or quite devoid of interest in the civic and social problems which were discussed in the Saturday Lunch Club. As for the Catholics outside the organization, most of them looked askance at my participation. To them the Saturday Lunch Club was "a radical bunch," but they never took the trouble to find out what radicalism meant or how the objectives of the Saturday Lunch Club compared with Pope Leo's encyclical "On the Condition of Labor."

Among the founders of the Club was Willis Mason West, head of the Department of History at the University of Minnesota and the author of many textbooks in that field. Shortly before I left St. Paul, he had decided that he was tired of teaching and would be happier as a farmer in northern Minnesota. Within five years, he revised this judgment and returned to the state university. Shortly before he left the university for the farm, the members of the Saturday Lunch Club gave him a dinner at which he was the beneficiary of several laudatory speeches. His first wife had been dead many years but she had left him six children. His second wife, who sat beside him at the dinner, had also presented him with half a dozen offspring. My own spoken tribute to him on that occasion closed with substantially the following language: "It is said of the great French Dominican, Pére Lacordaire, that on his death-bed he exclaimed: 'I die a repentant Monk but an unrepentant liberal.' Now, I have no doubt that Professor West will also die an unrepentant liberal but his chances of dying a repentant Monk are not so good."

Professor West is dead; so is the able journalist, Stiles Jones; the crusading attorney, ames Manahan, who induced the Interstate Commerce Commission to order a 20 per cent reduction in the price of the upper berths in sleeping cars; the incorrigible single taxer, C. F. Buell; and probably the majority of the older members of the Club whom I knew. In 1938 and also in 1939, I addressed the organization when I was on vacation in Minneapolis, but recognized few of those in attendance. At all times, the great majority of the members of the Club have been sincere patriots, lovers of their kind and devoted to social justice. Association with them was beneficial to me and, I think, to them likewise.

CHAPTER VIII

RETURN TO THE CATHOLIC UNIVERSITY: PUB-
LICATION OF *DISTRIBUTIVE JUSTICE*:
THE WORLD WAR

EARLY in 1913, I began to think seriously about transferring from the St. Paul Seminary to the Catholic University. Some of my friends encouraged me in this design,
particularly Rev. Dr. William J. Kerby, who was professor
of sociology at the Catholic University from 1897 until his
death in 1936. As already noted, I had followed some of his
courses as a graduate student in that institution. He always
entertained a somewhat exaggerated estimate of my ability
and usefulness. Three Bishops who had long been good
friends of mine likewise did all they could to promote the
project. They were James J. Keane, Archbishop of Dubuque,
who had been rector of St. Thomas Seminary during four of
my seven years there; James McGolrick, Bishop of Duluth;
and James O'Reilly, Bishop of Fargo. Cardinal Gibbons, as
chancellor of the University, strongly desired to have me on
the faculty. When I called on him in February, 1914, he cut
short my expressions of respect with a plea that I come to
the University as soon as possible.

For some two years, my intermittent requests to be relieved
of my duties at the St. Paul Seminary, were refused by Archbishop Ireland. Nor was the intervention of my friends more
successful. On one occasion when discussing with another
member of the Hierarchy my endeavors to win his assent

through episcopal intercession, the Archbishop exclaimed: "Positively, that man is bombarding me with Bishops!"[1]

However, the Archbishop's unwillingness to permit my departure from St. Paul was not without compensating features. Shortly before my period of study at the Catholic University came to a close, one of my instructors expressed the fear that as professor in Archbishop Ireland's seminary I would not improbably get into difficulty with him because of the differences in our economic views. Other friends of mine occasionally gave voice to the same apprehension. As I have noted in an earlier chapter, nothing of that kind ever came to pass. When, after more than a dozen years of teaching under his eye and direction, he remained reluctant to dispense with my services, I took some satisfaction in the record that I had made and in the failure of the fearful forecasts to which I have just referred.

Indeed, the Archbishop had more than once manifested his faith in my capacity and judgment. The incident which I like best to recall occurred in May, 1911. A few months previously the Archbishops of the United States, in response to repeated urging by their brother of St. Paul, had appointed three Bishops as a committee to make a study of the "losses" suffered by the Church in the United States. Archbishop Ireland had steadily contended that the number of American Catholics "who had fallen away," that is, ceased to be genuine professors of the faith, was much smaller than many prominent Catholics believed and asserted. In the main, he based this position upon his own experience, observation, and analysis of the facts; but his opinion was undoubtedly influenced to some extent by his love for America, her institu-

---

[1] When I told the Archbishop about Cardinal Gibbons' interest in the matter, he replied: "You may tell the Cardinal to mind his own business." Although he and Cardinal Gibbons were lifelong friends and practically always saw eye to eye on Church policies, Archbishop Ireland was invariably vigilant with regard to his own jurisdiction.

tions, and her people. Some of the estimates of the "losses" were, without doubt, much too high, particularly those made by persons whose American patriotism was less comprehensive and less wholehearted than that of John Ireland.

After the Archbishop's committee (of which he was not a member) had been organized, Archbishop Ireland asked me to undertake the direction of the investigation and all the other tasks that were involved in the endeavor to estimate the defections from the Church throughout her history in the United States. He emphasized the large opportunities that would naturally come to me in carrying out the assignment and made an earnest plea for my acceptance. Nothing in his words or manner suggested that he was giving an order or imposing an obligation. Three years were to be allowed for the completion of the work. To his evident surprise, I did not immediately accept but requested a few days for further consideration. Just before leaving New York for Europe, some three weeks later, I wrote the Archbishop, declining the assignment, giving as reasons my lack of familiarity with the technique required for such a study and my reluctance to interrupt my work in the field for which I had prepared myself and in which I believed I could accomplish more for the Church than in the proposed investigation. Undoubtedly, he was greatly disappointed at this response but he never referred to the matter again.

About a dozen years later, a priest student at the Catholic University took this problem as the subject of his doctoral dissertation. His study was published in 1925 under the title "Has the Immigrant Kept the Faith?" Undoubtedly, it is a better production than any that I could have turned out. So, the Archbishop's longfelt wish was realized. Had he lived to read this book, he would not have been disappointed at its conclusions. The author is now Bishop of Seattle, the Most Rev. Gerald Shaughnessy, S.M.

Probably the main reason for the Archbishop's reluctance to let me go to the Catholic University was his fear that professors in his seminary would get into the habit of looking forward to separating themselves from it, and regarding their work at the seminary mainly as an apprenticeship for a wider field at the Catholic University. Two of the seminary professors had already achieved this promotion, namely, Rev. Dr. Thomas E. Shields, who became professor of education at the Catholic University and founder of Catholic Sisters College, and Rev. Dr. William Turner who for several years occupied the chair of philosophy at the University and was appointed Bishop of Buffalo in 1919. The former died on February 15, 1921, the latter on July 10, 1936.

In June, 1915, Archbishop Ireland notified me that he had secured a man to conduct my courses at the seminary and that I was now free to leave for Washington. I took up my work at the University in the latter part of September of that year. It was that of professor of political science. Simultaneously, I conducted a class in economics at Trinity College. With the exception of two years, I have taught continuously at Trinity ever since, most of the time, however, in the Department of Political Science. At the beginning of the school year of 1916–1917, my professorship at the University was changed to that of moral theology, a position which I continued to occupy until 1937, when I became professor of sociology in the School of Social Science. Concurrently with moral theology, I taught a class in industrial ethics.

All three of these courses were of graduate, or postgraduate, rank. Those in moral theology led to the degrees of Licentiate (S.T.L.) and Doctor (S.T.D.) in Sacred Theology, while those in industrial ethics and sociology enabled students to pursue the degrees of Master of Arts and Doctor of Philosophy. In my classes of theology the number of students seldom was greater than ten, and with very few exceptions they were priests who had completed their four years of theological studies before entering the University. One reason why the classes were so small is found in the long time required to obtain degrees. During most of the years when I taught in the School of Sacred Sciences, two years were required for the licentiate and two years more for the doctorate. That meant two and four years respectively in addition to the four years of theological studies which the students had pursued for ordination to the priesthood.

PUBLICATION OF DISTRIBUTIVE JUSTICE

When I came to the University in September, 1915, I brought with me the rough draft of a book to be entitled *Distributive Justice* with the subtitle "The Right and Wrong of Our Present Distribution of Wealth." By the following June I had rewritten (or retyped) the manuscript, and the book was published in November.

As stated in the Preface, the volume aimed "to discuss systematically and comprehensively the justice of the processes by which the product of industry is distributed." Since the distribution is made among four well-defined economic groups, the question that I put before myself was "how much of the product ought to go to each of these groups in order that the distribution may be just?" Therefore, I considered in order, the claims of the landowner, the capitalist, the businessman, and the laborer. Following are the titles of the four sections, dealing respectively with these four agents of production and sharers in the product: I. The Morality of Private Landownership and Rent; II. The Morality of Private Capital and Interest; III. The Moral Aspect of Profits; and IV. The Moral Aspect of Wages. In each of these sections the discussion involved five topics or considerations: (1) the economics of our distributive system; (2) the injustices of the actual distribution; (3) the principles and rules of a just distribution; (4) unsound proposals for a better distribution; and (5) reforms which would bring about a just or a more nearly just distribution.

Briefly set down, the main conclusions of the study were as follows: The existing system is defective, sometimes gravely defective, in every one of its four aspects or institutions, namely, private landownership, private ownership of capital, the direction and ownership of business, and the wage system. Nevertheless, none of these institutions is essentially unjust. Rent-taking is not in itself against justice. Interest on loans in the existing industrial system is as well justified as interest on productive capital. While we cannot demonstrate that the latter is just, neither can we prove that it is unjust. It enjoys a presumptive justification which is sufficient practically. The profits of the businessman do not necessarily violate justice. Nor is the wage contract in itself wrong. The abuses and evils and injustices in our present economic arrangements require different methods for their abolition, according to the institution in which they are found; that is, according as they affect landownership, capital ownership, business management, and the employer-employee relation. No single formula or generalization can be devised which will answer intelligently the question "What Is a Just Distribution?" At the end of the volume, however, an attempt was made to answer it in the following four sentences:

The landowner has a right to all the economic rent, modified by the right of his tenants and employees to a decent livelihood, and by the right of the state to levy taxes which do not substantially lower the value of the land. The capitalist has a right to the prevailing rate of interest, modified by the right of his employees to the "equitable minimum" of wages. The businessman in competitive conditions has a right to all the profits that he can obtain, but corporations possessing a monopoly have no right to unusual gains except those due to unusual efficiency. The laborer has a right to living wages, and to as much more as he can get by competition with the other agents of production and with his fellow laborers.[2]

The two concluding paragraphs emphasize the difficulties of the study and the relativity of the problem of a just distribution:

No doubt many of those who have taken up this volume with the expectation of finding therein a satisfactory formula of distributive justice, and who have patiently followed the discussion to the end, are disappointed and dissatisfied at the final conclusions. Both the particular applications of the rules of justice and the proposals for reform must have seemed complex and indefinite. They are not nearly so simple and definite as the principles of Socialism or the Single Tax. And yet, there is no escape from these limitations. Neither the principles of industrial justice nor the constitution of our socio-economic system is simple. Therefore, it is impossible to give our ethical conclusions anything like mathematical accuracy. The only claim that is made for the discussion is that the moral judgments are fairly reasonable, and the proposed remedies fairly efficacious. When both have been realized in practice, the next step in the direction of wider distributive justice will be much clearer than it is today.

Although the attainment of greater justice in distribution is the primary and most urgent need of our time, it is not the only one that is of great importance. Neither just distribution, nor increased production, nor both combined, will insure a stable and satisfactory social order without a considerable change in human hearts and ideals. The rich must cease to put their faith in material things, and rise to a simpler and saner plane of living; the middle classes and the poor must give up their envy and snobbish imitation of the false and degrading standards of the opulent classes; and all must learn the elementary lesson that the path to achievements worthwhile leads through the field of hard and honest labor, not of lucky "deals" or gouging of the neighbor, and that the only life worth living is that in which one's cherished wants are few, simple, and noble. For the adoption and pursuit of these ideals the most necessary requisite is a revival of genuine religion.[3]

Distributive Justice received wide and favorable recognition.

[2] *Distributive Justice*. Reprinted through the courtesy of The Macmillan Company, 1927, p. 396.
[3] *Idem*, pp. 396–397.

Almost the only adverse reviews were written by socialists and single taxers. One of the most judicious and favorable critiques appeared in the *New Republic*, February 17, 1917, from the competent pen of Dr. Alvin S. Johnson. At the end of his review, he declared that I had presented "the most comprehensive and dignified existing treatise on the ethics of economic reform." The following paragraph is worth quoting in full:

Ethical judgments abound in economic literature, but these are derivative from common sense, not from any logical system of ethics. This is the fault of the ethical systematizers as well as of the economists. Few ethical authorities have had sufficient knowledge of economic facts to adapt ethical principles to the economic field; few economists are abreast of the best modern work in ethics. To this rule the most notable exception among contemporary writers is Dr. Ryan. His economic scholarship is unimpeachable; survey his writings, and you are forced to the conclusion that among the economists of today there are not many who can match him in command of the literature and in sanity of judgment. He would not make a good mathematical economist, one infers from his handling of certain aspects of the interest problem and of "economic causation"; but a man may be an excellent economist without mathematical gifts. Dr. Ryan's ethical scholarship is also sound. It is essentially a Catholic ethics that he professes, and therefore conservative. This makes it all the more significant that Dr. Ryan's book should be worthy of adoption as a manual of radical economic reform.

My good friend, Dr. Carlton J. H. Hayes of Columbia University (whose acquaintance I had not yet made) included the following sentences in the long review that he wrote for the *American Political Science Review*, November, 1917:

A book may be temporarily valuable merely because it is timely, informing, and somewhat novel. It cannot be a masterpiece unless, in addition to these qualities, it has logical and literary excellence. Dr. Ryan in *Distributive Justice* is a master of clarity, precision, and sanity. Primarily an economist, he writes not in the jargon of the professional but so simply as to be immediately apprehended by laymen.

Ten years after its publication I revised the work, making some additions and some eliminations. The new edition was published in May, 1927. Among the principal additions were those presenting new statistical material, a discussion of the decision of the Supreme Court in 1923 nullifying the minimum-wage law of the District of Columbia and a chapter entitled "Toward Industrial Democracy." This chapter presented an expansion of what I had said in one of the chapters of *Socialism: Promise or Menace,* concerning the necessity of enabling wage earners to become also owners of the instruments of production.[4]

At the present time the work calls even more urgently than in 1926 for another revision, to take account of new statistical material, recent developments in economic practices, institutions, and opinion, and pronouncements by the Popes and by the American Hierarchy which have been made since 1930. However, I would not change any of the statements of principles, nor, except in very rare instances, any of the applications of principles. In the editions already published there are a few purely economic propositions and a few reform proposals which need some measure of revision, for example, the land question does not now seem to be as important as when I wrote the book and some of the recommendations for taxation of land, as noted in Chapter VII, have been rendered unnecessary by the tendency of land values to fall rather than to rise. Some new measures of reform require presentation and discussion, particularly with regard to our chronic and mass unemployment. With these changes and possibly a few others the book, I confidently believe, will retain for some time to come a large amount of usefulness.

Distributive Justice is unquestionably the most important book that I have written. Moreover, it is probably the most

[4] See Chapter VII. *Supra.*

nearly adequate work that has been produced by anybody for the province with which it deals.

THE WORLD WAR

At the beginning of the War of 1914–1918, my sympathies immediately went to the Allies. While I placed the proximate responsibility for the outbreak upon Austria, Germany, Russia, France, and England in this order, my attitude toward the two groups of belligerents was determined only in a very slight degree by my interpretation of "war guilt." The main reason why I wanted the Allies to win was that a victory by the Central Powers would bring much more suffering and injustice upon the peoples of the world than would the triumph of France and Great Britain. Despite the grave injustices and the amazing stupidity embodied in certain provisions of the Treaty of Versailles (of which I shall have more to say later on) I cling to my original position in this matter. I still think that victory for the Allies was at least a lesser evil than would have been a victory for imperial Germany, plus Austria, Turkey, and Bulgaria. In this place, it is not necessary to recount the specific facts and reasons which impelled and even now impel me to this conclusion.

When the United States entered the war, April 6, 1917, my reaction was one of regret and sadness. Perhaps I should have felt happy, or at least reconciled, if I had been convinced that American intervention was necessary to prevent a complete German triumph; but I do not recall that I gave much thought to this consideration in 1917. I acquiesced in the declaration of war because I assumed that the President and Congress were in a better position than I to make the right decision.

The proposals for ending the war and re-establishing peace sent by Pope Benedict XV to the belligerents, August 14, 1917, seemed to me to be entirely reasonable. I include here a summary of them because it has been evident for many years now that their rejection by the belligerents was the greatest mistake and the greatest tragedy that has been committed by responsible statesmen in modern times, perhaps in the entire history of mankind:

(1) The fundamental point must be that the material force of arms shall give way to the moral force of right, whence shall proceed a just agreement of all upon a simultaneous and reciprocal decrease of armaments. (2) Taking the place of arms, the institution of arbitration, with its high pacifying function, according to rules to be drawn in concert, and under sanctions to be determined against any state which should decline either to refer international questions to arbitration or to accept its awards. (3) The true community and freedom of the seas. (4) As for damages . . . we see no other way . . . than by setting up the principle of entire and reciprocal condonation. (5) Territory now occupied [to be] reciprocally restituted. Therefore, on the part of Germany, there should be total evacuation of Belgium, with guarantees of its entire political, military, and economic independence towards any power whatever; evacuation also of French territory; on the part of the other belligerents, a similar restitution of the German colonies. (6) The same spirit of equity and justice must direct the examination of the remaining territorial and political questions, and particularly those which concern Armenia, the Balkan States, and the territories which form part of the former kingdom of Poland, which in particular, by reason of her noble historical traditions and the sufferings endured, specially during the present war, has a just claim on the sympathies of all nations.[5]

The response of the Central Powers to the Papal plea I regarded as evasive and almost discourteous. That of President Wilson did not strike me as convincing. His reasons for not accepting the Pope's proposals were plausible, but they involved too many assumptions. Even his conception of Benedict's fundamental stipulation was inaccurate and did the Papal position less than justice. To say that "His Holiness in substance proposes that we return to the *status quo ante bellum*," was to introduce a facile phrase which in the circumstances

---

[5] See *The Pope Speaks*. Harcourt, Brace and Company, 1940, pp. 285–289.

could easily carry with it misleading connotations. At any rate, it was an oversimplification. If the Pope's specific recommendations had been adopted by all the belligerents, the new Europe might well have been so different from the *status quo ante* as to render the dispute about a return to it relatively unimportant. Apparently the main reason for the President's rejection of Pope Benedict's proposals was stated in the following sentence:

We cannot take the word of the present rulers of Germany as a guarantee of anything that is to endure, unless explicitly supported by such conclusive evidence of the will and purpose of the German people themselves as the other peoples of the world would be justified in accepting.

Nevertheless, peace negotiations in the spirit and the atmosphere that were possible in 1917 might well have enlisted the wholehearted support of the German people. Not improbably they would have overthrown and adequately curbed their "irresponsible government." While we cannot be certain that these things would have come to pass, we can be well assured that if President Wilson and the other statesmen on both sides who rejected the Papal proposals could have foreseen the present awful condition of Europe they would have given the Pope different answers. Enlightened by such a look into the future, President Wilson would have seen in the Pope's proposals the most hopeful basis for attaining the noble ends which he stated in the following sentences:

Punitive damages, the dismemberment of empires, the establishment of selfish and exclusive economic leagues, we deem inexpedient and in the end worse than futile, no proper basis for a peace of any kind, least of all for an enduring peace. That must be based upon justice and fairness and the common rights of mankind.

In February, 1918, I published an article in the *Catholic World* entitled "Freedom of Speech in Wartime." Were our country at war today and I writing on the same subject, I should not recede from any of the positions taken in that production. Following is its most important paragraph:

The question of freedom of speech in wartime presents two aspects, the legal and the moral. Under the former comes the alleged constitutional right to oppose by speech and publication the military policies of our Government. Men have vociferously proclaimed that such a right is guaranteed to them by that provision of the Federal Constitution which declares that "Congress shall make no law . . . abridging the freedom of speech or of the press." The espionage law, which prohibits spoken or printed words tending to discourage recruiting and the operation of the selective draft, and which has been utilized to send such exponents of free speech to jail, is angrily asserted to be in violation of this article of the Constitution. As pointed out by Louis F. Post, however, there is another article in the Constitution which empowers Congress to declare war, and to make all laws which shall be necessary and proper for carrying its war powers into execution. On their face, these clauses give Congress full authority to enact the espionage law, or any other law which restricts freedom of speech to the extent necessary to prosecute the war. The freedom of speech protected by the Constitution is stated in very general terms. It is not declared by the Constitution to be unlimited. Whether and how far it may properly be limited by statute law in particular cases, can be determined only through other provisions of the Constitution, and through the meaning that was authoritatively attached to the right of freedom of speech when the Constitution was adopted. Both these tests seem to justify the restrictions which Congress has already placed upon freedom of expression in the present war. In any case, the power to interpret the Constitution authoritatively has been located by that document itself in the Federal Supreme Court. It has not been confided to the fragile judgment of war-opponents, conscientious or otherwise. These zealous defenders of the Constitution should utilize the remedy provided by the Constitution. They should take their grievance to the courts.

About the middle of December, 1918, I spoke in advocacy of a league of nations at a meeting of the Knights of Columbus in Louisville, Kentucky. This was one of the very first addresses delivered in the United States on this subject. As we know, the Covenant of the League of Nations was not embodied in the Treaty of Versailles until some five months later.

In the May, 1919, issue of the *Catholic Charities Review*, I said in an editorial:

The sum of the argument is this: states are bound to one another by as definite, as urgent and as far-reaching obligations of charity as those which govern individuals; in the present international crisis these obligations of charity clearly require the United States to make those relatively slight sacrifices which are necessary to save the peoples of Europe from experiences perhaps worse than those of the war, through which they have just passed; and the only means in sight by which this can be accomplished is the League of Nations.

More than twenty-one years after the publication of this editorial, I stated my attitude toward the League in a pamphlet entitled "The Obligation of Catholics to Promote Peace" and "The Rights of Peoples," published in September, 1940, as follows:

Unfortunately the international organization set up at Versailles was greatly handicapped from the beginning. The League of Nations was dominated by a few of the powerful and victorious states and was conducted in much the same vengeful spirit that these same states had embodied in the treaty of peace. Probably this fact was mainly responsible for the opposition of American Catholics to American membership in the League. Had, however, the United States entered the League, it might have exercised sufficient influence to change the principal injustices of the peace treaty and to develop an effective instrument of world peace and world justice. Of course, we cannot be certain that American participation would have produced these beneficent results. Of three things, however, we can be certain: (1) that American participation could have caused the whole post-war history to be different and infinitely better; (2) the incompetence of the League could not have been greater with America in than it has been with America out; (3) the representatives of the United States in the League would have been able to prevent their associates from inflicting injury upon our own country.

The temptation to elaborate each of these three points is very great, but it must be resisted in this place. Nevertheless, we wish to summarize very briefly the practical implications of these three propositions: (1) American membership in the League would have prevented the collapse of the German Republic and the triumph of Hitler; (2) with America in the League, conditions and developments in Germany, Russia, and Italy and some other countries could not have been worse than they are and have been since the end of the World War; (3) the assumption that the representatives of European countries would have shown themselves to be so much more clever than the American members, that our interests would have been gravely endangered, receives no support from what we know about the intelligence and skill of our countrymen. It is curious and paradoxical that some of our most active jingoes disclose an inferiority complex when they think of American representatives sitting face to face with those of other countries at a conference table.

CHAPTER IX

THE BISHOPS' PROGRAM OF SOCIAL RECON-STRUCTION: THE NATIONAL CATHOLIC WELFARE CONFERENCE

B ETWEEN February, 1918, and June, 1919, more than sixty programs under the title, "Social Reconstruction," or some variation of it, were drawn up and published by prominent groups of persons in Italy, France, Great Britain, and the United States. The authors of these pronouncements assumed that the war had made the world safe for political democracy and that the peoples of the world were now ready to establish a regime of economic democracy and social justice. Hence they undertook with varying degrees of comprehensiveness to show just how this end could be attained.

The great majority of the programs came from religious bodies and labor unions; about half a dozen were issued by business organizations.

These pronouncements were well described and summarized in a publication entitled *Reconstruction Programs,* by Estella T. Weeks, published in New York in 1919 by the Woman's Press. Their general nature, aims, and spirit are stated in the Introduction to this little volume.

For over half a year now [says Miss Weeks], the challenging tocsin of "Win the War" has been stilled, and the slogan "Reconstruction" has taken its place. . . . Mankind—and even more, womankind—has found in itself a tremendous new moral force sufficient to stir hundreds of millions to daily, hourly, putting forth of the best in them in a *common cause*, spurred by an idealism of democracy vital to live as well as to die for. . . . The most significant note that echoes in practically all the programs studied is a consciousness of the new spirit abroad in the world. New conceptions of human liberty, justice and opportunity are being voiced. . . . Reconstruction must be made a crusade.

The fervent faith and large hopes of a better world expressed in the foregoing sentences were not realized. None of the reconstruction programs was adopted in any country. If the authors could have foreseen what a small part of their proposals would be in operation twenty-two years later, they would undoubtedly have been greatly discouraged and disillusioned.

Some ten or twelve of the sixty-odd reconstruction programs had appeared before December 1, 1918, when I accepted an invitation to address a gathering of the Knights of Columbus at Louisville. The ablest and most comprehensive of them was the "Social Reconstruction Program" of the British Labor Party, the authorship of which was generally credited to Mr. Sydney Webb, the distinguished Fabian socialist. Inasmuch as it pointed to complete Socialism as the ultimate goal, its favorable reception by the public seemed to me to indicate the need of a positive program from a Catholic source. Why should I not try my hand at the task? After summarizing briefly the pronouncement issued by Cardinal Bourne, Archbishop of Westminster, and the programs of the British Labor Party, of the American Federation of Labor, of twenty British Quaker employers, of the United States Chamber of Commerce, and of the British Interdenominational Conference of Social Service Unions, I stated that I should not attempt "to formulate a comprehensive scheme of reconstruction," but should confine my attention "to those reforms that seemed to be desirable and also obtainable within a reasonable time, and to a few general principles which should become a guide to more distant developments."

When I had almost finished the production, I realized that it was much too long for an address on such an occasion. Therefore, I put it aside and prepared the speech on the League of Nations.

A few days after I had put aside the rough draft of the piece on social reconstruction, the Rev. Dr. John O'Grady, who was then secretary of the Committee on Special War Activities of the National Catholic War Council, happened to see it on my desk, and learned that I had no idea when or where it would be published. "Let me have it," he said; "I want to bring it to the attention of my committee." Inasmuch as he seemed to be in a hurry to get the production, I refrained from rewriting it and merely dictated with a few verbal corrections the contents of the pencil draft to the operator of a typewriting machine and added a final carefully written paragraph. When he read it to the members a day or two later, Dr. O'Grady had no difficulty in getting the committee's approval of it for publication by the National Catholic War Council. Soon after that event, the Administrative Committee of the National Catholic War Council accepted the production and issued it with less than half a dozen verbal changes on February 12, 1919. It should be noted that the National Catholic War Council was composed of the Catholic Archbishops of the United States and that the Administrative Committee was its executive agency. The members of this Committee were Peter J. Muldoon, Bishop of Rockford and chairman; Joseph Schrembs, Bishop of Toledo; Patrick J. Hayes, afterward Cardinal-Archbishop of New York; and William T. Russell, Bishop of Charleston. All of them have passed away except Bishop Schrembs, who is now Archbishop-Bishop of Cleveland. Following is a copy of the Foreword, signed by the members of the Administrative Committee:

The ending of the Great War has brought peace. But the only safeguard of peace is social justice and a contented people. The deep unrest so emphatically and so widely voiced throughout the world is the most serious menace to the future peace of every nation and of the entire world. Great problems face us. They cannot be put aside; they must be met and solved with justice to all.

In the hope of stating the lines that will best guide us in their right solution the following pronouncement is issued by the Administrative Committee of the National Catholic War Council. Its practical applications are of course subject to discussion, but all its essential declarations are based upon the principles of charity and justice that have always been held and taught by the Catholic Church, while its practical proposals are merely an adaptation of those principles and that traditional teaching to the social and industrial conditions and needs of our own time.

It should be noted that the official title of the program was: "Social Reconstruction: A General Review of the Problems and Survey of Remedies."

The main proposals and recommendations of the document may be summarized as follows:

(1) Minimum-wage legislation; (2) insurance against unemployment, sickness, invalidity, and old age; (3) a sixteen-year minimum age limit for working children; (4) the legal enforcement of the right of labor to organize; (5) continuation of the National War Labor Board, for this and other purposes affecting the relations of employers and employees; (6) a national employment service; (7) public housing for the working classes; (8) wartime wages and a long-distance program of increasing them, not only for the benefit of labor but in order to bring about that general prosperity which cannot be maintained without a wide distribution of purchasing power among the masses; (9) prevention of excessive profits and incomes through a regulation of rates which allows the owners of public utilities only a fair rate of return on their actual investment, and through progressive taxes on inheritance and income, and excess profits; (10) effective control of monopolies, even by the method of government competition if that should prove necessary; (11) participation of labor in management and a wider distribution of ownership through cooperative enterprises and worker ownership in the stock of corporations; (12) establishment

of cooperative stores in order to eliminate unnecessary middlemen, reduce prices to the consumer and train the participants in business methods and in the capacity for cooperation.

Undoubtedly the "Bishops' Program" received much more public attention and discussion than any of the other programs for social reconstruction. Catholics, Protestants, journalists, economists, and labor leaders gave it a large measure of praise. The most conspicuous dissents from this general acclaim were provided by the *National Civic Federation Review* and the famous (or infamous) "Lusk Report" on *Revolutionary Radicalism*. In volume four, number eleven, of the former, the editor, who was the late Ralph M. Easley, wrote:

> But it must be remembered that this "manifesto" is not the view of the Catholic Church; it is only the expression of opinion of the gentlemen signing the document and has no official sanction.

In the September 25, 1920, number of the same publication, P. Tecumseh Sherman published a long article in which he strove to show that the endorsement of the legal minimum wage and of social insurance by the "Bishops' Program" was neither economically sound nor in exact accord with Catholic doctrine. Mr. Easley's pronouncement is obviously superficial and incorrect, while Mr. Sherman's has been refuted and discredited by the logic of subsequent events.

At the end of the first of the four very large volumes constituting the "Report of the Joint Legislative Committee Investigating Seditious Activities, filed April 24, 1929, in the Senate of the State of New York" (the "Lusk Report"), we read the following:

> A certain group in the Catholic Church with leanings toward Socialism, under the leadership of the Rev. Dr. Ryan, professor at the Catholic University of Washington, issued in January, 1918, a pamphlet called "Social Reconstruction; a General Review of the Problems, and a Survey of Remedies." . . . Where the socialistic tendency of the committee shows itself most clearly is in what is said under the heading

of "Cooperation and Copartnership." This statement is of sufficient importance to be quoted.[1]

The quotation comprises the well-known paragraph of the "Bishops' Program" which declares that the majority of the workers "must somehow become owners, or at least in part, of the instruments of production," describes the methods by which this goal can be reached and points out that it "would not mean the abolition of private ownership." When the Lusk Committee called this proposal "socialistic" it identified and stigmatized itself as one of the most benighted bodies ever created by a state legislature. It implicitly proclaimed that American wage earners should never become anything but wage earners. Of course, this doctrine is directly contrary to that laid down by Pope Leo XIII and Pope Pius XI. Probably the chairman, Senator Clayton R. Lusk, was both ignorant of and indifferent to any pronouncement by the Popes, but the three or four Catholic members of the committee should have known better than to sanction this extraordinary reference to the "Bishops' Program." To be sure, the "Lusk Report" was published in 1920, while the encyclical *Quadragesimo Anno* did not appear until 1931; but the encyclical *Rerum Novarum* had been in existence almost thirty years.

Perhaps the most effective refutation of the foregoing and a few other charges against the orthodoxy of the "Bishops' Program" was provided by a letter from Bishop Muldoon, published in the *Nation*, April 11, 1919:

However much men may differ about certain minor details contained in the Programme, it is based upon the immutable principles of justice and charity which the Church holds, has ever held, and will ever hold. The duty of the Universal Church is to instruct the citizens of each state in the application of these principles. And although at times the Church has found it difficult to make its voice heard above the clamor of materialism, yet she has ever been watchful for a suitable

---

[1] Vol. I, p. 1139.

opportunity to impress her lessons of justice and charity upon all peoples, but especially upon captains of industry. That opportunity came at the close of the war. To us it appeared that the world, and in particular the United States, was willing to listen to representatives of the Church, which throughout all the ages has striven not only to protect the workman but to further his progress in all ways consistent with Christian morality. In this you have the reason why the Bishops have brought forth once again the old, old principles of justice which the Church is bound to preserve and to teach as best she may.

Four or five years after he had written the foregoing letter, I asked Bishop Muldoon whether any of the American Bishops regarded the program as too radical or too advanced. He replied in the negative, adding, however, that a Bishop who entertained such a view might have hesitated to avow it to him, on account of his authoritative sponsorship of the document. Nevertheless, Bishop Muldoon seemed to be persuaded that the amount of dissent from the program was insignificant among the members of the American Hierarchy.

On re-reading the reviews of and comments on the "Bishops' Program" more than twenty years later, one finds in most of them the belief that it would have a great and beneficent influence upon social thought and social action in the near future. By some of the commentators this belief was expressed in terms of optimistic enthusiasm. As we now know, all such hopeful forecasts met with disappointment. For more than a decade, social thinking and social action were chilled and stifled in an atmosphere of pseudo prosperity and thinly disguised materialism.

About the only effective opposition to this degeneration was offered by the Department of Social Action of the National Catholic Welfare Conference. After the great depression got under way, and particularly following the appearance of the encyclical *Quadragesimo Anno* in 1931, there occurred a revival of interest in the "Bishops' Program," which continued to grow until the year 1939 when a new edition became necessary. It was called the Twentieth Anniversary Edition.[2] In the Introduction by Most Reverend Edward Mooney, Archbishop of Detroit, and chairman of the Administrative Board of the National Catholic Welfare Conference, it is noted that of the twelve proposals of the "Bishops' Program" summarized in a preceding paragraph of this chapter, all but the last two have been either wholly or partially translated into reality. Indeed, some little progress has been made even with regard to these two. Continuing, the Introduction declares:

The proposals and recommendations of the "Bishops' Program" were, indeed, far-reaching for the time when they were written. But viewing the document in the light of present-day discussion, we are immediately struck by two omissions: the program says little or nothing about the problem of unemployment, and disclaims any intention "to formulate a comprehensive scheme of reconstruction." There are two explanations for the former omission. In the first place, the country had not seen any serious unemployment in the four years immediately preceding the publication of the program. There was then no warning that an industrial recession was coming in 1920. In the second place, there was then no indication of the great technological improvements that were to appear some three years later. The substitution of machines for men had not yet attained the pace at which it has proceeded from 1922 until the present moment. When the "Bishops' Program" was published there was no definite reason for thinking that the country was on the eve of a period of chronic unemployment. Nevertheless, the "Bishops' Program" demanded an increase in labor's share of the national income and a decrease in excessive profits both as a measure of social justice and as a preventive of widespread unemployment and recurring industrial depressions. Today anyone can discern the prophetic truth of that statement.

This discussion of the "Bishops' Program" may be fittingly closed with the presentation of two other recent pronounce-

[2] At the instance of Senator LaFollette, this was promptly printed as *Senate Document*, *No. 79*, of the first session of the 76th Congress.

ments. The statement on the "Church and Social Order" issued February 7, 1940 by the Archbishops and Bishops of the Administrative Board of the National Catholic Welfare Conference, advocates many of the measures recommended in the earlier document; for example, a wider distribution of ownership, a better distribution of the national income between capitalists and wage earners, social insurance against unemployment, sickness, accident, old age, and death, participation by the workers in the management, profits, and ownership of business, the right of labor to a living wage before the capital owner receives profits, and the right of labor "to bargain collectively through its own chosen representatives." The other declaration which I wish to quote was made by Robert H. Jackson, the Attorney General of the United States, at the annual meeting of the National Conference of Catholic Charities in Richmond, October 17, 1938:

Liberal political thinking in America has been profoundly influenced by the "Bishops' Program of Social Reconstruction," issued by four Bishops of the Church, including Cardinal Hayes, shortly after the close of the World War. Too modestly disclaiming that it was a "comprehensive scheme of reconstruction," it sought to serve as "an imperative call to action" for "reforms that seem to be desirable and also obtainable within a reasonable time." But the leaders of public life chosen at that time were bent on restoring "normalcy." They had no ear for advice or reform. What suffering might have been spared to men, had the voice of the Bishops been heeded by those who came to power in 1920, instead of having to wait for the disaster-born administration of 1933.

THE NATIONAL CATHOLIC WELFARE CONFERENCE

This heading is not intended to imply that the paragraphs under it will present a comprehensive description of the organization bearing this title. Only one department of it is pertinent to the production upon which I am now engaged. It seems appropriate, however, to include a brief account of the organization's origin. The paragraphs quoted below are taken from an article in the *American Ecclesiastical Review,* October, 1928, written by the late Most Rev. Austin Dowling, Archbishop of St. Paul, and at the time chairman of the Administrative Committee of the National Catholic Welfare Conference:

In February, 1919, seventy-seven Bishops of the United States met in Washington to celebrate the Golden Jubilee of Cardinal Gibbons. At that meeting the now Cardinal Cerretti appeared and expressed the wish of His Holiness, the then Pope, Benedict XV, that the Bishops should make plans for an annual meeting whereat they would take common counsel on matters of general import and establish definite departments that would, under their supervision and direction, carry the work assigned. The Bishops immediately and unanimously decided to act in accordance with the Holy Father's request. To form such an organization a survey committee of Bishops, known as the General Committee on Catholic Affairs and Interests, was appointed by the Chairman, Cardinal Gibbons, with orders to make a survey and to report at the next meeting of the Bishops to be held the following September.

In the meanwhile, on 10 April, 1919, the Holy Father, Benedict XV, having received word of the action of the Bishops at their February meeting, wrote a letter to all the Bishops of the United States in which he congratulated them on the action taken, pointed out how the progress of Catholicism is promoted by these frequent assemblies of the Bishops: how through the wisdom gathered from such assemblies "the wise direction of the Bishops" may be helpful to the social and educational movements of the day.

This General Committee on Catholic Affairs and Interests, after diligent labor and country-wide conference, reported at the September meeting. Ninety-three Bishops attended. That meeting resolved that an organization of the Bishops be formed to be known as the National Catholic Welfare Council. It further decided that "an Administrative Committee, composed of seven members of the Hierarchy, be elected by the National Catholic Welfare Council to transact all business between meetings of the National Catholic Welfare Council and to carry out the wishes of the National Catholic Welfare Council as expressed in its annual sessions."

It will be noted that in the last paragraph, Archbishop Dowling refers to the new organization as the National Catholic Welfare *Council*. At the annual meeting of the Hierarchy in 1923, the name was changed to the National Catholic Welfare *Conference*. "The General Committee on Catholic Affairs and Interests," appointed by Cardinal Gibbons at the meeting of the Bishops in February, 1919, consisted of Bishops Muldoon, Schrembs, Glass, and Russell, who then constituted the Administrative Committee of the National Catholic War Council. It will be observed, therefore, that the National Catholic Welfare Council grew out of and succeeded to the National Catholic War Council. When the general committee made its report to the Bishops in September, 1919, it recommended the establishment of the following departments "to carry on efficiently the work of the National Catholic Welfare Council": (1) Education (2) Press and Literature (3) Social and Charitable Services (4) Societies and Lay Activities (5) Missions, Home and Foreign. Before the next meeting of the National Catholic Welfare Council (held September 22–23, 1920) the name of the Department of Social and Charitable Services had been changed to the Department of Social Action. Slight modifications have also been made in the titles of the departments having charge of the press and lay activities; the Department of Missions was never set up; four new departments have been organized, namely, Executive, Legal, Catholic Action Study, and Youth. The total number of departments is now eight.

Between the February and the September meetings in 1919, the general committee had appointed subcommittees to assist it in preparing its report to the Bishops. The group to which was assigned the subject, "Social and Charitable Services," suggested that the division to be set up for this field be called the "National Bureau of Social Service," and suggested for the bureau about a dozen important activities. Most of these fell under the head of sociology and social work rather than labor and industry. These proposals were embodied in the report of the general committee.

The Department of Social Action was organized in February, 1920. For seven years, it comprised two divisions, one dealing with social work and citizenship, the other with industrial relations. The chairman, and authoritative head, of the department, was Most Reverend Peter J. Muldoon, Bishop of Rockford and former chairman of the Administrative Committee of the National Catholic War Council. The director, and immediate executive, of the Chicago division, was Dr. John A. Lapp, an able authority on sociology and political science. I was appointed director of the division located at the headquarters of the N.C.W.C. in Washington. My first act in this position was to secure as assistant director, Rev. R. A. McGowan, a young priest who had been a member of my class of industrial ethics at the Catholic University in the scholastic year of 1915–1916 and who had subsequently served as army chaplain.

This is as good a place as any to put down, after more than twenty years of close personal and professional association, my estimate of Father McGowan. The Department of Social Action, the Catholic Church in the United States, and the cause of social justice, are indebted to him in far greater measure than I could adequately describe. Although I have been and still am his superior in the department and the responsible director of its activities, I recognize that he has done by far the greater share of the work, both in planning and execution, and originated the majority of the decisions. I cannot recall any important instance where his judgment was mistaken. Moreover, he has furnished most of the new ideas for the department. So pleasant and amicable have been our personal relations that my recollection does not cover any occasion on which a word of blame, complaint, or annoyance passed between us. Many a time I have thanked God that Father McGowan happened to be unassigned and living in Washington when I was required to find an assistant director for the Department of Social Action.

Operating within the Department of Social Action are the Rural Life Bureau and the Family Life Section; closely affiliated with it are the Rural Life Conference; the Catholic Association for International Peace and the Catholic Conference on Industrial Problems. With the exception of the Rural Life Conference all these organizations are directed by members of the staff of the department.

For several years now the principal fields of activities of the Department of Social Action have been industrial relations, citizenship, rural welfare, and international relations. The types of specific activities under these heads comprise publications, correspondence, lectures, appearances before committees of Congress, co-operation with other bodies in the pursuit of common social objectives, suggestions for the organization of study clubs and outlines for conducting their meetings, and the promotion and conduct of industrial conferences. More than one hundred and fifty pamphlets and several books have been published by the department; the correspondence has become enormous and the amount of information distributed to inquirers is almost equally great; members of the staff give lectures or other forms of addresses on appropriate subjects to various kinds of organizations with considerable frequency; they testify on bills under consideration by committees of Congress whenever they can do so consistently with their other duties and their interest in the proposed legislation. Not the least important activity of the department has been co-operation with similar bodies in the Federal Council of Churches of Christ and the Central Conference of American Rabbis in the organization and carrying out of industrial conferences, for example, on unemployment.

The Catholic Conference on Industrial Problems has held upwards of eighty-five two-day conferences in some thirty-five cities from the Atlantic to the Pacific and from St. Paul to New Orleans. Finally, the department has helped to organize, provide speakers for, and participate in Priests' Summer Schools of Social Action, the majority lasting four weeks, in ten different dioceses, and two National Congresses of Social Action held respectively in Milwaukee in 1938 and in Cleveland in 1939.

The Milwaukee congress was held under the patronage of Archbishop Stritch. It was attended by thirty-five Bishops, seven hundred and fifty priests, and several thousand lay persons. There were five general sessions and seventeen sectional meetings. At each of the latter the problems of a particular industry or profession or economic group were discussed by three speakers. In almost every instance the third speaker was a Bishop or priest who set forth the Catholic teaching with regard to the industry or group that was under discussion. For example, Bishop Muench dealt with "Agrarianism in the Christian Social Order"; Rev. Frederick Siedenburg, S.J., explained Catholic social teaching in relation to the automobile industry; Bishop Lucey offered remedies from the encyclicals for "Proletarian and Industrial Insecurity"; Rev. John M. Hayes, D.D., discussed "Catholic Principles and the Meat Packing Industry." Some of the other industries considered at the sectional meetings were the building trades, needle trades, printing trades, railroad industry, and the steel industry. By far the greater part of the economic life of the country was considered in these sectional meetings.

On the day following the close of this great conference, two meetings were conducted at the same place by several hundred priests for the discussion of social action by the clergy. Among the topics discussed were: sermons on social problems; radio addresses; lectures; study clubs; labor schools; literature and the press; employers, employees, and legislation. The methods and proposals considered at these meetings were directed toward bringing priests into active participation in social action, not merely through speaking and writing, but through actual contact with industrial operations.

Near the close of the Milwaukee congress a statement of basic principles was presented by the Most Rev. Edwin V. O'Hara and the Most Rev. Karl J. Alter, respectively, the chairman and vice-chairman of the Department of Social Action. Following are the most important propositions:

That a prominent aim of industry should be to provide stable employment so as to eliminate the insecurity and the other social ills that arise from excessive changes of employment and residence.

That as machinery is introduced into industry, workers thereby displaced should be guaranteed adequate protection.

That employment should be available for workers at not less than a family living income.

That a Christian Social Order in America will look forward to some participation by employees in profits and management.

That a wide distribution of ownership of productive property should be encouraged by legislation.

That collective bargaining, through freely chosen representatives, be recognized as a basic right of labor.

That minimum wage standards be set up by law for labor unprotected by collective bargaining.

That there must be an increase of wealth produced, if there is to be an adequate increase of wealth distributed.

That a Christian Social Order involves decent housing for all the people.

That a Christian Social Order, organized on the basis of self-governing industries and professions, according to the plan proposed by Pius XI in his encyclical, *Quadragesimo Anno,* will establish social justice and promote industrial peace.

That a Christian Social Order can be maintained only on the basis of a full acceptance of the teachings of Jesus Christ.

Surely, the foregoing propositions are devoid of vagueness, platitudinousness or "pussyfooting." Every one of them is definite, specific, courageous, and progressive. Twenty years ago, or even ten years ago, this series of "basic principles" could not have been produced by any equally representative assembly of American Catholics. Indeed, no gathering of anything like the magnitude of the Milwaukee congress could have been assembled at either of these periods, and obviously not at any earlier period. More strikingly than any possible array of other evidence, this congress manifests the immense progress made by Catholics in this country in their appreciation of the importance of Catholic industrial teaching and the necessity of diffusing it in a systematic manner. To the Department of Social Action of the National Catholic Welfare Conference belongs a very great part, probably the greater part, of the credit for this beneficent change in thinking and in action. Since its establishment, the department has probably done more to promote the study and propagation of Catholic social principles, particularly as found in the great encyclicals of Popes Leo XIII and Pius XI, than all other influences combined.

A few Catholics have attacked the department and tried to discredit its actions and utterances, on the ground that neither it nor its officers are accurate exponents of Catholic social doctrine. This sort of criticism has come mainly from two sources: ultraconservative but socially ignorant persons, and industrialists who dislike some of our statements on wages, labor unions, industrial democracy, etc. For two practical reasons this opposition has been ineffective: first, our position was easily shown to be in accord with authoritative Catholic teaching, as found in Papal encyclicals; second, the chairmen of the department, Bishops Muldoon, Lillis, and O'Hara have never regarded those criticisms as valid, or requested us to modify our interpretations of Catholic social doctrine.

Looking back over the history of the Department of Social Action, I realize that my part in it has been one of the most satisfying and fruitful experiences of my life.

CHAPTER X

IN DEFENSE OF CIVIL RIGHTS AND LIBERTIES

THE paragraph quoted in Chapter VIII from my article on "Freedom of Speech in Wartime," defended
whatever restrictive legislation should be found necessary to
promote efficient execution of the war measures adopted by
our government in 1917 and 1918. Nevertheless, some two
years after the appearance of this article, I became an active
member of the Joint Amnesty Committee which worked
over a period of some three years (1921–1923) to obtain the
release of the so-called "Political Prisoners." These were
men who had been convicted during the years 1917 and 1918
of violating those provisions of the espionage and compul-
sory-service laws which proscribed actions or utterances
which would tend to interfere with the successful conduct
of the war.

After the conflict had ended, I saw no reason, either of
patriotism or of morality, to justify the further detention of
prisoners whose only political offense had consisted in writing
or speaking against American participation in the war, or
criticizing the manner in which it was carried on, or retaining
membership in some organization which included a few
other men who had so written or spoken. It seemed to me
that the objects of these wartime acts had been fully attained
through the incarceration of the offenders for the duration of
the war. The attitude which I took at that time on this question is fully set forth in the following article which I published
in the *Catholic Charities Review*, May, 1922:

In Christ's description of the Last Judgment, as recorded in the 25th chapter of the Gospel according to St. Matthew, one of the tests whereby the sheep will be separated from the goats is this: "I was in prison and you came to Me." There are still confined in various Federal prisons about 100 political prisoners. These men are all serving sentences on charges of having violated the Espionage Act and the Selective Service Act. The offences for which they are detained all consisted of words spoken or written. None of them is now serving time for any act of violence.

Freedom of speech is not an absolute right, either in morals or under the civil law. Since a man can effectively interfere with the conduct of war by his vocal organs or by his pen, as well as by his arms or his hands, he may be as reasonably restrained from, and punished for, acts of the former kind, as of the latter kind. The assumption that men should be permitted to say what they like regardless of the effects, is illogical and indefensible.

Nevertheless, these political prisoners should all be released without further delay. This, for two reasons: First, because they have already expiated whatever guilt attaches to them. Two or three years' imprisonment is surely sufficient retribution for such utterances as, "this is a capitalistic war," or "we ought not to enlist in an army which will shoot down our brothers in Europe." Very few of the speeches and expressions for which these men were sentenced contained anything stronger than the words just quoted. In the second place, it is overwhelmingly probable that the majority of those still in prison did not even commit the acts for which they were convicted. Ninety-eight men belonging to the I.W.W. were found guilty at one time in Chicago, August, 1918, by a jury which deliberated only twenty-five minutes. Major Alexander S. Lanier, who was commissioned by the Military Intelligence Department of the Government to review the records in all the I.W.W. cases, declared that these men were convicted in "a wave of hysteria," and that if the American people knew the facts, "they would demand that every one of them be released."

The responsibility for keeping these men in prison rests immediately upon the Department of Justice. Apparently the Department assumes that most, if not all, of the prisoners should be denied liberty as a warning to others who might be tempted to speak or write against the Government's conduct of a war. Inasmuch as the next war in which the United States will be engaged, is very uncertain as regards time, the relation between the present detention of these men and the mental operations of men who might be tempted to imitate them during an indefinite war in the indefinite future, is neither direct, important, nor obvious. The position taken by the Department of Justice in these cases can be adequately explained only on the hypothesis of belated war hysteria. All the other nations that were engaged in the war have long since freed all the men that they had imprisoned on charges similar to those for which our political offenders are still held in prison. Is our Government less just and more vindictive than other governments? Or, do our officials require a longer time to emancipate themselves from the benumbing and perverting influence of war psychology?

In a letter to me about one month earlier, Major Lanier said:

It is a great wrong to keep these men in prison. Many of them were absolutely innocent, as you say, of any offense whatsoever, and were convicted solely because they were members of a revolutionary and deservedly unpopular organization. Political prisoners, four years after the cessation of hostilities, is a very grave reproach to our Government, and is doing more harm than good.

Major Lanier's reference to the main reason why those men were convicted and sentenced, has application to many situations other than those which arose during the World War. Many times since then men have been sentenced to prison, or otherwise deprived of their civil rights, not because they had violated a legal statute, but because they were regarded as dangerous, or at least as "undesirable" persons to have at large. Lawmakers, law administrators, and juries have dealt with them, not in conformity with the provisions of the statutes or the Constitution but according to the principle or the practice of lynch law. Even a President of the United States yielded to this prejudice and adopted this method. In a letter to me, under date of September 25, 1922, President Harding wrote: "The decisions have been delayed because I thought it undesirable to pardon men with I.W.W. tendencies in a time when the nation was greatly threatened by the existing industrial strikes."

In other words, men who, according to the principles of law, deserve to be at liberty may be kept in jail, lest their freedom become a social or industrial nuisance.

The last group of the political prisoners (those sentenced in Sacramento) was released by President Coolidge at Christmas, 1923. Whether he would have moved more promptly and taken a more rational view of the whole problem than President Harding if their places had been exchanged, we do not know. What we do know is that Mr. Coolidge's act of clemency, toward the end of 1923, was much less contentious and much more "safe" than it would have been in 1921 or 1922. At any rate, the incident exemplified the well-known "Coolidge luck."

What has just been said about the infliction of illegal or extralegal penalties upon undesirable persons, brings to mind the expulsion of the socialists from the lower house of the New York legislature early in the year 1920. There were five of these, all representing districts in New York City. They were expelled merely as members of the Socialist party, because they "belonged to and were affiliated with a disloyal, seditious and revolutionary organization." Inasmuch as a legislative body is constitutionally empowered to keep out or to throw out any elected member for any reason, or for no reason, the action of the New York legislature in this case was not illegal. It was merely extralegal and arbitrary. At the committee hearing which was followed by the act of expulsion, the socialist members "on trial" were represented by my erstwhile antagonist in the debate on Socialism, Morris Hillquit. Here is a copy of a letter which I wrote him on that occasion:

January 26, 1920

My Dear Mr. Hillquit:

When I was in New York Friday I telephoned your residence with the intention of congratulating you on the very able and altogether magnificent fight that you have been making at Albany on behalf of fair play and representative government. What I wanted to say to you then I say now.

You and your associates are combating the most brazen and insidious political outrage that has been committed in this country since 1877. I agree with the social and political principles held by your five clients as little today as in the days when you and I crossed swords in the pages of *Everybody's Magazine,* but I hope I still believe in justice, in democracy, in the reign of law.

Possibly my desire to see your present triumph is not altogether unselfish, for I see quite clearly that if the five Socialist representatives are expelled from the New York Assembly on the ground that they belong to and avow loyalty to an organization which the autocratic majority regards as "inimical to the best interests of the State of New York," a bigoted majority in, say, the legislature of Georgia may use the action as a precedent to keep out of that body regularly elected members who belong to the Catholic Church. For there have been majorities in the legislature of more than one Southern State that have looked upon the Catholic Church exactly as Speaker Sweet looks upon the Socialist party.

With best wishes for your health, I remain

Sincerely yours,

John A. Ryan

The position which I took in this matter evoked both praise and condemnation. Among the expressions coming under the former head, I prize most highly a letter from the late Frank I. Cobb, the brilliant editor of the *New York World.* I quote a part of it:

I have been astonished to find that in New York there is a great deal of Catholic support of Speaker Sweet, in his attempt to throw the socialists out of the Assembly. Catholics who support this outrage have evidently forgotten the Know Nothing campaign that was once directed against them, and which might be resumed at any time by the same kind of evangelical fanatics who are sustaining the Anti-Saloon League.

Your own position in the matter is so sound, that you will never have to apologize for it.

While I have never had "to apologize for it," I did write a few letters by way of explanation and justification, only one of which will be mentioned here. The late William D. Guthrie, a distinguished Catholic lawyer of New York City, wrote me, "deploring" my letter to Mr. Hillquit, and expressing the opinion that I was wrong in viewing "the action of the New York Assembly as a menace to constitutional liberty." As chairman of the Committee on Political Reform of the Union League Club of New York, a notoriously reactionary and opulent organization, Mr. Guthrie presented a report to the Club February 12, 1920, in which the suspension and imminent expulsion of the five socialists were approved and strongly defended. The main argument in the report was to the effect that the five socialists were members of a "disloyal" organization; but the report was unable to cite any law, constitutional or statute, federal or state, which made "disloyalty" a ground for refusing to seat a duly elected candidate, or for expelling him. The report did, indeed, appeal to one favorable precedent, namely, declarations by the Committee on Elections of the House of Representatives in 1867 and 1868. Perhaps the less said about the actions of Congressional committees in those partisan days of "Reconstruction," the better.

Here is the closing sentence of my reply to the letter sent me by Mr. Guthrie: "You and I know that the plot to unseat the socialist members has in the main been actuated, not by motives of patriotism and love for Christian institutions, but by a mixture of practical politics and industrial interests." One of the many indications that might be cited in support of the quoted assertion is the fact that Mr. Sweet, the Speaker of the Assembly, who was the most powerful factor in the expulsion, prevented, in the legislative session of 1919, the enactment of a minimum-wage law and an eight-hour law for women workers and of a law to insure wage earners against sickness. Mr. Sweet called these measures "bolshevistic." As a manufacturer, he probably considered them "inimical to the best interests of the State of New York," which was the language he later used with reference to the Socialist party.

Speaker Sweet was right in this characterization, but he was wrong in promoting the arbitrary act of expulsion, the "legislative lynching," as it was stigmatized by the *New York World*. On this specific point I desire to quote from an article which I published in the *Catholic Charities Review*, May, 1920:

Should not men who belong to such an organization as the Socialist party be excluded from our legislative halls? Even though no charge was proved against the five expelled men except that of membership in the Socialist party, is not this a sufficient offense to warrant the action taken by the Assembly? The answer to the first of these questions is "yes," to the second, "no." If it were possible to do so without endangering the political rights of other minorities it would be desirable to make members of the Socialist party, as now organized, legally ineligible to any public office. But this should be done by law, by statute, by a formal legislative enactment. When these five socialists were elected, there was in existence no such law. Whether the bill enacted into law since the expulsion will stand the test of constitutionality, remains to be seen. The crime of the New York Assembly consisted in *disfranchising by arbitrary action in the case of certain individuals* a party and five electoral constituencies before the organization had been outlawed by a *formal and general statute*.

The difference between the two methods is the difference between autocracy and law. While the Assembly, as every other legislative body, has apparently the constitutional power to exclude members for any reason or for no reason, it ought to exercise this great power guardedly, without abuse, and in harmony with the spirit of constitutional rights and liberties. The Assembly violated all these rules of fairness, and created a precedent which can easily be used and abused for the oppression of other minorities than the Socialist party. Acting upon the principle established by the New York Assembly, any legislature may expel the members of any minority group, party or religion on the plea that the majority of the legislature regards such an organization as an undesirable element in the social and political life of the state. This precedent can properly be used against the members of a labor union, a reform association, or a religious denomination. We Catholics, who are in a minority in almost all the states of this country, should be the last to sanction the creation of such an arbitrary and unjust precedent.

My whole objection to the action of the Assembly is, therefore, against the method and procedure rather than the results. I do not believe that the end justifies the means. The question of method is fundamental. It underlies all our constitutional guarantees of individual liberty, all our bills of rights. A benevolent and wise despot may sometimes disregard these forms and guarantees without serious injustice to individuals or the community; but we do not want to take the risk of giving such power to any man, or any group of men, even to a legislative body. We feel safer when we know that the legislative body attains a given end by observing the approved forms of law, by taking the responsibility of enacting a general statute, instead of dealing arbitrarily with a particular instance. This is the lesson of long and bitter experience.

The bill referred to in the first of the three paragraphs just quoted, was vetoed by Governor Alfred E. Smith on May 19, 1920. In support of his action, he wrote an extremely able memorandum, the gist of which was that the provisions of the law could be so abused and perverted in administration as to deprive citizens of their "basic rights to representation on the ballot. . . ."

The hazard to which the Governor referred is the only consideration, in my opinion, which can reasonably be urged against legislation which would outlaw the Communist party today and prevent its members from holding public office. Nevertheless, the ingenuity of legislators ought to be equal to the task of drafting a bill which would do just that and nothing more, and which could not be abused, perverted, or misapplied in administration, for example, so as to penalize non-Communist groups or individuals whom public officials regard as "disloyal," "dangerous," or "undesirable."

The bill to outlaw the Socialist party was one of a series of six disapproved by Governor Smith. They were popularly called the "Anti-Sedition" bills. Some of them originated with the legislative committee which had brought about the expulsion of the five socialist members, while others were fathered by Senator Lusk, the chairman of the Joint Legislative Committee Investigating Seditious Activities. This was the group that perpetrated the four folio volumes (aggregating about 4,500 pages) referred to in Chapter IX.

Although the Lusk Report must have cost the State of New York tens of thousands of dollars, it has for a long time now been consigned to practical oblivion, if not "damned to everlasting infamy." Probably less than one per cent of those who read what I am writing here have ever seen that ill-starred and egregious production. Its condemnation of me and my "socialistic" friends and the "socialistic" proposals in the Bishops' Program, looks pretty silly today.

As one who has noted with deep regret Alfred E. Smith's adoption of reactionary political and economic views in recent years and his connection with such an organization as the "Liberty League," I am glad to give heartfelt recognition to the magnificent contributions which he made to social and industrial betterment, political reform, and genuine liberalism, while he was Governor of New York. In the light of these invaluable services to the needy classes and in view of his influential leadership and example as chief executive of the Empire State in a sordid and reactionary decade, his subsequent defection deserves to be forgotten. Instead of submitting additional words of my own on this subject I shall quote three paragraphs from the eloquent tribute published by Dr.

Edward T. Devine in the *Survey* for May 29, 1920. It is headed "To Governor Smith:"

You had a great chance last week, and you made the most of it. Hereafter the New Yorker who travels, when shamed by the names of Lusk and Sweet and Stevenson, will be able to point to your vetoes and hold up his head. Probably you would think it a joke to be compared with John Milton or Daniel Defoe or Sidney Smith, though you have yourself, in one of these messages, quoted the words of Benjamin Franklin. But the fact is that all of these men owe their high place as prose writers partly to the accident that in their time also there were men like the authors and instigators of the Sweet-Lusk bills, who gave them just such chances as you had to defend freedom and to denounce bigotry. . . .

You have killed all these vicious bills, but you have done much more. At some future session the legislature may try to pass these or similar bills over your veto. Your vigorous and pithy remarks will make any such performance difficult. It will not be surprising if the bills are never heard of again.

What you have done, at any rate, is more than to kill these bills. You have punctured an absurdity. You have restored a sense of proportion. You have spoken words of truth and soberness at a time when untruth and insanity are still abroad. You have stripped the mantle of patriotism from the charlatan; you have made the patrioteer appear the ridiculous creature that he is. You have brought public discussion in this state back into the domain of reality and common sense. You have made it difficult for a legislative committee, discredited in its own political field, to regain its lost prestige by a foray into an economic field for which it is even more obviously disqualified at the start.

Harlan F. Stone was appointed Attorney General of the United States in April, 1923. (Since 1925 he has been an associate justice of the Supreme Court.) One of his first acts as head of the Department of Justice was to adopt a policy which had the effect of greatly discouraging such attitudes and actions as those which had been responsible for the Lusk Report, the expulsion of the five socialists, and the long delay in freeing the political prisoners. I described this policy and its implications in the *N.C.W.C. Bulletin* for June, 1923, in an article entitled "The End of Hysteria." It is reproduced here in full because it holds some lessons for present and possibly future situations. Here is the article:

The Attorney General of the United States made an announcement on May 13 which deserves much more attention than it has received. It has a much wider significance than its wording would lead the average reader to infer. The statement was simply to the effect that Attorney General Stone would himself direct the reorganization and the operations of the Bureau of Investigation of the Department of Justice, and that the Bureau would be employed henceforth for the purpose of aiding the lawyers of the Department of Justice in the preparation and prosecution of cases brought to their attention.

Within the compass of this innocuous statement is contained an official reversal of one of the major policies followed by the Bureau of Investigation for more than five years. That policy consisted in the very active investigation and pursuit of revolutionary persons who were held to be a menace to the Government of the United States. These activities may be said to date from the appearance of Attorney General Palmer before the appropriations committee of the House of Representatives about two years prior to the end of the Wilson Administration. On that occasion, Mr. Palmer asked for an appropriation of some three million dollars in order to combat what he declared to be an organized conspiracy to overthrow the government. Having obtained from Congress the money for this purpose, he carried out the notorious raids upon aliens at the end of 1919 and early in 1920. Some ten thousand aliens were taken into custody on the ground that they believed in or were threatening the overthrow of the government by violence. Less than six hundred of them were finally found to be subject under the law for deportation. And nearly all of these were sent out of the country merely for membership in certain organizations which had been adjudged illegal. No conspiracy to overthrow the government was found to exist. The dangerous material seized in the raids consisted of four pistols, some stage muskets used in amateur theatricals, four iron balls which dissolved in water, and large quantities of "revolutionary documents." The raids were accompanied and followed by enormous hardships to hundreds of those who were arrested.

In his report to the Second Session of the Sixty-seventh Congress,

Senator Thomas J. Walsh thus summarized the illegal actions committed by the Department of Justice in these wholesale arrests: The Bureau of Investigation had no authority to make arrests in deportation proceedings; a large percentage of the warrants authorizing the arrests were "in plain violation of the Fourth Amendment to the Constitution of the United States;" the searches carried out by the agents of the Department of Justice were without authority in law, as also was the issuance of search warrants in these proceedings. About two years after making this report, Senator Walsh in a review of Louis F. Post's book, *The Deportations Delirium of Nineteen-Twenty,* drew this terrific indictment of the Palmer raids:

"Louis F. Post's book is a narrative of incidents illustrating a curious and revolting phase of post-war psychology. It is a ringing indictment of both the American Government and the American people—the former for acts of heartless oppression, compared with which the Acadian dispersion was a mild-mannered performance, and the latter for the indifference with which the most hideous injustices perpetrated by high officials in perfect contempt of constitutional guarantees were regarded."

While the Palmer raids were the first and last of their kind, the spirit which provoked them remained in the Department of Justice under the administration which succeeded that of Mr. Palmer. For the last three years, the Bureau of Investigation of the Department has devoted an immense amount of time and energy to the investigation of revolutionary movements and persons, and radicalism, generally. The number of Communists and Communist sympathizers in the United States was magnified enormously by spokesmen for the Bureau. The public was reminded periodically that the revolutionary performers in the United States were so numerous and their activities so dangerous as to require constant watching and unceasing planning to thwart their destructive purposes. Possibly most of this activity on the part of the Bureau of Investigation was undertaken and carried out in good faith. The hysteria concerning Bolshevism and "red" revolution which was aroused during the last year of the war continued long afterwards in official as well as in unofficial circles. Every well-informed person now knows that the revolutionary groups in the United States were at no time significant or dangerous, either in numbers or in any other respect. But the investigating and persecuting activities of the Department of Justice, together with incessant propaganda, both official and unofficial, kept a large part of the American people in constant fear of violent revolution or at least of violent attacks upon the Government.

This unnecessary and misdirected activity produced two evil results. First, grave injustice was done to thousands of innocent and ignorant foreign-born residents of the United States, while other thousands received a decidedly unfavorable impression of American justice and American freedom. In the second place, the words "revolutionary," "red," "radical," "Bolshevist," were used in such a confused way as to bring discredit upon reform movements, and persons interested in industrial reform. The connection between the violent revolutionist and the industrial progressive was established by some such process as this: Bolshevist = Communist = Socialist = "red" = radical almost any one who criticizes existing industrial or political arrangements or conditions.

Attorney General Stone's announcement with reference to the Bureau of Investigation marks the end of official complicity in these abuses, and in this confusion of popular thought. It marks an official return to sanity. The members of the Bureau, the investigators, are to be henceforth "law school graduates." The detectives, with their psychology of suspicion and their methods of espionage, are passing from the stage. Even if the new Attorney General should perform no other noteworthy act during his term of office, his administration would deserve well of the American people.

The only criticism that I would make now of the foregoing production is that its heading was too comprehensive. "The End of Hysteria" had not really arrived. What I thought was the end was only an intermission. Hysteria will seize a certain proportion of the people whenever new political or economic movements become so formidable as to constitute an apparent menace to existing political or economic institutions. It becomes particularly pervasive and intense when the danger is exaggerated through misleading propaganda by a combination of fearful patriots and unscrupulous champions of powerful economic interests. Shortly after the World War the triumph of Bolshevism in Russia produced sufficient hysteria to make possible the notorious "red raids" conducted by Attorney General Palmer, and the expulsion of the socialists from the New York legislature. In 1938 and 1939, the trepidation over Communist activities brought about the introduction of some seventy anti-alien bills in the Seventy-sixth Congress, on the theory that all Communists were aliens if not vice versa. At least nine-tenths of these bills were unnecessary and unreasonable. Not more than two or three of them were enacted. In the spring of 1940, the hysteria about "Fifth Columnists" stampeded the House of Representatives into passing a bill by a vote of eight to one which ordered the immediate deportation of Harry Bridges, the powerful West Coast labor leader, in the face of the fact that in 1939 James M. Landis, Dean of the Harvard Law School, had found after a prolonged hearing, a lack of sufficient evidence to show that Bridges was a Communist. This action of the House of Representatives provided an exact parallel to the expulsion of the socialists from the New York Assembly. Both actions contravened the forms of law. In this connection, I am introducing a copy of a letter, written July 6, 1940, to Senator William H. King, chairman of the Committee on Immigration of the United States Senate:

Dear Senator King:

Some of us are so greatly disturbed over the action of the House of Representatives in passing the Bill for the forthright deportation of Harry Bridges that we are requesting the opportunity for a hearing on the Bill before the Sub-Committee of the Senate to which it has been referred. We regard this Bill as a grave infringement of the spirit as well as the letter of the Bill of Rights. In all probability, it violates the due process clause of the Fifth Amendment; for the Supreme Court has held in at least two cases that the word "person" in the Fifth Amendment includes aliens, even natives of China (Wong Wing v. U. S., 163 U. S. 238, and Li Sing v. U. S., 180 U. S. 495). In its present form the Bill would deport Harry Bridges without a hearing or any kind of proceeding that could be regarded as due process.

Even if it be not unconstitutional, the Bill is revolutionary, arbitrary, and extremely dangerous as a precedent. If Harry Bridges can be deported in this fashion, so can any other alien whom Congress does not like, when it succumbs to the factitious hysteria of the moment. Congress should hesitate long before it sanctions this unwarranted innovation and creates this horrendous precedent.

Harry Bridges is a pest and a nuisance. While he has stimulated the unionization of large groups of workers on the Pacific Coast and obtained for them considerable economic benefits, he has done much more harm than good to the cause of organized labor as a whole. Nevertheless, he is as much entitled to the protection of the Constitution and of the regular forms of law and judicial procedure as any other alien. The Fifth Amendment does not say that *no person shall be deprived of life, liberty or property without due process of law,* "except aliens who have become undesirable." In fact, the Bill of Rights was designed in no small degree for the benefit of such unpopular persons as Harry Bridges. Respectable persons seldom, if ever, need the protection of the due process clause. It is the unrespectable, the unpopular, the despised minorities, the politically weak and the socially helpless who stand most in need of this protection. The Bill of Rights is based upon the fundamental, ethical principle that even members of the foregoing classes are human beings, endowed with a moral and indestructible dignity of personality, and requiring civil protection for the fundamental rights of personality. In this respect, the United States differs sharply and completely from Totalitarian countries. In the present critical situation, we ought scrupulously to refrain from any act which would enable the Totalitarian states to point at us the finger of scorn and to assert that we care no more than they for individual human rights.

Sincerely yours,

John A. Ryan

Although the Committee on Immigration did not grant the requested hearing, it did adopt a just and rational procedure. Instead of reporting the Bill to the Senate, it referred the question of deportation to the Attorney General of the United States, thus ensuring a judicial inquiry into the alleged Communism of the pestiferous Mr. Bridges. This was a happy and just solution.

Sometime between 1920 and 1925, I became a member of the American Civil Liberties Union and accepted a place on its national committee. The main object of this organization has always been to defend the constitutional rights of citizens and aliens to freedom of expression and assembly. In the majority of instances the beneficiaries of its activities have been such relatively weak persons as "radicals," "foreigners," "socialists," and "Communists." Those against whom it has defended such groups have sometimes been private illegal associations such as the "Vigilantes," but in most cases they have been law-enforcement officials, such as, sheriffs, mayors, and policemen. Invariably the A.C.L.U. has merely endeavored to protect its clients against oppression and to ensure for them that due process of law, that is, the right to a hearing and a fair trial, which is guaranteed by our state and federal constitutions. As would naturally be expected, the majority of those assisted by the A.C.L.U. have been persons accused of Socialism, Communism, or some other equally unpopular affiliation.

Of course, I was aware of this fact but instead of deterring me from becoming and continuing to be a member, it had the opposite effect; for I knew that the constitutional guarantee of "due process of law" was intended to protect all these "subversive" elements as well as the more respectable members of American society. Nevertheless, my membership in the organization gave pain to some of my fellow Catholics. Apparently they held that a Communist or a person regarded as such by a local vigilance committee, ought not to have the benefit of this constitutional guarantee but should be summarily dealt with by a local group of superpatriots or by a little band of policemen equipped with rubber hose or similar "persuasive" instruments. Obviously, this is the naked principle of lynch law.

Notwithstanding the mistakes made by A.C.L.U.—and they have not been few or isolated—its unwavering endeavors to protect the constitutional rights of the poor, the weak, the despised, and the unpopular have made it one of the most effective champions in America of civil and social justice.

Among the mistakes just alluded to, one of the most notorious has been the propagation of an unfounded and illogical theory of free speech. This has been due mainly to the doctrinaire ideas of the director, Roger N. Baldwin. He has defended the alleged right of anyone, citizen or alien, to advocate murder, assassination, or the overthrow of government by force and violence, so long as the advocate stops there and does not translate these beliefs into actions. I have already given the reasons why I regard this position and this distinction as illogical and indefensible.

While I knew all about these peculiar views of Mr. Baldwin, I realized that they were not often cited and, therefore, did not interfere seriously with the good work of the organization on behalf of the helpless and the unpopular. I also was aware that some superpatriots called Roger Baldwin a Communist and asserted that the A.C.L.U. was "dominated by Communists," or "led by Communists," but I knew that these charges were barefaced calumnies. As a matter of fact, the executive officers and the national committee taken together never included more than two or three Communists and for several years now not more than one Communist. At its latest annual meeting, the A.C.L.U. adopted a rule which prohibits the inclusion of even one Communist on its governing body.

Nevertheless, I resigned from the A.C.L.U. and its national committee sometime in 1935: not because I had come to disapprove of its main objectives or to be fearful about associating with some misguided but honest radicals, not even because my membership might be productive of "pharisaical scandal," but simply and solely because the organization had gone into the field of "academic freedom." In a letter to Roger Baldwin, I pointed out that this was none of our business, that we should confine our activities to cases involving *civil* liberties and that violations of academic freedom might safely be left to the Committee of University Professors which had been set up to deal with the latter subject. I called attention to the absurdity, for example, of my membership on the national committee of an organization which might undertake to defend a professor at the Catholic University who has been dismissed for teaching heresy!

The executive committee begged me to reconsider my determination to resign but gave no indication of changing its policy of intervening in the province of academic freedom. Hence, there was nothing left for me to do but to insist upon the acceptance of my resignation.

Chapter XI

ATTITUDE TOWARD PROHIBITION

HERE is the text of the Eighteenth Amendment to the Constitution of the United States:

Section 1. After one year from the ratification[1] of this article the manufacture, sale, or transportation of intoxicating liquors within, the importation thereof into, or the exportation thereof from the United States and all territory subject to the jurisdiction thereof for beverage purposes is hereby prohibited.

Section 2. The Congress and the several States shall have concurrent power to enforce this article by appropriate legislation.

Section 3. This article shall be inoperative unless it shall have been ratified as an amendment to the Constitution by the legislatures of the several States, as provided in the Constitution, within seven years from the date of the submission hereof to the States by the Congress.

The implementation of the amendment was provided by the Volstead Act. Vetoed by President Wilson, October 27, 1919, the bill for the Act was, within two days, repassed by overwhelming majorities in both houses of Congress. June 7, 1920, the Supreme Court of the United States placed upon the Act the stamp of constitutionality.

As specified in the Act, "intoxicating liquors" comprised all liquids "containing one half of one per centum or more of alcohol by volume which are fit for use for beverage purposes." Probably the most important enforcement sections of the Act are the following:

No person shall on or after the date when the Eighteenth Amendment to the Constitution of the United States goes into effect, manu-

[1] Ratification was completed January 16, 1919.

facture, sell, barter, transport, import, export, deliver, furnish or possess any intoxicating liquor except as authorized in this Act, and all the provisions of this Act shall be liberally construed to the end that the use of intoxicating liquor as a beverage may be prevented.

It shall be unlawful to have or possess any liquor or property designed for the manufacture of liquor intended for use in violating this title or which has been so used, and no property rights shall exist in any such liquor or property.

After February 1, 1920, the possession of liquors by any person not legally permitted under this title to possess liquor shall be prima facie evidence that such liquor is kept for the purpose of being sold, bartered, exchanged, given away, furnished, or otherwise disposed of in violation of the provisions of this title.

Some Catholic opponents of prohibition maintained for several years an attitude which I regarded as disingenuous. Instead of honestly and forthrightly asserting that the legislation was not morally obligatory, they criticized and ridiculed it in such terms as to lead their hearers and readers to draw that very conclusion. Other Catholic antagonists adopted a more straightforward course, contending that the Volstead Act was devoid of moral quality because it was a "purely penal" enactment. In Catholic ethical teaching a "purely penal" law is one whose obligation is not single but "disjunctive;" that is, it binds the citizen either to comply with its terms or faithfully to accept the penalty specified for its violation. This concept found a place for a long time in civil law, as well as in canon law and moral theology.[2]

With the first of these two positions I had little patience. It struck me as evasive and, in some instances, lacking in courage. The second contention, that the Volstead Act was "purely penal" and, therefore, not directly binding in conscience, I recognized as honest and plausible but rejected as untenable. For many years, indeed, I have looked upon the

[2] See *Blackstone's Commentaries on the Laws of England*, 1, p. 57, and any manual of moral theology.

theory of "purely penal" laws as of doubtful validity, or at least, of limited application. Here is a recent statement of my position in this matter:

> It seems, however, that the practical obligation of a purely penal law is attenuated almost to the vanishing point. If the violator of the law is not obliged to make known his transgression, nor to waive his legal right of defense, his duty of "accepting the penalty" is merely that of submitting to the sentence of the court. That is, he must not break jail nor evade payment of a fine. When the offender evades apprehension, he escapes all moral obligation; when he successfully contests prosecution, he likewise remains free from moral accountability; when he is convicted, his moral obligation is merely that of omitting actions from which in most cases he is physically restrained by the sheriff or the policeman. In a word, the moral obligation of a purely penal law is next to nothing, its moral sanction, i.e., the effectiveness of the moral element in preventing violations, is practically nothing.[3]

In the *American Ecclesiastical Review*, April, 1924, I published a short article under the heading "Are Our Prohibition Laws Purely Penal?" In the first part of this production I refuted the preposterous proposition that *all* civil laws are "purely penal!" I drew the conclusion that the Eighteenth Amendment was not "purely penal" and that it had "the same validity as any other civil law." As to the Volstead Act, I said that those provisions of it which forbid a person to manufacture, possess, or transport liquor for his own use or to give it to his friends "are tyrannical and unjust interferences with the liberties and rights of the citizen." I then added this paragraph:

> Therefore, the person who day after day carries on the business of bootlegging is guilty of a grave violation of an important, morally binding law. It is difficult to see how he can be absolved in the tribunal of penance unless he promises to discontinue his illicit occupation. Does the person who purchases liquor from him likewise sin gravely? Probably he does not, unless his patronage be more or less continuous.

[3] *Catholic Principles of Politics.* The Macmillan Company, New York, 1940, pp. 188–189.

If it is given only on rare occasions, the cooperation can probably be regarded as lacking the degree of importance necessary to constitute a mortal sin.

An article which I published in the *Catholic World* in May, 1925, set forth at considerably greater length the conclusions just summarized. Here are the most important:

> The Eighteenth Amendment and those provisions of the Volstead Act which forbid the sale of intoxicating liquor and which prohibit acts involved in or immediately connected with the sale of intoxicating liquor are binding in conscience. . . . On the other hand, the non-commercial and private manufacture, possession and transportation of liquor for consumption by oneself or one's friends, remain lawful in the field of conscience and morality . . . Inasmuch as the law which they (bootleggers and saloon-keepers) violate has to do with a grave matter, it is difficult to see how they can carry on their traffic without committing a sin which is grave. . . . The person who buys liquor only occasionally and for his own use cannot be held to cooperate so gravely in the evil traffic that each purchase renders him guilty of grave sin. On the other hand, it is difficult to see how these acts can be regarded as entirely free from moral guilt.

These conclusions were based upon the assumption that federal prohibition of the liquor traffic was not an unjust interference with individual liberty; for it had approved itself to the public authorities as the best method of abolishing or reducing grave social evils. I admitted that if the legislators were mistaken in this judgment the prohibition laws were unjustified, but I contended that they and the laws were entitled to the benefit of a legal and moral presumption that no such mistake had been made. If this presumption is to be overthrown, I said, "a vastly greater amount of evidence will have to be brought forward than has thus far appeared." Nevertheless, I gave it as my own opinion that state prohibition or the Canadian system, or a combination of both, "would in the long run have proved more effective."

In consequence of these two articles, not a few Catholics

assumed that I was in favor of national prohibition as a public policy. Of course, the inference was unjustified and illogical, and indicative of loose thinking. To say that a certain civil law has moral validity is one thing; to declare that it is politically or socially wise is quite another thing. As a matter of fact, I had taken the contrary position in the years 1918 and 1919 in three editorials in the *Catholic Charities Review*. While they all antedated the Volstead Act, I never repudiated or changed my mind about any of them subsequently. Following are the most significant sentences in the first editorial (April, 1918):

The prohibitionists show a disregard for individual liberty in their attempt to establish national prohibition. There seems to be no sound reason why the people of each state should not be permitted to decide this question for themselves. There is no national exigency demanding uniformity of legislation on this subject. . . . The states that prefer to have liquor can enjoy that condition without hindering the desire of other states to have prohibition. The latter already have the power to protect themselves against the contaminating influence of the former by excluding liquor shipments entirely. Yet their representatives in Congress have sought to impose prohibition on the liquor states by means of an amendment to the federal Constitution. They wish to confer and impose the benefit of prohibition upon those benighted states that have not sense enough to adopt the measure themselves. This is essentially the same attitude of undemocratic paternalism and superior tyranny that, as we noted above, is taken by the professional prohibitionists toward individual drinkers.

In the second editorial (June, 1918), I reaffirmed this position and quoted a letter from an angry subscriber which contained this delectable effusion:

None but the unthinking will be deceived by the oft-refuted booze rot in your April number, but it is a pity you saw fit to publish such illogical stuff. It sounds very much like the inexhaustible shallow prattle of one of those beer-foam philosophers of Baltimore, but no matter where it came from I could smell the beer on it quite distinctly, and read the same stuff on the brewers' journal and other liquor organs, time and again. When my subscription expires, please stop sending me the magazine. If I want pro-booze arguments, I can get all I want of them, and get them first-hand, and put up in better style, from the booze press, and they have the additional merit of being what they profess, booze organs.

The last of the three editorials was written after the ratification of the Eighteenth Amendment and a few months before the enactment of the Volstead bill (February, 1919). In the opening paragraph I said that the wisdom and the justification of national prohibition were not at the moment practical questions, that we should have to "wait and see" whether it would prove efficacious. The question that was still within the realm of actuality, I said, was whether the Anti-Saloon League would succeed in its efforts to get into the enforcement act (the Volstead bill) a clause forbidding the manufacture and possession of liquor for personal use. This extreme proposal I denounced as an unjustifiable exercise of legislative authority.[4]

In the latter part of the year 1926, I revised the *Catholic World* article, quoted above, for inclusion in my book *Declining Liberty and Other Papers,* which appeared in April, 1927. The revision presented a fundamental modification of my attitude toward the morality of the prohibition legislation. Previous to 1926, I had held that these ordinances enjoyed the presumption of moral validity as regularly enacted measures which provided an effective form of liquor legislation. By 1926, that presumption seemed to me to have been negatived by the consequences of the legislation. Hence I put the following paragraph into the book cited above:

Six years of experience with the legislation have changed its moral aspect. There is now grave reason to doubt that the conditions necessary to justify this degree of interference with individual rights really existed. The degree of success which attended state and local prohibi-

[4] Ryan, *Questions of the Day.* The Stratford Company, Boston, 1931, pp. 30-32.

tion prior to the national legislation, the degree of success achieved by the Quebec system, and the degree of failure which has characterized the attempt to enforce national prohibition, constitute sufficient evidence to warrant a reasonable and prudent man in holding that the Eighteenth Amendment was an unnecessary, unwise and unjust enactment.[5]

Soon after this statement appeared, some persons who had criticized my previous position, asserted that I had "changed my mind about the morality of prohibition." Obviously, this was inaccurate and unfair. It reflected a lack of precise thinking. The change in my views involved not ethical principle, but the application of a principle to a new set of facts. Before 1926 the legislation was, I held, morally valid and binding on the citizens because it was regularly enacted to promote the public welfare and because, in the absence of evidence to the contrary, it seemed to promote that end; therefore, it enjoyed the presumption of moral binding force. If this general principle is not accepted and observed, then no civil statute possesses certain moral validity, and a citizen who is so disposed may question and disobey any civil law without incurring moral blame. This position is directly contrary to the Catholic teaching that, in general, civil laws are moral laws and bind in conscience.

My position in 1926 was, in brief, that prior to that time the legislation had been morally obligatory because it seemed to be in the public interest, but that the experience of the preceding three or four years had exposed it as harmful. Hence the Volstead Act had lost its validity and moral binding force upon the citizen. In other words, the presumption of validity previously enjoyed by that statute had by 1926 been evidently destroyed by the new facts and developments.

I still think that this position was correct; therefore, I still believe that the law was binding in conscience up to 1926 (or

[5] *Idem*, p. 34.

thereabouts) and that subsequent to that date its binding force ceased to exist.

After 1926, I made no significant statement on the morality of prohibition until April 3, 1929, when I published an article in the *Commonweal* entitled "Who Shall Obey the Law?"[6] In his inaugural address, March 4, 1929, President Hoover had declared:

> If citizens do not like the law their duty as honest men and women is to discourage its violation; their right is openly to work for its repeal.

Replying to this and one or two other assertions on prohibition in the inaugural address, I pointed out that no civil statute expresses any such *legal* duty as Mr. Hoover asserted, and that the President of the United States has no competence to define *moral* duties. Here are the most significant paragraphs of the article:

> The unforgivable offense committed by the Eighteenth Amendment is the fact that it is a legislative statute rather than an enabling act. National prohibition could have been brought about by an amendment empowering Congress to legislate the liquor traffic out of existence. Had this course been taken, the amendment would undoubtedly have been adopted and Congress would undoubtedly have enacted such legislation. This procedure would have been democratic, even though unwise. The unwisdom could have been corrected through subsequent repeal of the law by a majority of the two houses in Congress. In that event, the President's demand that the people observe the prohibition law until they could muster a majority for its repeal would have had a considerable appearance of reasonableness. . . .
>
> Until the prohibitionists are willing to take statutory prohibition out of the Constitution, until they are willing to convert the Eighteenth Amendment into a mere enabling act, they stand convicted of toryism and contempt for democracy. Until they do this, their invocation of "the will of the people" and similar slogans on behalf of the prohibition laws will remain a kind of blasphemy and a very real hypocrisy. They themselves will continue to deserve the contempt of all genuine be-

[6] Reprinted in *Questions of the Day*.

lievers in democracy and the Eighteenth Amendment will continue
to be

> A fixed figure for the hand of scorn
> To point his slow, unmoving finger at . . .

Despite the President's admonition and censure, the law-abiding
opponents of prohibition may possess their souls in patience. They can
derive consolation and courage from the reflection that they are
battling for fundamental democracy, for majority rule, for the van-
quishment of fanaticism, intolerance and toryism, for security against
prohibition of tobacco, against the Puritan Sabbath, against compulsory birth control for the poor, against sterilization for "social in-
adequates," and against all the other tyrannies that the self-righteous
and superior sections of our population would impose upon their
"inferior" fellow-citizens. Every one of these outrageous proposals is
due fundamentally to the same attitude of mind and the same disposi-
tion of will that produced the Eighteenth Amendment. In a word, the
"honest men and women" who actively oppose prohibition in all
lawful ways can rightfully feel that they are engaged in a great crusade
for fundamental liberties, for liberties that are not a whit less sacred
and precious than those which were fought for by the men who made
the American Revolution.[7]

About six weeks later, President Hoover returned to the
subject of violations of the prohibition legislation in an address before the representatives of the Associated Press assembled in New York City. Apparently, he had in mind my
article in the *Commonweal*. At the request of the *New York
Herald Tribune,* I wrote a reply which was published in that
paper, April 23, 1929. Here is my statement:

There are two propositions in the President's speech which must fill
every thoughtful citizen with alarm and astonishment. The first is
ethical, the second political. "No individual," he says, "has the right to
determine what law shall be obeyed and what law shall not be enforced." What about the right of the individual conscience? Must a
man obey a civil law which he believes to be wrong? Apparently the
President would not only deny the moral supremacy of conscience but

[7] *Op. cit.,* pp. 6, 7, 8, 10.

cast opprobrium upon those honored names of men and women who in every country and in every age have dared to put their conceptions of right above their fear of political penalties. President Hoover aligns himself in effect with those who hold that the State can do no wrong. He bids us bow our knees before the Omnipotent State. This is neither good ethics nor good Americanism.

His other astonishing proposition is: "If a law is wrong its rigid enforcement is the surest guaranty of its repeal." Neither the superficial plausibility nor the hackneyed character of this assertion is a guaranty that it is in accord with the facts of life and experience. Our Blue Laws —to take only one illustration—show that the people can sometimes get rid of tyrannical laws by other methods than formal repeal; that repeal may be impossible and general disobedience may be the only remedy. Long after the great majority of the people of the United States shall have declared for repeal of the Eighteenth Amendment thirteen thinly populated states could thwart the will of the majority, regardless of the extent to which the Amendment had been enforced. Would the President have the majority submit eternally to a fanatical minority in deference to an exploded theory of political policy?[8]

In an editorial published about the middle of May, the *Commonweal* reported that my article printed in the issue of April 3, had been "as widely commented upon as anything ever written for the *Commonweal.* . . ." So far as I can recall, most of the comments were favorable. The most conspicuous exceptions were furnished by Thomas J. Heflin, Senator from Alabama, several non-Catholic papers, and two professionally anti-Catholic periodicals. Referring to me as "an appointee of the present Catholic King of the Vatican City, an appointee of the Catholic Pope-King of the Vatican City or Catholic kingdom," Mr. Heflin attacked particularly this statement: "That the citizens are obliged to obey civil laws, even those that they do not like, is true in general, but not necessarily true in every case." Having read this sentence to his fellow senators (that is, to the very few who had remained in the chamber) he exclaimed:

[8] *Op. cit.*, pp. 11-12.

Now what do you think of a theologian in America, of a priest, taking that position in a free government—that the Catholic citizen, for that is what it means, may decide for himself what law he will obey in the United States and what law he will violate?[9]

None of the diatribes printed in the anti-Catholic journals deserves notice. Of the criticisms carried in the non-Catholic religious papers, only one will be considered here. It was written by Harry Earl Woolever, editor of a news distributing agency called the National Methodist Press, and was published in several of the various regional editions of the *Christian Advocate*. Mr. Woolever denounced my *Commonweal* article as "the most vicious attack yet made against national prohibition . . . the most un-American and harmful attack which has been made against the Constitution of the United States since the ratification of the Eighteenth Amendment . . . one of the most vicious attacks which have been made against American institutions in a generation."[10] Incidentally, he misrepresented my position by attributing to me the statement that the provisions of the prohibition law "never had a shadow of validity in morals." Senator Heflin repeated this untrue assertion a few days later. In my article, I had restricted the quoted words to *some* of the provisions of the Volstead Act, namely, those which prohibit the manufacture, transport, or possession of liquor by the citizens for their own use.

The *Congregationalist* published two editorials, April 25 and May 23, 1929, which were pleasingly different in tone and content from Mr. Woolever's production. In a letter replying to the first editorial, I said that it "differed from almost all the other unfavorable criticisms, inasmuch as it was evidently intended to be fair." Nevertheless, I closed the letter with the following paragraph:

[9] *Congressional Record*, May 8, 1929.
[10] *Christian Advocate*, April 18, 1929.

The prediction, or the threat, of dire consequences to me and my fellow priests on account of the reaction which utterances such as those in my *Commonweal* article may provoke, does not move me at all; for I have faith in the abiding sanity of the American people. To "the whirlwind" which, you say, I am due to reap, I would address the words of King Lear: "Blow, winds, and crack your cheeks! rage! blow!"

When I wrote these sentences, I had no idea or hope that the "abiding sanity of the American people" would be manifested in the repeal of the Eighteenth Amendment within five years, that is, December 5, 1933. Few, if any, others cherished any such expectation. For example, Chester Rowell asserted "the complete practical impossibility of making any substantial change in the law." Probably most persons who would have liked to see the Eighteenth Amendment and the Volstead Act repealed, still accepted the forecast made by the late Professor Howard L. McBain less than a year before the appearance of my article:

> Political prophecies are perilous; but it is highly improbable that the Eighteenth Amendment will ever be ripped from the side of the Constitution, or even be substantially altered, by the Constitutionally prescribed method of amendment.[11]

The next and the last important statement that I made on the prohibition question was read at a hearing before the Judiciary Committee of the House of Representatives, February 26, 1930. On that occasion, I defended the following propositions: the presumption of beneficial effect assumed for the Volstead Act during the four or five years immediately following its enactment has been overthrown by subsequent experience which shows that the act is injurious to public welfare; the Act violates personal liberty and personal rights and promotes widespread insincerity, as is strikingly shown in the conduct of those multitudes of citizens "who drink whenever they

---

[11] *Prohibition, Legal and Illegal.* The Macmillan Company, New York, 1928, p. 171.

get the opportunity, have no scruple about violating the prohibition law and yet support it with their voices and their votes"; the prohibition legislation, its administration, and its main supporters exhibit the spirit of toryism, strikingly so, in the attitude that prohibition is good for the working classes and may properly be imposed upon them by the superior classes; the Eighteenth Amendment is fundamentally undemocratic because it has the form of a compulsory statute rather than an enabling act for Congress; the Amendment should be repealed and the sale of liquor consigned to public agencies preferably under the management of the several states. My statement closed with this paragraph:

When a determined majority of the American people decide that they no longer want national prohibition, they will fine legal ways to end it, despite the undemocratic barriers erected by tories, fanatics, industrialists and autocrats. No doubt, it will be a long, hard struggle but those who take it up can sustain themselves with the assurance that, as I have written elsewhere, "they are engaged in a great crusade for fundamental liberties, for liberties that are not a whit less sacred than those which were fought for by the men who made the American Revolution."[12]

This statement obtained wide publicity. From the seventy-five clippings that I have preserved, I infer that some account of the statement was carried by the great majority of the secular papers of the United States, north, south, east, and west. So far as I know, the editorial attitude toward it was mostly favorable. One of the important exceptions was published by the *Christian Advocate* of Pittsburgh. It was probably written by a man already quoted in this chapter—Harry Earl Woolever. Referring to my appearance before the Judiciary Committee, he said:

The wets called as a chief champion the man who, because of his relation to the Roman Hierarchy and his influence among Romanists, has

[12] *Catholic Charities Review*, April, 1930, p. 101.

done more to overthrow the influence of President Hoover's efforts in behalf of law observance than any other individual, alien or American. Father John A. Ryan, professor of moral theology and industrial ethics at the Catholic University of America and director of the Social Action Department of the National Catholic Welfare Conference, is the doughty champion chosen by the wets.

While I would fain accept this estimate of my influence in this situation, I have no means of knowing whether it is correct. What the evidence seems to show unmistakably is that my statement before the Judiciary Committee was even more effective than my *Commonweal* article and that taken together, these productions made a considerable contribution to the movement, which, less than four years later, brought about the repeal of the Amendment and the Volstead Act. More than seven years have passed since repeal and I still rejoice over my part in that achievement. While I am not completely satisfied with its results, I believe that they are far superior to the conditions under the last seven or eight years of prohibition. And that so far as is humanly possible the abuses of the present situation can be corrected by democratic processes consistently with individual rights and social welfare.

CHAPTER XII

VISITS TO IRELAND

IN JUNE, 1922, I embarked for Ireland, mainly for the purpose of making a hurried survey of recent economic and political developments. Eleven years had gone by since my preceding visit to the land of my ancestors. In the meantime, there had occurred the unsuccessful insurrection of Easter Week, 1916, the successful two-year conflict between the Irish Republican Army and that curious and notorious military band of hirelings, known as the "Black and Tans," the negotiation of a treaty of peace between the British government and the representatives of Dáil Eireann (the parliament elected by the adherents of the insurgent Irish Republic) which authorized the establishment of the Irish Free State. The last-named event was formally and officially completed by the vote in the Dáil Eireann ratifying the treaty on January 7, 1922.

My desire to make a peaceful study of Irish conditions was unexpectedly and violently thwarted. Before our boat reached Cobh (Queenstown) we learned of a rebellion against the Free State authorities by some of the groups that had opposed ratification of the treaty. They had voted against ratification because the treaty did not provide for an independent Irish republic. When I got off the boat at Cobh, I found that town controlled by the Insurgents. The same was true of the city of Cork, whither I had gone to get a train for Dublin. There I learned that the Insurgents had destroyed the railway bridge at Mallow, thus making impossible direct travel to the capital. Hence, I was obliged to make the journey through Waterford, a very roundabout route. To reach that city required a full afternoon; to complete the journey to Dublin took all the next forenoon. Trains over the direct route, via Mallow, normally made the trip in five hours.

When I reached Dublin, I found that my contemplated visit to an uncle in Tipperary was then impossible because the railway leading to that county had been torn up by the Insurgents. During the three weeks that were required to repair the railway, I remained in Dublin, occupying a good deal of the time in writing a series of articles on the civil war (euphemistically known afterward as the "Trouble," or the "Troubles"). Before I went to bed, on my first night in Dublin, I had become aware of sporadic shooting which seemed to be for the most part sniping by isolated Insurgents at the Free State military and police. The mild alarm that I felt over this "excitement" quickly left me when I observed that the wall at the head of my bed in Vaughan's Hotel was composed of brick about one and one-half feet in thickness. Realizing that no missiles from ordinary firearms could penetrate that barrier, I fell asleep immediately. Thereafter, I scarcely ever gave the matter a thought, although the intermittent nocturnal shooting continued during all the three weeks that I spent in Dublin. On the morning following my first night there, I searched the papers anxiously for accounts of casualties. I found no such news. So far as I could learn, the bullets fired during those curious activities failed to hit any human being during the score of nights when I was compelled to hear them.

One of the most gratifying experiences that I had in those weeks was to see British soldiers strolling about the city with nothing else to do. On my two preceding visits to Ireland both the military and the police were exercising authority as employees of the English government. Now the place of the

Royal Irish Constabulary had been taken by the Civic Guards of the Irish Free State, while the army of the Crown had been displaced by the army of the Free State. Now the British soldiers walked the streets of Dublin, having no more civil power than I or any other foreigner. They were merely waiting for transports to return them to England. Within a few weeks they had all departed. In the meantime, the people of Dublin regarded them with as much indifference, while treating them with as much courtesy as they extended to any other group of strangers. This phenomenon struck me as a most practical and impressive proof that the old, bad order had passed away and that the people of Ireland were once more masters in their own house.

Through the kindness of the late Frank P. Walsh, I possessed letters of introduction to most of the men who had been leaders in the organization of the Irish Republic and the Dáil Eireann. By the time I arrived in Dublin, a few of them were leading the Insurgents against the newly established Free State. The principal names that I can now recall in this category were Eamon de Valera and Harry Boland. A few days after my arrival, the latter was mortally wounded by the Free State soldiers while resisting arrest. I stood on the sidewalk and saw his funeral procession pass down O'Connell Street to Glasnevin Cemetery. Mr. de Valera I did not meet until some sixteen years later.

Most of those to whom Mr. Walsh's letters introduced me were prominent officials in the Free State government. I recall now the president, Arthur Griffith; the commander of the Free State Army, Michael Collins; George Gavan Duffy, one of the negotiators of the treaty; Richard Mulcahy who took Collins' place as head of the army when the latter was killed in ambush by a band of Insurgents; William T. Cosgrave who became president of the Free State upon the sudden death of Arthur Griffith; and several other members of the government who were somewhat less prominent. Most of them I had the great pleasure of meeting at a dinner party, given for the late Rev. R. J. Tierney, S.J., and myself by Dr. and Mrs. Robert MacLaverty at their distinguished residence in Merrion Square. In the parlor after dinner, I had a long talk with Arthur Griffith, in the course of which I asked him what was the greatest number of men under arms at any one time fighting the "Black and Tans." His answer was: "About two thousand!" In other words, through the guerilla warfare which had been perfected under Collins, Griffith, and others, two thousand Irishmen defeated the forces of the British Empire and compelled Lloyd George to enter negotiations for a treaty of peace. As Michael Collins expressed it to Harry Boland, "we bluffed the British Empire." Probably nothing quite equal to this achievement can be credited to any other people in modern times.

Griffith was widely regarded as a somewhat cold, even dour personality. He certainly looked that part. Nevertheless, on the occasion of my first meeting with him, in his office, I saw tears come into his eyes as he listened to my description of some Insurgent depredations which I had seen from the train on my way to Dublin.

Michael Collins joined the group at the MacLaverty home about an hour after the dinner. He came into the room very unobtrusively, remained about half an hour, and left as quietly as he had come. If either his arrival or his departure had been perceived by the members of the Insurgent forces then hiding in Dublin, he would not have got away peacefully. I can see him now, in his new uniform as commander in chief, with his stalwart figure, his handsome face, his wonderfully winning smile, his very boyish manner, and his rich west Cork brogue. (No, not "accent," it was no such pale fraud; it was an honest and wholesome brogue.) I recall particularly the moderation and sense of proportion which he displayed in discussing some exceptionally diabolical performances of certain Insurgent gangs. As I listened and observed, the thought came to me that, despite his meager thirty-two years, this man was and would be a tower of strength to the Free State. Alas! Within a month both he and Arthur Griffith had passed out of the world of doctrinaire politics, rebellions, and pillage. As already noted, Collins was killed by the Insurgents in his native county, while Griffith died quite as suddenly but from natural causes—if we can include in this category a broken heart.

In his historical novel, *The Invisible Army*,[1] my Irish cousin, Desmond Ryan, thus refers to Michael Collins, as he appeared to many during the war against the "Black and Tans":

Barely two or three years ago this young man was unknown. Unknown to the readers of his escapes. Unknown to those who were thrilled by a sudden legend sweeping from the Dublin gossips and the British Secret Service to fill the columns of the world's press. But the London-Irish had known the son of the Clonakilty farmer listening to the Hyde Park orators with intent ear and twinkling eye, shocking staid enthusiasts among the exiles with his whirlwind manner and expletives, an alert and dashing figure on the hurling or football field, orating in the political clubs or hanging over the galleries of the London theatres. Then in the restless days after the Insurrection he had emerged. Why, none knew. A curious power emanated from him, and by some inborn genius he had gone onward, unaided, to the leadership of the Invisible Army. Dan Hogan had Michael Collins well recorded in his memory and saw in that one personality the inspiration of all the calculated defiance which broke down prison discipline, hunger-struck, clamoured for guns and drilled for preference outside police barrack doors.

Arthur Griffith told me an amusing story apropos of the eagerness and failure of the British Intelligence Service to apprehend Collins in those exciting and perilous days. The narrative was dramatically interesting to me because Collins

[1] Pp. 97, 98.

was in the room at the time, although he was unaware of what Griffith was saying. One night in Dublin a certain British officer heard a newsboy calling out: "Picthers of Michael Collins, only a shillin'." Inasmuch as Collins had more than once passed close to British officers and soldiers un-recognized, partly because photographs of him seemed to be nonexistent, or, at least, very scarce, this particular military servant of His Majesty's government joyfully seized the opportunity to obtain one. Having paid the newsboy a shill-ing, he received in return a sealed envelope. Opening it, he found it empty. And to the newsboy, who had withdrawn to a discreet distance, the angry officer shouted: "You young rascal, there is no picture in this envelope." To which the unabashed vendor replied: "Oh! is he gone agin?" Character-istically Irish!

Austin Stack, one of the most prominent leaders of the Insurgents in the civil war said publicly after that unhappy event: "Michael Collins was almost a great man."[2] He might well have left out the "almost;" for Michael Collins *was* a great man. This judgment will hardly be rejected by any impartial person who follows Collins' career from his days as a mere clerk in the London post office through his partici-pation in the Easter Week "rising," his exploits in the fight against the "Black and Tans," his part in negotiating the treaty, and his subsequent conduct as head of the provisional government and commander in chief of the Free State forces. And the end of it all came when he was only thirty-two!

The person whom I saw most frequently in Dublin during my stay there in 1922 was Mrs. Alice Stoptord Green, widow of John Richard Green, the English historian. When the Free State was established, she became one of the first members of the Senaad Eireann (senate of Ireland). She was then in

[2] Quoted in *The Invisible Army*, by Desmond Ryan. Arthur Barker, Ltd., London, 1932, p. 214.

her late seventies, and had written several authoritative volumes in the field of Irish history. Although the widow of an Englishman and the daughter of a distinguished clergyman of the Church of Ireland (Episcopalian) she was a very loyal and sincere Irishwoman. One day she informed me that she had never met a Catholic priest nor smoked a cigarette until she was forty years of age. "And," she added, laughing, "I do not know which of these acts gave some of my friends the greater scandal." When her husband died, she left England, came back to Ireland, and remained there until her death a few years ago. During the "Troubles," however, she was very pessimistic. One day she exclaimed: "I am afraid we'll never get out of this. We are so impulsive; even so mercurial." My reply was: "Nonsense, Mrs. Green. I was born and grew up in an entirely Irish community in the United States. They were normal, average Irish, but they were quite as stable and hardheaded as the average Yankee. So, I do not share your fears concerning the present civil disturbances here or the capacity of the Irish people to emerge safely."

In an article which I wrote for *America* about this time, I predicted that by August 15 the Insurgent bands would have been dislodged from every city and town in Ireland. When the middle of August arrived, I was able to write to that journal that my prediction of a month earlier had been "substantially and almost literally fulfilled."[3]

Reading again today the paragraphs in which Desmond Ryan describes the last days of that deplorable conflict, I find therein this sentence: "By August 12, the Free State Army had swept all before them, with many wounded and a small but growing death-toll."[4] So, I was happily right and Mrs. Green was fortunately wrong.

[3] *America*, August 19 and September 16, 1922.
[4] *Unique Dictator, A Study of Eamon de Valera*. Arthur Barker, Ltd., London, 1936, p. 212.

The document officially known as "Articles of Agreement for a Treaty Between Great Britain and Ireland," was ratified in the Dáil Eireann, January 7, 1922, by a vote of sixty-four to fifty-seven. At the general election held June 16 of the same year, the candidates for membership in the first Free State parliament who favored the treaty numbered eighty-nine, while the opponents were only thirty-five. The opposition to the treaty was based upon two main grievances: the oath to the King and the authority to be exercised over legislation and legislative processes by the Governor General in the name of the King. Following are the provisions of the treaty covering these two matters:

1. Ireland shall have the same constitutional status in the Community of Nations known as the British Empire as the Dominion of Canada, the Commonwealth of Australia, the Dominion of New Zealand and the Union of South Africa, with a Parliament having powers to make laws for the peace, order and good government of Ireland and an Executive responsible to that Parliament, and shall be styled and known as the Irish Free State.

2. Subject to the provisions hereinafter set out the position of the Irish Free State in relation to the Imperial Parliament and Government and otherwise shall be that of the Dominion of Canada, and the law, practice and constitutional usage governing the relationship of the Crown or the representative of the Crown and of the Imperial Parliament to the Dominion of Canada shall govern their relationship to the Irish Free State.

3. The representative of the Crown in Ireland shall be appointed in like manner as the Governor-General of Canada, and in accordance with the practice observed in the making of such appointments.

4. The oath to be taken by Members of the Parliament of the Irish Free State shall be in the following form:

"I . . . do solemnly swear true faith and allegiance to the Constitution of the Irish Free State as by law established and that I will be faithful to H. M. King George V, his heirs and successors by law, in virtue of the common citizenship of Ireland with Great Britain and her adherence to and membership of the group of nations forming the British Commonwealth of Nations."[5]

[5] *Op. cit.*, p. 280.

In the debate on the treaty in the Dáil it was asserted "that the Constitution of the Irish Free State would have the King of Great Britain as head of Ireland," and that members of the parliament would "swear allegiance to that Constitution and that King."[6] As a matter of fact, the Constitution of the Free State which was adopted a few months later did not "have the King of Great Britain as head of Ireland" nor was the oath taken by the members made to the King as King. Article Two of the Constitution declared that "all powers of government and all authority, legislative, executive and judicial in Ireland are derived from the people of Ireland and the same shall be exercised in the Irish Free State (Saorstat Eireann) through the organizations established by, or under, or in accord with this Constitution," and the form of the oath as quoted above expressed allegiance to the King "in virtue of the common citizenship of Ireland with Great Britain and her adherence to and membership of the group of nations forming the British Commonwealth of Nations." So, the oath was not taken to the King of Great Britain in that capacity but to the King in his position as head of the British Commonwealth of Nations of which the Irish Free State was a member. Indeed, one of the articles of the famous "Document Number 2" which Mr. de Valera wanted instead of the treaty that actually was negotiated and ratified, contained this sentence: "That for the purposes of the association, Ireland shall recognize His Britannic Majesty as head of the association." On the other hand, it is too bad that the British government was unwilling to accept "Document Number 2." Professor Alison Phillips, who is described by Desmond Ryan as "none too sympathetic" with Irish aspirations made the following statement sometime later:

It is possible to regret that the British Government, having once made up its mind to surrender, did not frankly recognize the Irish Republic on some such terms as these. To have done so would not have

[6] *Op. cit.*, p. 155.

exposed the Crown to any greater humiliation than it has suffered, nor Great Britain to any dangers from which the actual treaty preserves her, while Ireland might have been spared the ruin, desolation and bloodshed of another year of fratricidal strife.[7]

With regard to the other main objection offered by those who opposed ratification, namely, the provision which was implicit in the treaty and explicit in the Constitution adopted for the Free State, to the effect that no bill passed by the parliament would have force as law until the Governor General had signed it in the name of the King, the simplest comment is that this was an empty form. According to the treaty, the Irish Free State had the same relation to the British government as had the Dominion of Canada; but the Governor General of the Dominion of Canada never or practically never refuses to give the royal assent to bills enacted by the Canadian parliament. Despite this reservation in the name of the King, the parliament of the Free State was as independent of Great Britain in the enactment of laws as though the Free State were a republic. In the years which followed his accession to the headship of the Free State in 1932, Mr. de Valera brought about the abolition of both the oath and the office of governor general, without any serious objection from the British government. What he and his party were able to accomplish in this respect despite their defeat in the civil war, they could obviously have achieved in the absence of a civil war as soon as they came into power. From every point of view the civil war was unnecessary.

The first of the articles which I wrote for *America* while in Dublin in July, 1922, includes the following paragraphs. After declaring that the "idealists" looked upon their armed contest with the Free State forces as a great and heroic struggle on behalf of a "principle," I continued:

In their minds the principle at stake is the right of the nation to

[7] *Op. cit.*, pp. 206–207.

complete political independence. Many times since my arrival in this country have I heard the exclamation, "There is too much idealism in Ireland!" There is much talk about "the soul of the nation," "selling the nation for ignoble peace and comfort," "continuing the nation in the bonds of political slavery," and similar rhetoric and buncombe which convey no realistic idea, but which unfortunately have a real power to delude and mislead persons who do not take the trouble to analyze either the content of these bombastic phrases or the realities of the present political situation. To a political realist this sort of idealism is a gross perversion. The "idealists" are engaged in the attempt to clothe political principles with the sanctity of ethical principles or religious principles. To give up, even temporarily, the armed struggle for a republic is to their minds morally wrong. It is as immoral as to compromise with murder, or theft, or adultery. To accept the Free State is as bad as to accept a corrupted form of religious faith. Obviously this is pure fanaticism.

The person who is able to distinguish between political forms and principles on the one hand and the forms and principles of religion and morality on the other hand, will not permit himself to forget that the former are merely means to human welfare. Keeping in mind this fundamental truth, he will realize that in some situations human welfare can be better promoted by partial independence than by complete independence. The latter is not an end in itself. Whether it is the best means to the real end, namely, human welfare, depends upon the facts of the existing situation. In Ireland today the pertinent facts are that through the Free State the Irish people can safeguard and promote their welfare, physically, intellectually, morally and spiritually, quite as thoroughly and as extensively as they could if they had an independent republic. . . .

Not less extraordinary than this perversion of an ideal is the attempt made by the Republicans to justify their position by political arguments. Admitting that the majority of the people desire the Free State, they contend that this choice is morally invalid because it was made under duress, under threat of a resumption of war by the British Government. Do the Republicans, then, offer the people a perfectly free choice? Not at all. The British Government said in effect: "Accept the Free State, or we shall renew the war of the Black and Tans." The Republicans say in effect: "Reject the Free State, or we shall subject you to the ravages of civil war." Probably very few Irishmen have been deceived by this sophistry. The fact of the matter, and the reason of the matter, is that the people have a right to choose between the alternatives that are before them; they have a right to make a choice of evils. That right they exercised in deciding for the Free State. To deny them the right of choosing what they regard as the less of two evils, is to deny the essential principle of self-determination and of democracy. To assert that they had not a sufficient degree of moral and psychological freedom to perform a morally valid human act, is to utter a rather obvious falsehood.[8]

William T. Cosgrave and his associates in the Free State government were brilliantly successful in their trying and difficult task of putting down the sporadic outbreaks which continued for a few months after the substantial collapse of the Insurgent warfare in August, 1922. No less brilliant and successful were their endeavors to obliterate the traces of damage and destruction perpetrated during the civil war and to place the Free State upon a solid basis of law and order accompanied by as large a degree of economic prosperity as was humanly possible of attainment. Since Eamon de Valera came into power in 1932, his government has introduced a large number of economic and social reforms, especially in slum clearance and housing. Moreover, the de Valera administration has brought about the adoption of a new Constitution for Ireland (December 11, 1936). The latter contains no reference to an oath of allegiance or to a "representative of the Crown or of the Imperial Parliament." With not a little pleasure and pride, I quote a few short paragraphs from this Constitution. First, I present the Preamble:

In the Name of the Most Holy Trinity, from Whom is all authority and to Whom, as our final end, all actions both of men and States must be referred,

We, the people of Eire,

Humbly acknowledging all our obligations to our Divine Lord, Jesus Christ, Who sustained our fathers through centuries of trial,

[8] *America*, August 19, 1922, p. 416.

Gratefully remembering their heroic and unremitting struggle to regain the rightful independence of our Nation,

And seeking to promote the common good, with due observance of Prudence, Justice and Charity, so that the dignity and freedom of the individual may be assured, true social order attained, the unity of our country restored, and concord established with other nations,

Do hereby adopt, enact, and give to ourselves this Constitution. . . .

And here is the greater part of Article 45:

1. The State shall strive to promote the welfare of the whole people by securing and protecting as effectively as it may a social order in which justice and charity shall inform all the institutions of the national life.

2. The State shall, in particular, direct its policy towards securing:

i. That the citizens (all of whom, men and women equally, have the right to an adequate means of livelihood) may through their occupations find the means of making reasonable provision for their domestic needs.

ii. That the ownership and control of the material resources of the community may be so distributed amongst private individuals and the various classes as best to subserve the common good.

iii. That, especially, the operation of free competition shall not be allowed so to develop as to result in the concentration of the ownership or control of essential commodities in a few individuals to the common detriment.

iv. That in what pertains to the control of credit the constant and predominant aim shall be the welfare of the people as a whole.

v. That there may be established on the land in economic security as many families as in the circumstances shall be practicable.

The administrations of both Mr. Cosgrave and Mr. de Valera have shown a high order of statesmanship. No person with Irish blood in his veins need apologize for the political capacity of his race as shown in the homeland from 1922 to the present hour.

My next visit to Ireland was made in 1932, mainly for the purpose of attending the International Eucharistic Congress in Dublin. The religious devotion and piety of the Irish people were manifested with an intensity and on a scale that surprised and delighted their fellow Catholics in Europe and from the United States. The closing ceremonies of the Congress in Phoenix Park were witnessed by at least three-quarters of a million people, the great majority of whom had walked three miles each way in order to participate. The final ceremony was the bestowal over the radio, of the Papal Benediction by Pope Pius XI from Rome. When I informed the Holy Father that I had heard the words of his blessing in Dublin the preceding Sunday his eyes lit up and he inquired in the language we were using "War es klar?" I responded that the broadcast was perfectly clear.

Shortly before I arrived in Dublin that summer, the controversy on the Land Annuities had been precipitated by the recently elected de Valera government. In two articles which I published in the *Commonweal,* September 28 and October 5, 1932, I took the position that the action of the Irish government in discontinuing the payment of the annuities was contrary to both legality and morality. In consequence of these articles several hundred readers of the *Commonweal* canceled their subscriptions, just as several hundred other readers had done with the magazine *America* on account of my article on the civil war ten years before.

Instead of entering upon a lengthy description of the dispute and quoting from my *Commonweal* articles, I present the account of the matter given by Desmond Ryan:

What was the Land Annuities dispute? Like its twin, the oath dispute: both very simple and very technical. In both cases lawyers and constitutional experts are still arguing, and Mr. Cosgrave and Mr. de Valera's daily organ, the *Irish Press,* are still battering each other with statistics, quotations and document this and document that. Five eminent Irish lawyers backed Mr. Cosgrave. Seven eminent Irish lawyers backed Mr. de Valera's contention that Ireland was not legally liable, and the twelve of them played hide-and-seek through all the clauses of the hastily drafted Irish Treaty, and in and out of Mr. Lloyd George's 1920 Government of Ireland Act, and all the archives of the Irish Free State.

The Land Annuities had been paid without question by the Cosgrave Government from 1923. Between 1870 and 1909 some 18 Land Acts had been passed by the British Government to give the Irish farmers ownership of the land on which they had been for generations merely tenants. For generations, in the Irish view, this land had been plundered from the Irish people by massacre, rapine, famine and persecution. Eventually, to the British mind, British statesmen ransomed the sins of their ancestors with a generosity unexampled in history. The land-lords were bought out from 1891 with land stock, public securities issued by the British Government, and the British Government was legally liable to the holders of the stock. Before the Irish Free State was established, the Land Commission collected them, as one of the departments of the British administration. Under the 1920 Government of Ireland Act the Land Annuities were assigned to both Governments, North and South. Under different agreements between the Cosgrave and British Governments it was agreed that the Free State should pay over the money to the British Treasury. The Free State Government did so. The de Valera contention has been that these agreements were secret and not formally ratified by the Dáil. Mr. Cosgrave and his party deny this, and retort that it was a pity Mr. de Valera wasn't there when they mentioned it in the Dáil.[9]

In the boat which took me and several hundred other Americans to the Eucharistic Congress in Dublin, the usual concert was given the second last night of the voyage. My contribution was a recitation of Joseph I. C. Clarke's stirring ballad entitled "The Fighting Race" but more commonly known as "Kelly, and Burke, and Shea." Here is an account of that performance of mine, written by a journalist who was in the audience:

I take you to the concert! Picture Dr. John A. Ryan, the noted theologian and economist, reciting poetry! You have heard him so often at banquets and meetings, discussing economic and other serious questions that you probably find it no easy task to imagine him in any other role. And yet as Father Ryan told in poetry, the story of the Kellys, Burkes, and Sheas, many wept.

Father Ryan put his whole heart and soul into the declamation. We saw a new Father Ryan. We saw a Father Ryan proud of his lineage,

[9] *Unique Dictator*, Desmond Ryan, pp. 243-244.

proud of his Faith, putting everything his Irish heart could draw upon into that poem. One knew that his heartstrings were being played upon by himself, for he was thinking of his heritage and what his ancestors in the Faith had suffered and accomplished.

My latest (I hope not my last) visit to Ireland was made in the summer of 1938 when I was on my way to The Hague to read a paper at the International Catholic Peace Congress. While tarrying in Dublin, I was a guest of the late Frank P. Walsh and Mrs. Walsh at a banquet in their honor given by Mr. de Valera. Although he was quite well aware that I had more than once in magazine articles taken a critical position toward his administration, he did me the honor to give me a seat only two places from him on his right and requested me to offer the invocation both at the beginning and at the end of the meal. While seated there, I asked Mr. de Valera the English pronunciation of the word which describes his title as head of the government, *Taoiseach*. In reply, he gave the phonetic spelling "theeshach." I then asked whether the term had about the same meaning as premier or prime minister. He replied: "No, not quite, it is more the equivalent of 'chief' or 'leader'." "Oh," said I, "*Il Duce* or *Der Fuehrer*." Laughing quietly, he said: "Well, yes."

The dinner was a magnificent affair, held in a vast hall in Dublin Castle with large-size portraits of some thirty or forty men who had held the office of lord lieutenant of Ireland, looking down upon those seated at the table. The contrast between the government of Ireland under British domination and the present regime could not have been more strikingly portrayed. In this splendid room, where for many centuries the lord lieutenants and their friends had dined as the ruling representatives of the English Crown, there were now seated Irish rebels and the sons and daughters of Irish rebels, presided over by the chief executive of a free Ireland.

CHAPTER XIII

INTERNATIONAL QUESTIONS

EARLY in the year 1922, I came upon a book which had been published a few weeks previously, entitled, *America and the Balance Sheet of Europe* by John F. Bass and Harold G. Moulton. This was the first of a long list of productions which I was to read on the general subject of German reparations and inter-Ally war debts. Worthy of particular mention are the two decisive volumes by John Maynard Keynes, *Economic Consequences of the Peace* (1920) and *A Revision of the Treaty* (1922), and five volumes published by the Brookings Institution and written by members of the staff of that organization, namely, *Germany's Capacity to Pay* (1923), *The Reparations Plan* (1924), *The French Debt Problem* (1925), *World War Debt Settlements* (1926), and *War Debts and World Prosperity* (1932). The facts and conclusions set forth in Bass and Moulton's book flashed upon me almost as a revelation. Subsequent works in this field, such as the seven mentioned above, in the main, amplified the facts and confirmed the conclusions.

The "London Settlement" of the reparations problem which was communicated to Germany by the Allied Powers, May 5, 1921, fixed the obligation of that country at the astounding sum of one hundred thirty-two billion gold marks (thirty-three billion dollars). As we look back at the subsequent history of the reparations, including the repudiation of about five-sixths of this fantastic sum, we wonder how responsible statesmen could have been so blind. We ask ourselves whether a more realistic and more charitable attitude might not have prevented the fiscal collapse of Germany in the 1920s and the rise of Hitler in the 1930s.

Returning to the Bass and Moulton volume, I call attention briefly to the most decisive and most illuminating facts set forth therein on the reparations controversy. The crucial question, said the authors in effect, is not how much Germany can pay but how much the Allies are willing to take. Obviously they would not accept payment in German paper money. Only three kinds of payment or "transfer" could have been satisfactory: labor and goods ("payments in kind"), gold, and industrial products. Owing to the competition with their own laborers, merchants, and manufacturers, which would be produced by the first method of payment, neither the French nor the Belgians were willing to permit more than an infinitesimal fraction of the total reparation payments to be made by German labor, and the same was substantially true concerning proposed payments by direct transfer of goods; with regard to the second method, it is sufficient to point out that the entire supply of gold in Germany in 1921 would have sufficed only for discharging the interest obligation for a little more than half a year; finally, only a small part of the annual installment of reparations could have been made indirectly through the export of German industrial products, for the simple reason that Germany's creditors did not desire any considerable increase of imports competing with the products of their own industries. Said Bass and Moulton:

The simple truth is that the insistence of Allied nations that Germany must pay to the limit of her capacity is the supreme inconsistency of the ages. At the very time when the governments of all the Allied nations are demanding that Germany pay in full, under threat of military penalties, one can scarcely pick up a trade or financial journal without reading accounts of the menace of reviving German competition in all the markets of the world. . . .

In conclusion, the nature of the reparations dilemma cannot be better epitomized than in the words of a well-known Anglo-Saxon businessman: "We believe Germany should be forced to pay; we doubt whether she can pay; but if we find that she can, by jingo we won't let her."[1]

Exactly the same dilemma appeared in the situation concerning payments due the United States by the Allies on account of money borrowed during and immediately following the Great War. Although Congress reduced these debts in 1923 by 43 per cent on the average, the great majority of the debtor countries discontinued their annual payments on the reduced sums within a few years. In fact, no German reparations and only an insignificant amount of Ally debts have been paid since 1931.

CANCELLATION OF WAR DEBTS AND REPARATIONS

In 1926, I took part in a debate with the late Senator Burton of Ohio on the question of war-debt cancellation. I pointed out that our attempt to collect any significant portion of these obligations would necessitate: discontinuing the practice of indefinite lending abroad; curtailing our exports and, therefore, our production of certain important kinds of goods; and a drastic reduction of our tariffs in order to let in sufficient foreign products to provide the annual sums due from the debtor nations. To be sure, some of them could probably have paid the annual installments in full if they were permitted to send us certain kinds of goods; for example, Great Britain by operating her factories at full capacity could export to us millions of dollars' worth of textiles. Had that arrangement been seriously contemplated or threatened, the Congress of the United States would undoubtedly have raised the tariff barrier still higher. In other words, we did not want to be paid in the only fashion in which payment could be made.

[1] *America and the Balance Sheet of Europe*, by Bass and Moulton. The Ronald Press Company, 1921, pp. 215, 221.

✦ Therefore, it seemed to me that the only realistic and honest way of dealing with the question of inter-Ally debts was through all-round cancellation, subject to two conditions, however: first, that the claims of the Allies upon German reparations should likewise be canceled; second, that all the nations concerned should adopt and enforce a policy of disarmament, outlawry of war, and revision of the Treaty of Versailles.[2]

These suggestions brought a considerable reaction in the form of more or less severe criticism. I was accused of "playing England's game," being "entirely too free with American claims and property," etc., etc. Probably the majority of the critics had little or no understanding of the economics of debt payment by one nation to another. They did not realize that no considerable amount of such payments can be made except in the form of goods; or if they were aware of this situation they refused to face the fact that our country would refuse to accept annually the enormous increase of imports which would be entailed. By evading that issue some of the critics were enabled to indulge freely in their indoor sport of "twisting the lion's tail." Among the latter were many men who ought to know better or to show more intellectual honesty; for example, members of the United States Senate and the House of Representatives.

At any rate, the proposal which I made in the debate with Senator Burton was not taken seriously by any member of Congress, so far as I know, except the late Senator Borah. But he did not urge it assiduously or consistently. If it had been adopted by the nations concerned, the subsequent history of Europe might have been vastly different and much less deplorable. At any rate, cancellation would have been realistic and might have made some contribution to a

[2] Cf. Ryan, *Declining Liberty and Other Papers*. The Macmillan Company, New York, 1927, pp. 148–160.

regime of international sanity. What the creditor nations have actually obtained is virtual cancellation either by repudiation or by moratoria. German reparations will not be paid and the same is true of the debts owed by the Allies to the United States. All these claims have "gone with the wind." Nevertheless, we still hear statesmen denounce England, France and Italy for nonpayment "of their honest debts." In judging these vocal performances, we are confronted by a dilemma: those who utter them are either abysmally ignorant of economics or they are guilty of rather crude intellectual dishonesty.

In 1924, I published a pamphlet entitled "Christian Charity and the Plight of Europe." Following are the main violations of charity which I cited in relation to the war and its aftermath: (1) Austria's demands upon Serbia in July, 1914, on account of the assassination of the Crown Prince; (2) the refusal of the belligerents to accept Pope Benedict's proposal for peace in 1917; (3) President Wilson's subsequent failure to adhere to the proposition which he had enunciated January 22, 1917, that the best settlement of the war would be a "peace without victory;" (4) the reparations provisions of the Treaty of Versailles; (5) the invasion of the Ruhr by France; (6) the refusal of Great Britain and the United States to accept the proposal by John Maynard Keynes that all inter-Ally indebtedness incurred for the purposes of the war be canceled; (7) the failure of religious teachers before, during, and after the war to apply the moral principles of Christianity to international affairs, and their concessions "to a conception of patriotism which is essentially pagan;" and (8) the failure of American Catholics to keep themselves "unspotted from the jingoism and un-Christian nationalism which are not the least detestable elements in the war's miserable heritage."

CAPPER-JOHNSON BILL

On April 20, 1926, I appeared before a committee of the House of Representatives in opposition to the so-called Capper-Johnson Bill, because, as I interpreted its terms, this measure would enable the President to become "absolute dictator of all male citizens between the ages of eighteen and forty-five" upon a declaration of war by Congress, authorize the President in peacetime to "mobilize for war and absolutely to control under martial law all mines, factories, railroads, industries, banks, all money, all churches, colleges and schools, all organizations of women, boy scouts, campfire girls, and all services over which the government control becomes for any reason whatsoever in the opinion of the President, advised by the general staff, necessary to the termination of an emergency which is deemed likely to bring about war;" likewise, empower the President in such an emergency "to fix by his fiat alone the wages and salaries of all workers in the United States whether employed in war industries or in industries operated for private gain but declared essential to the civilian population;" finally, endow the President "with absolute power under the same conditions to fix wholesale and retail prices on commodities which he declares to be essential either to the government or to the civilian population."

Whether I should be willing to have these extraordinary and all-comprehending powers conferred upon the President in and for a time of actual war, I do not know. I should want to see what kind of war we were engaged in before forming an opinion. When I made the statements just quoted, there was not even a feeble threat of war anywhere on our horizon. Moreover, there were under way then some promising movements for the stabilization of peace in Europe. On the occasion which I have just described, I also opposed any considerable increase in the navy on the ground that America was not in the slightest danger of attack by hostile powers for the next ten years. Since the ten-year period expired in 1936, my forecast was vindicated; nevertheless, important measures had been taken to strengthen the navy before that date. As we now realize, this procedure was wise and statesmanlike.

THE CATHOLIC ASSOCIATION FOR INTERNATIONAL PEACE

The Catholic Association for International Peace was formed in the year 1927. Its stated objects and purposes are:

To study, disseminate and apply the principles of natural law and Christian charity to international problems of the day;

To consider the moral and legal aspects of any action which may be proposed or advocated in the international sphere;

To examine and consider issues which bear upon international goodwill;

To encourage the formation of conferences, lectures and study circles;

To issue reports on questions of international importance;

To further, in cooperation with similar Catholic organizations in other countries, in accord with the teachings of the Church, the object and purposes of world peace and happiness.

The ultimate purpose is to promote, in conformity with the mind of the Church, "The Peace of Christ in the Kingdom of Christ."

The Association has carried on its work mainly through annual and regional meetings and the publication of books and pamphlets. It embraces more than a dozen committees and subcommittees through which the publications are prepared, approved, and produced. Probably the most important of the committees are those on Ethics, History, International Law and Organization, Economic and Social Relations, Agriculture, National Attitudes, Nationalism, Cultural Relations, Latin America, and Peace Education. Of the books published, the most important is the *Catholic Tradition of the Law of Nations;* of the pamphlets, perhaps the following are most worthy of mention: "International Ethics," "Causes of War," "Latin America and the United States," "Europe and the United States," "The Ethics of War," "International Economic Life," "The Church and Peace Efforts," "The World Court and Arbitration," "Peace Statements of Recent Popes," and "The World State." "International Ethics" was the first of the publications. It took the form of a report to the Association by the Committee on Ethics of which I have been chairman from the beginning. This pamphlet has had a very wide distribution and apparently has proved useful and enlightening.

THE NATIONAL COUNCIL FOR THE PREVENTION OF WAR

For several years in the 1920s, I served on the executive board of the National Council for the Prevention of War. Although I was fairly active in that position and strongly approved the main objectives and policies of the Council, the time came when I realized that I could continue my membership no longer. Over my repeated protests, the executive board decided to intervene in the controversy and conflict between the government of Mexico and the Catholic Church. The first two or three pronouncements issued by the Committee on Mexican Relations, convinced me that these zealous men and women were not equipped either with the knowledge or the temperament to carry on the difficult and delicate work that they had undertaken.

While I never questioned the sincerity and earnestness of either the leaders or the majority of the ordinary members, I was not unaware that many of them were fundamentally pacifists. But their pacifism did not, in the years when I was with them, cause any unpleasant complications. Had I been a member when the Council took a strong stand against President Roosevelt's recommendation to Congress in 1939, to lift the embargo on the sale of arms in favor of

Great Britain and France, I am certain that I should then have withdrawn. The organization likewise fought against the program for national defense adopted by Congress in 1940. Judging from the utterances of its leaders during the last year or two, the National Council for the Prevention of War has become hopelessly isolationist. This is a far cry from the hopeful days when I was glad to join with my fellow members of the executive board in applauding the Treaty of Locarno, the Kellogg Pact, the proposed World Court, and even the imperfect League of Nations.

NATIONAL ISOLATIONISM VS. INTERNATIONAL MORALITY

Because I still have faith and hope in world peace through international action, and because I still believe that the precepts of the moral law bind nations as well as individuals, I reject and detest isolationism under any and every disguise. For these reasons likewise, I desire and hope for a British victory over Hitler and Mussolini. In this connection, I submit some excerpts from productions of mine published since the beginning of the war. The first was a radio address, delivered October 15, 1939, and entitled "The Misleading Issue of Neutrality." Here are three of its paragraphs:

Some of the utterances by isolationists, both inside and outside of Congress, suggest the inference that our country has no obligations of love and charity to any other country. These men advocate not only political but moral isolation. They contend that the injustice inflicted by the Hitler government upon the peoples of Poland, Germany, and Austria, and the manifold injustices which it will inflict over wider areas if it is successful in this war, are no moral concern of ours. They remind us unpleasantly of Cain, who demanded: "Am I my brother's keeper?" They imitate the Priest and the Levite, who passed by on the other side, "remaining neutral" to the suffering, the helplessness of the man, who "went down to Jericho and fell among robbers." The person who asserts that we should be impartial and indifferent with regard to the conflict between the Hitler government and the Allies, repudiates not only Christ's gospel of brotherly love, but the principles of natural morality.

States, no less than individuals, are subject to the moral law. And they are bound not only by the precept of justice but, likewise, by the precept of charity. In the present crisis our country is morally obliged to do all that it reasonably can to defeat Hitler and destroy Hitlerism. Victory for this evil genius and his evil principles, in this war, would mean the destruction of Christian civilization throughout a large part of Europe. This tragic result would follow inexorably from the Nazi philosophy and the Nazi policies which have been pursued during the last five years. . . .

The moral question confronting America is not that of "punishing villains in Europe," whether living or dead. It is the question of contributing so far as we reasonably can contribute, to the valiant effort now being made by Britain and France to prevent the triumph of paganism and barbarism in Europe. Hitler is a madman and a monster. As Rev. Robert I. Gannon, S. J., said recently, "Hitler is the most pestilential and altogether infuriating character of all times." One has to go back to Attila or to Genghis Khan to find men comparable with this "pestilential and infuriating character." And his capacity for evil is much greater than was that of either Attila or Genghis Khan.

The other quotations are taken from an article which appeared in the *Commonweal,* March 22, 1940, was reprinted as a pamphlet, and subsequently included as a chapter in the little volume compiled by the "Committee for Defending America by Aiding the Allies." The title of this book is *Defense for America.* In the *Commonweal* my article bore the caption, "Confusions About the War," while the pamphlet and the chapter in the book were entitled "The Right and Wrong of War." Here are two paragraphs from this production:

The extreme pacifist position, that war as such is always wrong because it involves violence, does not deserve formal discussion. With the position of some recent Catholic authorities, that in our day war is practically never justified because of its awful consequences, I have considerable sympathy; but if Hitler and his government intend to substitute paganism for Christianity not only in Germany but in the foreign territories which they have annexed in the last two years and if they are aiming at world domination, then I have no hesitation in saying that a successful war against this immoral Nazi program would be the lesser evil. In other words, such a war would be justified, despite the enormous ensuing destruction of life and property. . . .

The main propositions and conclusions stated in the foregoing paragraphs may be summarized as follows: no war can be just on both sides; in some wars both sides may be acting unjustly. Notwithstanding the use of unjust means or the pursuit of some unjust ends by a belligerent, a noncombatant may lawfully desire victory for that belligerent as the lesser evil. In describing the conditions of a righteous war, the word "motive" is almost always unnecessary and is sometimes misleading. The term "end" is more satisfactory. A "just cause" is practically identical with a "just end." That the Allies have a just cause is proved by the ends which they are seeking and the good effects which are bound up with their success, and also by the enormous evil effects which would derive from their defeat. Some of the reasons offered to justify an attitude of mental neutrality, or even of sympathy with the Nazis, are shallow, unrealistic and ethically invalid.

CHAPTER XIV

MINIMUM-WAGE LAWS OUTLAWED:
CHILD LABOR: LABOR UNIONS:
PUBLIC OWNERSHIP

I HAVE already noticed two facts concerning the constitutional aspect of minimum-wage legislation: the validation
of the Minnesota statute by the highest court of that state,
and the nullification of the District of Columbia law by the
Supreme Court of the United States. Between these two
events, the highest courts in all the other minimum-wage
states, but one, had upheld the legislation for their respective
jurisdictions, and the favorable decision by the Oregon
court had been, on appeal, sustained by a vote of four to four
in the United States Supreme Court.[1]

The confidence produced in the minds of the friends of the
legal minimum wage by these decisions was suddenly destroyed on April 9, 1923, when the Supreme Court imposed
the stamp of unconstitutionality upon the District of Columbia statute.[2] Five members of the Court, Justice Sutherland
writing the opinion, asserted that the law was arbitrary and
an unreasonable restriction upon freedom of contract as
protected by that clause of the Fifth Amendment which for-
bids Congress to deprive any person of "life, liberty, or
property without due process of law." The restriction was unreasonable because: the law "exacts from the employer an
arbitrary payment," not in proportion to the "value of the

[1] *Stettler v. O'Hara*, April 9, 1917.
[2] *Adkins v. Children's Hospital.*

service rendered," but in view of "the extraneous circumstance that the employee needs to get a prescribed sum of money to insure her subsistence, health and morals;" and the prescribed wage ($16.50 per week) ignores "the moral requirement . . . that the amount to be paid and the service to be rendered shall bear to each other some relation of just equivalence . . ."

Chief Justice Taft and Justices Holmes and Sanford dissented. Expressing the opinion of Justice Sanford as well as his own, the Chief Justice declared that a minimum-wage law is no more an unreasonable limitation upon freedom of contract than legislation prescribing maximum hours which the Supreme Court had already sustained in more than one case. Justice Holmes challenged the assumption that "liberty" in the "due process" clause included freedom of contract, pointing out that the earlier Court constructions of this clause

began within our memory and went no farther than an unpretentious assertion of the liberty to follow the ordinary callings. Later that innocuous generality was expanded into the dogma, Liberty of Contract. Contract is not specially mentioned in the text that we have to construe. It is merely an example of doing what you want to do, embodied in the word liberty. But pretty much all law consists in forbidding men to do some things that they want to do, and contract is no more exempt from law than other acts.

Owing to my awareness of the social philosophy entertained by a majority of the members of the Court, the decision did not strike me as a complete surprise; nevertheless, I looked upon it as entirely unnecessary and unjustified. At the request of the editors of various periodicals, I wrote half a dozen articles on its different aspects and implications. These productions were, soon after, reprinted as a pamphlet under the title, "The Supreme Court and the Minimum Wage." Here, I summarize the most important propositions that I urged against the reasoning of the Court: (1) aside from the citation of precedents (which proved unconvincing to the minority) the argument of the majority was neither legal nor juridical but ethical; (2) their ethical doctrine can be traced to the extreme individualism which characterizes our legal tradition and which, in turn, stems from the eighteenth century theory of natural law and natural rights and also from Puritanism;[3] (3) the assertion of the Court that the cost of living of the worker is an "extraneous circumstance," having no vital relation to the wage contract nor any ethical validity as a measure of proper compensation, is a direct contradiction of the Catholic doctrine on the ethics of wages particularly as enunciated by Pope Leo XIII when he declared:

> Let it be granted, then, that, as a rule, workman and employer should make free agreements, and in particular should freely agree as to wages; nevertheless, there is a dictate of nature more imperious and more ancient than any bargain between man and man, that the remuneration must be enough to support the wage earner in reasonable and frugal comfort. If through necessity or fear of a worse evil, the workman accepts harder conditions because an employer or contractor will give him no better, he is the victim of force and injustice.

In other words, the Court asserted that the livelihood of the worker has no ethical place in a legally fixed wage, while Pope Leo declared that the worker's requirements for a decent livelihood are the primary and most essential element in a just wage.

Upon the authority of the decision in the District of Columbia case, the Supreme Court, about two years later, with only Justice Brandeis dissenting, declared unconstitutional the minimum-wage law of Arizona.[4] Thereupon all the other existing state laws on the subject became null and void.

About a decade later, however, a few states passed new

---

[3] Here I have paraphrased some passages in Roscoe Pound's volume, *The Spirit of the Common Law*, pp. 13, 43, 100.

[4] *John W. Murphy et al. v. A. Sardell.*

minimum-wage laws which endeavored to meet the judicial objections to the earlier enactments.

The New York statute was typical. It prohibited the employment of any woman by any employer at an "oppressive and unreasonable wage" and defined such a wage as "one which is both less than the fair and reasonable value of the services rendered and less than sufficient to meet the minimum cost of living necessary for health." When a case under this law came before the Supreme Court[5] five justices held that the decision in *Adkins v. Children's Hospital* controlled the instant case, and, therefore, that the New York statute was unconstitutional, June 1, 1936. Chief Justice Hughes distinguished between the two cases and dissented from the opinion of the Court. In this action, he was joined by Justices Brandeis, Stone, and Cardozo, who, moreover, held that the decision in the Adkins case should be overruled.

A few days after this unfavorable decision was rendered, I criticized it severely in an address before the Catholic Conference on Industrial Problems in San Francisco. My criticism provoked a long reply from a prominent Catholic attorney of that city, the main contentions of which were that, not being a lawyer, I had no competence to discuss the reasoning of the Court; the Court's construction of "liberty" in the "due process" clause, was "the settled interpretation of the Constitution," and decisions since Adkins had virtually compelled the Court to follow that precedent in the New York case. In reply, I declared that my prolonged study of the "due process" clause and the decisions relating to it had rendered me better equipped to discuss the New York decision than the overwhelming majority of lawyers; denied that the precedents were either as old or as weighty as my legal critic had asserted, and inquired how the compulsory

[5] *Morehead v. People ex rel Joseph Tipaldo.*

character of the recent decisions could have been ignored by the dissenting justices, Brandeis, Stone and Cardozo.

However, the most practical and conclusive refutation of the objector's second and third propositions came from the Court itself, less than a year later, when it reversed itself by overruling the Adkins decision and holding the Washington State law constitutional.[6]

THE CHILD LABOR AMENDMENT

One of the sharpest controversies in which I have ever taken part was occasioned by the proposal for an amendment to the federal Constitution which would empower Congress to regulate child labor throughout the United States. The resolution for the amendment was submitted by Congress to the states for ratification in 1924. Up to that time (and, indeed, down to the present hour), the majority of the states had refused to enact laws adequate to combat the child labor evil. Moreover, the United States Supreme Court had pronounced unconstitutional two helpful statutes enacted by Congress. The first of these was the Keating-Owen Act (1916) which prohibited the transportation in interstate and foreign commerce of the products of establishments employing child labor; the second, known as the Pomerene Act (1919) levied a tax of 10 per cent on the net profits of concerns covered by the Keating-Owen Act. When both these laws had received from the Supreme Court the sentence of judicial disapproval, no method seemed left to solve the problem except a constitutional amendment. As proposed by Congress to the states, the resolution reads as follows:

Section 1. The Congress shall have the power to limit, regulate, and prohibit the labor of persons under eighteen years of age.

Section 2. The power of the several states is unimpaired by this

6 *West Coast Hotel Company v. Parrish*, March 29, 1937.

article except that the operation of State laws shall be suspended to the extent necessary to give effect to legislation enacted by the Congress.

At the request of the editor, I wrote an article for the November, 1925, issue of the *Catholic World,* which was later reprinted as a pamphlet. For the most part, this production endeavored to refute the objections to the amendment rather than to provide a positive exposition. It aroused a considerable measure of dissent and criticism to which I replied in several speeches, articles, and letters to the press. Some of the criticisms did me less than justice, while a few characterized my position as an approach to heresy, or at least as disloyalty to Catholic interests. Pressure was brought upon Bishop Shahan, rector of the Catholic University, where I was then teaching, to forbid me to continue discussion of the subject. Similar expostulations were made to the chancellor of the University, Most Reverend Michael J. Curley, Archbishop of Baltimore. Neither attempt was successful. At an annual convention of the International Federation of Catholic Alumnae I advocated ratification of the amendment in the forenoon session, and Archbishop Curley took the opposite stand in the afternoon. In the course of his remarks on this topic, the Archbishop said:

If Doctor Ryan does not agree with me, he is at perfect liberty to disagree. . . . I am not opposed to the Child Labor Amendment because it is Socialistic. Many who stand for the measure are not Socialists. President Coolidge is certainly no Socialist; nor is Dr. Ryan; nor is Senator Walsh of Montana.[7]

Some of the arguments against the amendment were naive and reckless; for example, that it was a "bill," that is, a contemplated statute whose provisions would, upon ratification by the states, immediately become fully operative, and that the resolution for the amendment had been pushed

[7] *The American Catholic Attitude on Child Labor Since 1891,* McQuade. Catholic University of America, Washington, D. C., 1938.

through Congress by powerful outsiders whose real object was to "sovietize and Russianize the family," rather than to abolish child labor. Only three of the arguments in opposition were really plausible: (1) Congress would inevitably, if not immediately, prohibit the labor of persons under eighteen years of age; (2) under the terms of the amendment, Congress could forbid boys and girls below this age to work on the parental farm or to perform domestic tasks; (3) Congress would likewise be empowered by the amendment to control the education of all children under eighteen years of age.

In reply to these contentions, I pointed out, first, the practical impossibility of establishing the eighteen-year limit while the great majority of the members of both the House and the Senate represented states that had refused to set up even a sixteen-year limit; second, that the hypothesis of Congress passing a prohibitory law against labor on the farm or in the household was even more fanciful; and, third, that to construe the word "labor" in the amendment as including the intellectual tasks of the schoolroom was artificial, far-fetched and wholly unwarranted, while the assertion that Congress would be empowered and compelled to provide school facilities for the children whom it forbade to work, was gratuitous. In his great speech in the Senate, January 8, 1925, the late Thomas J. Walsh refuted by an abundance of pertinent citations of court decisions the second and third of these arguments. Senator Walsh's speech was undoubtedly the ablest pronouncement made on either side of the controversy.

By 1926, it became evident that the amendment would not be ratified for some time. At the beginning of 1933 only seven states had acted favorably while thirteen had rejected the proposal. During that year, however, fourteen additional states ratified. Soon, there arose a revival of opposition, which became more general and more intense in 1934 than it had been a decade earlier. On April 13 of that year, the *Common-weal* published a contributed article which repeated most of the old misrepresentations. Replying to the misstatements of this article, I said, in a communication published in the same journal May 25:

We who were in close touch with the controversy on the Child Labor Amendment in the years 1924–1925, recognize all these assertions as old acquaintances. We are also aware that they all derive ultimately from two sources: first, the National Association of Manufacturers, whose very able General Counsel, James A. Emery, wrote one of the earliest pamphlets against the amendment. Mr. Emery is a Catholic, but for a quarter of a century or more he had appeared before congressional committees in opposition to every important measure of social justice introduced in Congress during that period. The other source is certain super-patriotic and pseudo-patriotic organizations which see in every effective piece of social legislation an attack either upon the Constitution or upon American political traditions and institutions. Yet thousands upon thousands of Catholics, as well as other Americans, have accepted unquestioningly this selfish and pernicious propaganda. Under its influence, these Catholics and these other Americans have come to look upon the Child Labor Amendment as the result of a clever and diabolical plot to transfer the control of children from the family to the federal government.

In closing, I wish to say that I knew practically all the principal promoters of the Child Labor Amendment and was fairly well acquainted with their activities in bringing the proposal before Congress. I have never known a group more honestly desirous of ending the evil of child labor. That was their single aim. Yet they have been and are still vilified as plotters against "the family, the home, the school and the church." Even the dead have not been spared. I knew Florence Kelley for almost a quarter of a century. As one of the vice-presidents of the National Consumers' League, of which she was general secretary, I worked with her on behalf of minimum-wage legislation and other laws for the protection of the weaker economic classes. I have never known any other person, man or woman, who labored with quite so much self-denial and effectiveness on behalf of "the least of these." Ex-Governor Smith and ex-Secretary Newton D. Baker have quite recently acclaimed her devotion to these causes in more eloquent language than any that I could command. Therefore, I should like to take this opportunity, Mr. Editor, to protest against the wholesale calumniation of both the dead and the living, perpetrated by certain opponents of the Child Labor Amendment, and I should like to point out that the Eighth Commandment has not been repealed.

By 1938, twenty-eight states had ratified the proposal; none has acted favorably since that year. Sentiment favoring the amendment has been weakened to a considerable extent through the enactment of the Fair Labor Standards Act of 1938. It will be recalled that the National Industrial Recovery Act, passed in June, 1933, included important provisions for the regulation of child labor. By February, 1935, most of the codes set up under the Act by the N.R.A. had established a minimum-age requirement of sixteen for employment in their respective industries. Soon after the N.I.R.A. was declared unconstitutional, May, 1935, many industries abandoned the child labor standards set up in the codes. So far as interstate commerce is concerned, this downward movement has been reversed through the Fair Labor Standards Act. Section 12 declares:

After the expiration of one hundred and twenty days from the date of enactment of this Act, no producer, manufacturer, or dealer shall ship or deliver for shipment in commerce any goods produced in an establishment situated in the United States, in or about which within thirty days prior to the removal of such goods therefrom any oppressive child labor has been employed.[8]

"Oppressive child labor" is defined in the Act as conditions

[8] On February 3, 1941, the Supreme Court of the United States (*U.S.A. v. F. W. Darby Lumber Co. and Fred W. Darby*) sustained all the provisions of the Fair Labor Standards Act. In passing upon the child labor section, the Court explicitly overruled the decision in *Hammer v. Dagenhart* (1918) which had invalidated the Keating-Owen Act. From 1918 until 1938, federal regulation of child labor through the interstate commerce clause was unconstitutional and unlawful; since February 3, 1941, it is both lawful and constitutional. The specific reversal by the Court of the verdict in *Hammer v. Dagenhart*, recalls the similar treatment accorded in *West Coast Hotel Company v. Parrish* (1937) to the decision which invalidated the minimum-wage law of the District of Columbia (*Adkins v. Children's Hospital* (1923)). As I noted with reference to this reversal in chapter XIV, above, "time moves on."

of employment under which any employee under the age of sixteen years is employed by an employer in any occupation, or any employee between the ages of sixteen and eighteen years, is employed by an employer in a particularly hazardous occupation. Since the child labor provisions of the Fair Labor Standards Act cannot apply to persons engaged in intrastate occupations, they fail to protect many thousands of child workers. Nevertheless, the Act does protect other thousands who have been neglected by the states that have failed to enact adequate child labor legislation.

LABOR UNIONS

In December, 1923, I gave an address at Lima, Ohio, on "The Need of a Constitutional Amendment for Social and Labor Legislation." A few weeks later, I repeated the speech in Buffalo, and in 1927 published it as a chapter in my book *Declining Liberty and Other Papers*. Noting that minimum-wage laws for women and eight-hour laws for men had been pronounced unconstitutional by the courts and that statutes providing for social insurance against sickness, accidents, and old age would probably meet the same fate, I advocated as "the obvious remedy" an amendment to the federal Constitution which should take substantially the following form:

The Congress and the several states shall have power to pass laws fixing minimum standards of welfare for the employment of workers, including hours of labor, wages, safety and sanitation, and provision for social insurance against sickness, accident, old age, and unemployment. Provided that the power granted to Congress by this section shall not be construed to prevent any state from enacting higher standards for the employment of labor within its borders than those established by the Congress.[9]

Of course, I could not foresee in 1927 that a decade later my proposed amendment would be rendered unnecessary

[9] Pp. 240–241.

through salutary changes in the personnel of the Supreme Court and in the opinions of some of the justices.

Between 1919, when the "Bishops' Program of Social Reconstruction" was issued, and 1929, when I began a long, sustained study of unemployment, I made many speeches and wrote many articles in defense of the right of labor to organize. My frequently expressed criticism of court injunctions in labor disputes was vindicated by the enactment of the Norris-Walsh-LaGuardia anti-injunction law on March 23, 1932. The policies and principles which I defended on labor's right to organize and the denunciations that I uttered against what I called "the open shop fraud" have obtained actual or virtual implementation in the National Labor Relations Act and its administration by the National Labor Relations Board. My advocacy of a new *status* for labor, that is, a condition in which the employee would be something more than a mere wage earner and would possess some share in management, profits, and ownership, has not been realized as rapidly as I had thought feasible and probable. I first advocated this reform in my debate with Morris Hillquit more than two and a half decades ago.[10] Some progress has been made indeed, but the total amount of achievement is disappointing. Nevertheless, no social prophecy is safer than the prediction that America will not find a tolerable solution of the labor question nor enduring industrial stability and peace until this program is pretty generally adopted. I shall have more to say on this subject in connection with the Papal encyclical *Quadragesimo Anno*.

PUBLIC OWNERSHIP OF PUBLIC UTILITIES

Early in the 1920s, I entered two organizations which have done valiant service in the movement for public ownership of public utilities, namely, the National Popular Government

[10] *Supra*, Chapter VII.

League and the Public Ownership League of America. For many years, I have been a member of the executive committee of the former and a vice-president of the latter. My prominence in these organizations exposed me occasionally to the epithet "socialist." However, this charge has not been made so frequently in recent years, particularly since the magazine *Public Ownership* (January, 1932) carried the following letter over my signature:

November 3, 1931

Dear Mr.—

The person who asked you how you could justify the presence of my name on the list of officers of the Public Ownership League of America in view of the Pope's declaration that a good Catholic could not at the same time be a true socialist, must be either ignorant or intellectually dishonest or given to slovenly thinking.

The only public ownership which this organization advocates is ownership of those industries known as public utilities, street railways, public light and power concerns, etc. Of course, you can call these proposals socialistic if you like, and even communistic, but that does not make them so.

Socialism means public ownership and operation of all or of practically all of the instruments of production and that is the kind of economic doctrine which our present Holy Father condemns in the encyclical from which you quote. The Pope also says: "It is rightly contended that certain forms of property must be reserved to the state since they carry with them an opportunity for domination too great to be left to private individuals without injury to the community at large." I am sure that this statement would be satisfactory to Carl D. Thompson, inasmuch as it authorizes all the "Socialism" that is sought by the Public Ownership League.

When you say that Carl Thompson "is a radical of the worst type," you do not alarm me at all, for I have myself been the object of equally vague and reckless epithets many times in the last twenty-five years. Whether the Socialist movement in the United States is now anti-Catholic, I do not know, nor does it much matter, for the organized American Socialist movement has dwindled into insignificance.

As stated earlier, I still believe in public ownership of

public utilities, but I have come to realize that the full program will not and, indeed, should not be put into effect quickly or according to a uniform pattern in all such industries. Moreover, public ownership does not necessarily imply public operation; nor is public operation a simple, single concept. Sometimes the publicly owned concern might advantageously be leased to a private corporation. Sometimes a public or semi-public corporation, such as the Port of New York Authority or the Tennessee Valley Authority, could perform the task more efficiently than a government instrumentality, such as the Post Office Department or a city department of waterworks. Public utilities are too varied in character and the problems of their operation are too complex to be dealt with by a single method or according to a uniform plan.

My interest in public utilities under private operation led me to comprehensive studies of valuation. In 1928, I published a pamphlet on "The Ethics of Public Utility Valuation," which presented most of the views that I had been advocating on this subject for several years, and dealt particularly with the decision of the Supreme Court in *McArdle et al. v. Indianapolis Water Company* (1926). The valuation sustained by the Court in that case was 50 per cent in excess of the actual cost of the company's property, plus the increases in land value which had occurred subsequently to the establishment of the corporation. According to the Court, this high valuation was warranted on the theory that "dominating consideration" should be given to present cost of reproduction. In the pamphlet I rejected the cost-of-reproduction theory as unfair to the consumers, and defended as the proper measure of valuation "the historical cost of the property." On this amount the owners of the property, I argued, had a just claim to a fair rate of return. On the other hand, the consumers could justly be required to pay charges sufficient to provide this fair rate of interest. When the Court sanctioned and required the higher valuation, it was in effect enabling the investors to receive interest on something that did not exist and compelling the consumers to pay a correspondingly excessive price for water.

So far as I am aware, no subsequent decision of the Supreme Court in a valuation case has given such great weight to cost of reproduction as in the Indianapolis case. Moreover, for a variety of reasons, valuation cases have come before the Court much less frequently in the last ten years than in the decade immediately preceding. In all probability the recent trend will continue for some years to come. However that may be, I still hold that historical cost as a general rule is the only measure of value that is at once fair to the investor and the consumer in the field of public utilities.[11]

In the years 1927 and 1928, I was engaged in controversies with Charles C. Marshall and a few other men in consequence of the former's open letter to Governor Smith, published in the *Atlantic Monthly,* April, 1927. In substance, Mr. Marshall asserted the existence of irreconcilable conflicts at many points between the Catholic Church and the Constitution of the United States, and that neither Governor Smith nor any other Catholic could be a loyal American citizen without reservations. It is probable that Mr. Marshall persuaded few persons that had not been already persuaded before he published his "Open Letter." Aside from my reply to Mr. Marshall in the *Commonweal,* my principal contribution to the controversy took the form of a reply to an article by Rev. Charles Hillman Fountain and appeared in *Current History* magazine, March, 1928. In the December, 1928, issue of the same magazine, I published at the request of the editors my judgments on the effect of religion on the presidential election of 1928. My conclusion was that if the religious factor had not been present in the

[11] The material in the pamphlet referred to above has been reprinted with considerable additions in my book *Questions of the Day*, pp. 134-180.

campaign, Governor Smith could easily have been elected. Following are the last two paragraphs of this article:

While I am disappointed and disillusioned on account of the injection of religious intolerance into the campaign, I am not discouraged. Nor have I the heart to attribute moral blame to the great majority of my fellow country-men and women who voted against Governor Smith mainly or exclusively because he is a Catholic. They are inheritors of a long anti-Catholic tradition, compact of misrepresentation and falsehood. They have never had adequate opportunity to learn the facts about the Catholic Church. But I cannot feel so indulgent toward the men who have exploited religious intolerance in the campaign from their pulpits, from the platform and by the written and printed word. Most of these men know better or are culpably ignorant. If the disgraceful history of the recent campaign in this matter is not to be repeated, there will be required a long, a comprehensive and an intensive campaign of education to enlighten them that sit in darkness.

Obviously, I am not pleased with the results of the election. As a Catholic, I cannot be expected to rejoice that some millions of my country-men would put upon me and my co-religionists the brand of civic inferiority. As an American, I cannot feel proud that the spirit of the Sixth Amendment to the Constitution is thus flouted and violated. As a believer in personal freedom and political honesty, I cannot feel cheerful over the prospect of four more years of the arrogant, despotic and hypocritical domination from which we are suffering by the grace of the Anti-Saloon League. As a democrat and a lover of justice, I cannot look with complacency upon a President-elect who, judged by his campaign addresses, believes that the economic welfare of the masses should be confided, practically without reservation, to the care of corporate business, in the naive faith that corporate business will dispense and hand down universal justice. This is industrial feudalism. Possibly it may turn out to be benevolent. In any case it will do violence to the most fundamental and valuable traditions of the America that we have known and loved.[12]

[12] *Questions of the Day*, pp. 98–99.

The two fearful prospects noted in this paragraph experienced different subsequent developments. "Domination" by the Anti-Saloon League lasted only four years longer and became considerably weakened during that time. The economic philosophy of Mr. Hoover proved disastrous during that same period; even today some of its evil effects remain.

Chapter XV

UNEMPLOYMENT AND THE GREAT DEPRESSION

FROM the year 1929 until the present hour I have given
more time to the study of unemployment, its causes,
effects, and implications than to any other subject in the field
of economics. During his campaign for election to the
Presidency, Herbert Hoover had visualized the near approach of the day when "poverty will be banished from this
land," and had held out hope that after his election there
would be a "chicken in every pot" and "two cars in every
garage." Despite these rosy prophecies, I wrote in December
of that year an article entitled "Unemployment: Causes and
Remedies." It was published in the *Catholic World* for
February, 1929. In the opening paragraph, I estimated the
number of unemployed at three million, which was one
million less than the estimate of Senator Wagner, made during the first half of 1928. Between the beginning and the end
of that year there had occurred, however, a notable increase
in business activity. The causes of unemployment I classified
as "particular" and "chronic." The former I subdivided into
seasonal, local, and technological causes. The principal
remedies for the unemployment due to particular causes I
put down as a comprehensive system of national, state, and
municipal employment services, public insurance against
unemployment, and expenditures for public works. In connection with the last-named measure, I praised the proposal
made by Governor Brewster of Maine at the convention of
governors held in New Orleans in December, 1928, which

contemplated continuous control and planning and expenditure of three billion dollars over a period of several years.

The "chronic" cause of unemployment, I designated as "general overproduction and underconsumption," which I summarily described in the following sentences:

> The vast majority, if not all, of our industries are capable of producing more goods than can be sold at profitable prices. Or, to describe the problem in terms of the consumer: those who would like to buy more goods have not the money; those who have the money to buy more lack the desire. As a consequence, the capacity for overproduction has become chronic and unemployment, or imminent danger of unemployment, has likewise become chronic.

Among the indications which I gave of this condition was the following quotation from an article by Ethelbert Stewart, United States Commissioner of Labor Statistics:

> We're up against a new system. The machine has put production ahead of population. What are we going to do with what we produce? The man who made two blades of grass grow where one grew before was a public benefactor then. But today we have all the hay we need, and more. The fellow who makes two stalks of wheat grow where one grew before isn't a public benefactor unless he creates new wants for his product and new ways of supplying them. . . .

The problem of finding a remedy for this unemployment was, I said, no longer a problem of production but that of increasing the consuming power of the masses. The means of bringing this about I specified as increased expenditures for public works, a universal minimum-wage law, and the five-day week.

A few months later, in October, 1929, I published four articles in the *Commonweal*.[1] While these articles covered much more ground than the *Catholic World* article, their main concern was what I had called chronic unemployment, but now denoted by the newer term, technological. In these

---

[1] Reprinted with additional material in my book *Questions of the Day*, pp. 180-217.

articles I presented a considerable number of facts and authoritative opinions to show the great extent of technological unemployment and the discouraging prospects. I quoted an optimistic statement in the report entitled "Recent Economic Changes" which had shortly before been issued by a committee under the chairmanship of Herbert Hoover: "Wants are almost insatiable; there are new wants which will make way endlessly for newer wants as fast as they are satisfied." While admitting the truth of this inconclusive generality, I pointed out that as a solution of unemployment it had two vital defects:

In the first place, it is quite unlikely that the requisite new commodities will be invented. More fundamental is the objection that this would be an undesirable kind of industrial society. The people of our age, even the wealthy, would not be benefited by new luxuries, and the masses ought not to be required to provide superfluous goods for the few, while they themselves are unable to obtain a reasonable amount of necessaries and comforts.

When I wrote those articles in August, 1929, I had no definite suspicion that the great depression was "just around the corner." As a matter of fact, it had set in imperceptibly by July, 1929, and was plainly evident the following November. The crash of prices on the stock exchange was an effect rather than a cause. It was a cause only insofar as it somewhat accelerated and temporarily intensified the downward movement of industrial activity. Of course, it made the depression spectacularly obvious. The depression would probably have been just as general, as profound, and as enduring in the absence of the orgy of speculation which reached its peak in the last days of October, 1929.

Since the beginning of 1930, I have written many articles and made many speeches on unemployment and the depression. In none of those productions have I departed from the main positions that I defended in my 1929 articles. Subsequent statements exhibit amplification, more facts, more cogent arguments, and greater emphasis on particular methods for meeting the current emergency. To illustrate the last-mentioned development, I would cite my long-continued advocacy of government spending as a means of providing employment and defeating the depression. Here I wish to present a specific, though brief, account of the earliest half-dozen of these articles and addresses. My later utterances can be summarized in a few sentences.

In the *Catholic World,* for July, 1930, I estimated the unemployed at five million and declared that the "industrial confidence" which President Hoover had sought to create and diffuse through the conferences of business and labor leaders, held the preceding November, had only temporarily checked the downward movement of industrial activity. I recounted the predictions of improvement made by the President in January, March, and May, and noted their continuous and complete refutation by the trend of business down to June. I attributed the depression and its persistence mainly to enlarged productive capacity and the lack of adequate purchasing power in the hands of the masses. As remedies, I endorsed the recommendation of the National Unemployment League that three billion dollars be expended by the federal government in road building, increased wages, and a thirty-five hour working week.

In an article in the *Commonweal,* September 3, 1930, I said that while President Hoover could not be blamed for the coming of the depression, he was distinctly culpable for disregarding the recommendation of Governor Brewster, in December, 1928, for a three-billion dollar public expenditure on public works to meet the problem of unemployment. I also criticized him for bringing about a reduction of one hundred and sixty million dollars in levies of income taxes and for recommending to the various government departments a reduction of expenditures. The first of these put money into the pockets of those who, in the main, would not spend it, while the second decreased the purchasing power of those who, in the main, were willing to spend.

In addresses before a meeting of the Catholic Conference on Industrial Problems, December 9 and 10, 1930, I denounced President Hoover's opposition to an increase in income taxes for unemployment relief and his assertion that such an increase would necessarily fall upon the workers and the farmers, and his further assertion that increased income taxes would deprive industry of new investments. I declared flatly that "those who have, must bear the burdens of those who have not," that stockholders cannot show any certain and permanent right to dividends as high as 6 or 7 per cent, and that the employment situation "is going to become worse before it becomes better." At a conference on "Permanent Preventives of Unemployment," in January, 1931, under the sponsorship of the Department of Social Action of the National Catholic Welfare Conference, the Social Service Commission of the Federal Council of the Churches of Christ, and the Social Justice Commission of the Central Conference of American Rabbis, I again denounced the provision made by the Hoover Administration for the relief of the unemployed as "shamefully inadequate;" referred to "our more than five million unemployed;" advocated unemployment insurance, higher wages, and a shorter working week, and stressed particularly the need of a five-billion dollar federal appropriation for public works.

During the remainder of the Hoover Administration, I repeatedly advocated federal relief for the unemployed and a huge appropriation by Congress for public works. By the latter end of 1932, I was specifying six billion dollars instead of five billion. In February, 1933, I advocated an outlay of from six to eight billion, and in May of that year, I said that

the $3,300,000,000 appropriation for public works pro-
posed by the Roosevelt Administration would not be adequate. In May, 1935, I declared that the amount of public
money actually spent to create purchasing between June,
1933, and the beginning of 1935 had been only two and one-
half billion dollars. Obviously, this meager sum could produce only a feeble degree of industrial recovery; hence I advocated an expenditure of five billion a year for the following
three years.

In the years 1934 and 1935, appeared the four Brookings
Institution volumes on the general subject of income and
economic progress.[2] It is not an exaggeration to say that
these studies have placed the theory of underconsumption and
oversaving upon a solid basis of economic evidence. Despite
the differences which Dr. Harold G. Moulton finds between
the Brookings version of that theory and the statement of it
by John A. Hobson, the resemblances are more significant
than the differences.[3] Inasmuch as I had adhered to Hobson's
theory for almost forty years, I welcomed these Brookings
volumes with joy. I was particularly glad to learn from
them that America's productive plant had been only 80 per
cent utilized in the busy year of 1929, although sufficient
labor had been available to operate the plant at full capacity.
In 1929 the idle machines and the idle men could have co-
operated for the production of several billion dollars worth of
additional goods, if only the potential consumers had been in
possession of sufficient purchasing power to demand this
enormous potential output.[4]

Since 1935, I have consistently and continuously defended
the theory of underconsumption, advocated higher incomes
for labor and the farmers, lower interest rates, and a smaller
share of the national income for the owners of capital. In all

---

[2] *America's Capacity to Produce*, 1934; *America's Capacity to Consume*, 1934; *The Formation of Capital*, 1935; *Income and Economic Progress*, 1935.

[3] *The Formation of Capital*, pp. 173–176.

[4] See note at end of this chapter.

that time, I have never ceased to champion large expenditures of public money for work relief and public works (W.P.A. and P.W.A.). Nevertheless, I have come to realize that the theory of "pump priming" has one definite limitation. Public works can "prime the pump" in the sense that so long as they are continued they cause an increase in private business and private employment. The ratio, I believe, is two and one-half men employed in subsidiary private industries for every one engaged upon the public project. After the stimulus of public works is withdrawn, however, private industry cannot continue at the pace that it has artificially acquired. Even if the government were to put into operation a program of public works so large that all the unemployed found either public or private jobs, private industry alone would not be able to continue this happy condition. Private industry would be unable to continue with full operation and full employment. The reason is to be found in the bad distribution, in the fact that the owners of capital still would receive more than they could spend, and that labor would obtain less than it would like to spend. In other words, the industrial pump would not stay primed, unless capital received less and labor more than under the present distribution.

The methods and measures which are now required to abolish unemployment can be summarily stated, as follows: raise as rapidly as practicable the minimum-wage rates in the Fair Labor Standards Act and gradually reduce the maximum hours from the present level of forty per week to thirty; bring about state minimum-wage laws for intrastate industries and even a federal law for these industries if it can be validly enacted under the "general welfare" clause of the Constitution;[5] bring about an increase in the incomes of the

---

[5] In one of the Supreme Court decisions, *Helvering and Edison Electric v. Davis* (1937), upholding the Social Security Act, we find these words: "Nor is the concept of the general welfare static. Needs that were narrow or parochial a century ago may be interwoven in our day with the welfare of the nation. What is critical or urgent changes with the times."

farmers; reduce interest rates by every feasible device, until they have reached 2 per cent; expend sufficient money on public works to provide employment for all who cannot find jobs in private industry and continue to do so until all the unemployed have been absorbed; as a rule, defray the cost of this program through higher taxes on incomes, inheritances, and excess profits, realizing that with full employment the national income could readily be increased by twenty-five or thirty billion dollars, which would be more than ample to provide with relative painlessness the additional tax payments.[6]

In an article in *Fortune,* November, 1935, entitled, "The Trouble With Capitalism is the Capitalists," Dr. Harold Glenn Moulton, president of the Brookings Institution, summarized the facts and conclusions presented in the four volumes cited earlier in this chapter. The article was reprinted as a pamphlet by the Maurice and Laura Falk Foundation, of Pittsburgh, under the title, "Economic Progress Without Economic Revolution." The following paragraphs from the article and pamphlet are reproduced here because they summarize the most important conclusions of the Brookings study and because they confirm, on the basis of "economic evidence," the theory of underconsumption which underlies the argument of the present chapter. The references are to pages in the pamphlet:

The obvious conclusion to be drawn at this point would be that American consumption is potentially much larger than actual production has ever been, and that the defect in the system lies in the element which connects the two to each other—the element of purchasing power. If the great mass of the population has incomes too small to enable it to buy what it wants and if an infinitesimal minority has incomes larger than it can spend, then consumption will be less than it could be and production also less. The rich, with the large incomes, will

[6] Cf. John Bauer, *National Welfare and Business Stability*. Harper & Bros., New York, 1940, Chap. V.

put into savings what they do not need to pay out for goods. Two-thirds of the entire savings ($15,000,000,000) made in 1929, for example, were made by that 2.3 per cent minority of the population having incomes in excess of $10,000. And since the proportion of the national income saved has tended, according to our findings, to increase in recent times with an increase in the concentration of wealth, the process may be expected to continue in aggravated form . . . (p. 12).

. . . the saving of money does not per se create a demand for capital goods. All it does is to furnish funds with which business enterprisers *may* employ labor and materials in the construction of new plant and equipment if the expansion looks profitable. But, by and large (business taken from competitors aside), expansion will only be profitable if the total market for the goods to be manufactured is also expanding. And the total market will only expand during a period of expanding consumptive demand. If an increasing percentage of the national income is diverted to savings channels, the flow of funds into consumptive channels may not be of sufficient magnitude to make it profitable for all the funds which have been diverted to investment channels to be profitably employed in the construction of new plant and equipment.

A flow of money savings into investment channels in excess of the requirements of the capital markets is a comparatively new phenomenon in the U. S. Until approximately the World War period, our capital requirements were characteristically larger than the people's savings. We made good the deficiency by borrowing abroad and by the expansion of commercial banking credit.

In the last twenty years, however, the situation has been profoundly altered. As a result of a higher average level of income, and particularly because of the concentration of income, the volume of money savings flowing to investment channels has so greatly increased that the balance has been shifted, and a maladjustment of basic significance has developed. Our capacity to produce consumer goods has been chronically in excess of the amount which consumers are able to take off the markets; and this situation is attributable to the increasing proportion of the total income which is diverted to savings channels. The result is a chronic inability to find market outlets adequate to absorb our full productive capacity (pp. 13–15).

CHAPTER XVI

THE ENCYCLICAL, *QUADRAGESIMO ANNO*: THE
ROOSEVELT REFORMS

ON MAY 15, 1931, in the office of the *New York Times,* I
listened to the transmission by radio from the Vatican
of the words of the encyclical issued that day by Pope Pius
XI. Long before the process was completed, I realized that
this was an exceptionally great Papal message on the social
question—powerful, comprehensive, traditionally Catholic,
and, in the true sense of the word, radical. I also derived great
comfort from the implicit approval which the Holy Father's
pronouncement gave to the socio-ethical doctrines which I
had been defending for almost forty years. Referring to the
new encyclical a few days later, Bishop Shahan, the rector of
the Catholic University, observed: "Well, this is a great
vindication for John Ryan."

The encyclical is designated in three different ways.
Quadragesimo Anno are the first two words of the Latin text
and may be regarded as the official title; the English equivalent is "Forty Years After." Both phrases connote the relation
of this encyclical to *Rerum Novarum,* or "On the Condition
of Labor," issued by Pope Leo XIII exactly forty years
earlier. The most expressive designation of the encyclical of
Pius XI is: "On Reconstructing the Social Order and Perfect-
ing It Conformably to the Precepts of the Gospel," which is
usually condensed into "On Social Reconstruction."

In an article which I published in the *American Ecclesiastical Review,* July, 1931, I presented and discussed "The
New Things in the New Encyclical." Of course, I did not

mean to imply that Pope Pius was enunciating new doctrines; I merely called attention to the new formulation and amplification of the traditional social teaching which had been set forth by Pope Leo XIII. Here are some of the new formulations made by Pius XI: the Church has a right to pronounce upon social and economic matters "insofar as they have a bearing upon moral conduct;" property has a social as well as an individual aspect and the task of defining its limits, where the natural law is not sufficiently definitive, "is the function of government;" the division of the output of industry between capital and labor "must be brought into conformity with the demands of the common good and social justice;" up to the present, the industrial product has not been "rightly distributed and equitably shared among the various classes of men;" the adult male worker has a right to a wage which will provide "ample sufficiency" for himself and his family and will enable him "to attain to the possession of a certain modest fortune;" wage earners should, wherever possible, become "sharers of some sort in the ownership or the management of the profits;" "a scale of wages too low, no less than a scale excessively high, causes unemployment."

The most important section of the encyclical is that which carries as a subhead the title of the whole document, namely, "The Reconstruction of the Social Order." The essence of the program is a system of occupational groups, or vocational groups, or guilds. In each industry the group should include all interested parties: labor as well as capital; employees as well as employers. Employers and labor and the other subdivisions of other occupations would keep their rights of separate assemblage and vote inside the occupational groups and their right of separate organization. These groups, says Pope Pius XI, would "bind men together not according to the position which they occupy in the labor market but according to the diverse functions which they exercise in society." The occupational groups would seek to modify competition by maintaining standards of fairness with regard to wages, hours, prices, and business practices; to avoid private industrial dictatorship by enabling labor to share in all industrial policies and decisions, and to exclude political or bureaucratic industrial dictatorship by keeping the immediate and day-to-day control in the hands of the agents of production. They would be prevented from injuring the consumer or the common good by governmental action, "directing, watching, stimulating and restraining, as circumstances suggest or necessity demands." This form of government control is different from and much less than that contemplated by collectivism. Moreover, the consumers could protect themselves through some form of representation in relation to the governing bodies of the occupational groups.

In a word, the occupational group system would aim to bring into industry sufficient self-government to reduce to a minimum the conflicting interests of the various industrial classes, to place industrial direction in the hands of those most competent to exercise it, and to permit only that amount of centralized political control which is necessary to safeguard the common good.

Not a few commentators and critics of the occupational group system have confused the Papal proposals with Fascism. As a matter of fact, Pope Pius XI presented in this encyclical a brief description of the Fascist "corporative organization," noting its substitution of the state "in the place of private initiative" and its "excessively bureaucratic and political character." The differences between the occupational group system and politico-economic Fascism have been neatly summarized by Rev. R. A. McGowan, assistant director of the Department of Social Action of the National Catholic Welfare Conference:

The first difference is that under a Fascist scheme of things, the government creates and controls the business, farmer and labor organizations; the organizations are not the people's own but the government's. The second is that government does most of the work and the government-created organizations do little. And the third is that the purpose is not justice and the organized and organic life of the people to rule their own work and ownership for the common good, but something else, usually national glory, war and empire.

Since the encyclical emphatically rejects both Socialism and Communism, the new social order which it proposes obviously has no affinity with any form of collectivism. On the contrary, it would decentralize the economic activities of the state and set up industrial self-government within the occupational groups, at the same time retaining a reasonable measure of supervision and direction by the government.

Could the occupational group system be fairly called capitalism? The answer depends upon our definition. Throughout the greater part of its history the dominating characteristics of capitalism have been: private ownership and operation of the means of production directed to the lowest practicable wage payments,. the highest obtainable receipts of interest and profits, and the maximum of economic domination. To be sure, a considerable minority of capitalists have not consistently sought all these ends, but I am discussing the system, the institution, as a whole, and its prevalent historical functioning. Obviously, the occupational group system, operating in accordance with the social and ethical principles laid down in the encyclical, would be alien to that kind of capitalism.

If, however, we discard the historical definition and think of capitalism merely as private ownership and operation of the means of production, then the occupational group system might be called a modified or reformed capitalism. But such a conception or classification, and such language is misleading rather than clarifying.

The great political and economic changes occurring throughout the world since the publication of *Quadragesimo Anno,* have strongly confirmed me in the conviction that only the occupational group system is capable of bringing to the nations political liberty, economic stability, and social justice. Not the least of its virtues is its fundamental democracy. Under it, men would be able to order their own economic lives. They would not be regimented by plutocratic or proletarian or political dictators. The intrinsic and indestructible dignity of the individual would be safeguarded against submergence in and subordination to the mass. The significance of the human person as a child of God and a brother of Christ would obtain, for the first time since the Middle Ages, effective recognition in economic institutions. The sacredness of personality has never been formally recognized in the maxims of historical capitalism. It is frankly rejected in the philosophy of Communism. It is treated as an exploded theory by many intellectuals. In the occupational group system it would again become a vital element in American thought and life.[1]

THE ROOSEVELT REFORMS

On March 4, 1932, I sat by a radio and listened to the inaugural address of Franklin D. Roosevelt as President of the United States. In common with the great majority of my fellow citizens, I had realized that the economic condition of the country was desperate, that millions of the people were discouraged and demoralized, and that the task confronting a new President was exceedingly grave and formidable. As the first sentences of Mr. Roosevelt's message came over the air, I began to feel moderately hopeful; as the speaker proceeded, this feeling increased steadily and rapidly; by the

[1] At the private audience, referred to in Chapter XII, which Pope Pius XI granted me in 1932, he spoke mostly about *Quadragesimo Anno*. I departed with the conviction that this encyclical was very dear to his heart.

time he had reached his closing paragraphs my hopeful-
ness had been transmuted into definite confidence and even a
mild measure of enthusiasm. Recognizing the maladjust-
ments of the economic system, and consequent distress of
millions of Americans, he placed the blame upon the shoul-
ders of the dominant economic groups who had known
"only the rules of a generation of self-seekers." While the
reasons which he offered for hope and the courses of action
which he promised to follow, were not stated in detail,
they were sufficiently definite and clear to convince men of
goodwill that he had rejected completely the theories and the
policies which had dominated the Hoover Administration.
The problem of unemployment, the notorious evils of the
banking and credit systems, and the plight of the farmers
were the most important matters that he discussed specifically. What he said on these topics suggested that he would
probably deal realistically with all the other acute economic
problems which then confronted and baffled the people of
the United States. Not the least satisfying features of the
inaugural address were its references to ethics and to courage.
Under the former head, these paragraphs are worth quoting:

Happiness lies not in the mere possession of money; it lies in the joy
of achievement, in the thrill of creative effort. The joy and moral
stimulation of work no longer must be forgotten in the mad chase of
evanescent profits. These dark days will be worth all they cost us if
they teach us that our true destiny is not to be ministered unto but to
minister to ourselves and to our fellow men.

Recognition of the falsity of material wealth as the standard of
success goes hand in hand with the abandonment of the false belief
that public office and high political position are to be valued only by
the standards of pride of place and personal profit; and there must be an
end to a conduct in banking and in business which too often has given
to a sacred trust the likeness of callous and selfish wrongdoing. Small
wonder that confidence languishes, for it thrives only on honesty, on
honor, on the sacredness of obligations, on faithful protection and on
unselfish performance. Without them it cannot live.

And under the head of "courage" the closing paragraphs are noteworthy:

We face the arduous days that lie before us in the warm courage of national unity; with the clear consciousness of seeking old and precious moral values; with the clean satisfaction that comes from the stern performance of duty by old and young alike. We aim at the assurance of a rounded, a permanent national life.

We do not distrust the future of essential democracy. The people of the United States have not failed. In their need they have registered a mandate that they want direct, vigorous action. They have asked for discipline and direction under leadership. They have made me the present instrument of their wishes. In the spirit of the gift, I take it.

In this dedication of a nation we humbly ask the blessing of God. May He protect each and every one of us. May He guide me in the days to come.

Practically all the reform measures enacted during the Roosevelt Administration have met with my hearty approval. Relief for the needy and helpless, minimum fair standards for work and wages, the right of employees to bargain collectively, larger incomes for labor and farmers, expenditure of public money for public works both to provide employment and to increase the purchasing power of the masses, reduction of the rate of interest both for the benefit of borrowers and in order to diminish the amount of national saving—all these seemed to me to be highly desirable means and ends. That all the ends were not fully attained through the legislation directed thereto is not surprising. The obstacles have been great and legislators and administrators are fallible human beings. Nevertheless, a comprehensive reading of American history will disclose that the reform measures enacted since the spring of 1933 constitute a greater advance toward a regime of social justice than the whole body of reform legislation previously passed since the adoption of the Constitution.

However, the enactment which interested me most and

from which I expected most, endured less than two years. The National Industrial Recovery Act was passed June 16, 1933, and was declared unconstitutional May 27, 1935. The National Recovery Administration provided for a forty-hour week, minimum-wage rates, right of labor to bargain collectively, fair business practices, a considerable measure of industrial self-government, and by implication it espoused and promoted the purchasing-power theory of business prosperity and economic welfare. More than once during those two years I pointed out the similarity between the institutions of N.R.A. and the constituent elements of the occupational group system. I contended that the plan recommended by Pope Pius XI was more radical, more democratic, and more desirable than N.R.A. as actually set up and functioning, and that the chief defect in N.R.A. structure was its failure, except in a minority of the industries, to give adequate representation to the employees. I still believe that if N.R.A. had been permitted to continue, it could readily have developed into the kind of industrial order recommended by Pope Pius XI.

N.R.A. met with a great deal of criticism on the one hand from ultra-liberals and on the other hand from the seekers after unlimited economic domination. One of the most plausible and persistent charges was that in actual operation N.R.A. favored the larger at the expense of the smaller business concerns. In order to deal specifically with this situation, on August 11, 1934, General Hugh Johnson, the national administrator, set up a committee of three, known as the Industrial Appeals Board. The members were Amos J. Peaslee, an international lawyer, John S. Clement, a manufacturer, and myself. We were empowered to deal with all grievances brought before us by businessmen, either against one another or against the National Recovery Administration. And we were instructed to give especial attention to the complaints of the smaller businessmen. So far as I can recall not more than two or three cases were brought by small men against large ones, or against the administration of N.I.R.A. The great majority of the petitions by the group of small men took the form of requests for exemption from compliance with the minimum-wage rates fixed for their respective industries. In the second case that we heard, a number of small producers using hand labor instead of machines, maintained that they could not pay labor twenty-eight cents an hour in competition with concerns that were equipped with up-to-date machinery. While we realized that they were thus handicapped, we refused their application on the ground that to grant it would cause the whole wage structure to collapse. We preferred to see a few inefficient concerns go out of business than to bring about a reduction in the wages of thousands of workers. In all similar cases, we followed the same rule. Because of this experience, I took a questioning attitude toward most of the charges that N.R.A. was discriminating against the small man.

One of the few reform proposals of President Roosevelt that failed of enactment was his plan for the reorganization of the federal judiciary. Here, I shall consider only that part of the plan which had reference to the Supreme Court. In February, 1937, the President sent to Congress a bill which would authorize him to appoint one additional justice for every existing member of the Court who had attained the age of seventy years. The bill stipulated, however, that not more than six extra justices could be appointed; hence the maximum membership of the Court could not exceed fifteen. The President sought this reorganization of the Supreme Court in order to prevent the judicial invalidation of reforms which had already passed Congress, and of others which were contemplated. In the first half of the year 1936, the Supreme Court had declared unconstitutional the Agricultural Adjustment Act and the Guffey Coal Act, in each case by a majority of six to three. Inasmuch as six of the sitting justices were past seventy years of age, the President under the terms of the bill would be entitled to appoint that number of new members. Added to the two under seventy who were favorable to the reform laws, they would constitute a majority of the enlarged Court.

Undoubtedly, the remedy proposed by the President was bold and drastic but it was not exactly revolutionary or unprecedented: it had been applied by other Presidents on a smaller scale.[2] I defended it in an address before the Civic Club of Manchester, New Hampshire, February 22, 1937, in an article in the *Commonweal,* April 16, 1937, and in letters to daily papers.

While I should have preferred some other method of correcting a situation which had become intolerable, I believed that nothing else would be available in time to prevent the nullification of important and beneficial economic and social legislation. Ever since the Supreme Court had invalidated (1923) the minimum-wage law of the District of Columbia, I had been exploring the possibility of a fundamental reform which would bring legislative measures for social justice into harmony with the federal Constitution. In Chapter XIV, I have given the text of a suggestion which I made in 1927 for a constitutional amendment for labor legislation. In the same year, however, I wrote that amendment of the Constitution was "a very tedious process and probably could not be carried through within the next twenty-five years."[3] On several occasions, therefore, I advocated the enactment of a law by Congress which would require the vote of at least seven of the nine justices to declare a law unconstitutional. I suggested that Congress might find authority for such a regu-

[2] Cf. article by Professor Edward F. Corwin in the *New York Times Magazine,* February 14, 1937.

[3] *Distributive Justice,* p. 368.

lation in Article 3, Section 2, Paragraph 2, of the Constitution which reads:

In all the other cases before mentioned, the Supreme Court shall have appellate jurisdiction, both as to law and fact, with such exceptions, and under such regulations, as the Congress shall make.[4]

Such a restriction, I held, would give realistic effect to the rule which the Court had professed to follow since the days of Chief Justice Marshall, namely, that "every possible presumption is in favor of the validity of an act of Congress until overcome beyond rational doubt." Commenting on this rule, Justice John H. Clarke observed:

It is difficult for men not steeped in legalistic thinking and forms of expression to understand how five judges can agree that an act of Congress is unconstitutional "beyond rational doubt" and that by clear and indubitable demonstration they have shown it to be so, when four of their associates, equally able and experienced judges, who have heard the same arguments on the same record, declare that to them "upon the basis of reason, experience and authority" the validity of the act "seems absolutely free from doubt."[5]

If this restriction had been in effect, the District of Columbia minimum-wage law, the New York ten-hour law, and certain other pieces of labor legislation would have been sustained, as well as the A.A.A. and the Guffey Coal Act. When the latter two measures had been declared unconstitutional, the seven-of-nine rule was advocated by Senator Norris.[6]

Many of the arguments urged against the President's reorganization proposal were honest and intelligent. Some of the honest arguments, however, did not evince a high degree of specific intelligence. Of these, I shall notice only one. It

---

[4] *Idem*, p. 370.

[5] *American Bar Association Journal*, November, 1923, p. 689.

[6] This proposal was introduced in Congress as early as 1823. For a brief account of it and subsequent instances, see *The American Doctrine of Judicial Supremacy*, Charles Grove Haines. University of California Press, 1932, pp. 469–475.

was expressed in the assertion that the President's proposal involved the destruction or annulment of those provisions of the Constitution which stood in the way of his reform measures. That view was too simple and unrealistic. There are no words in the Constitution which explicitly forbid Congress to pass such laws as the A.A.A. which the Court had declared unconstitutional, or the National Labor Relations Act and the Social Security Act which then seemed to be inevitably doomed to the same judicial treatment. The clauses in the Constitution upon which the Court based its unfavorable decisions are composed of general terms, which cannot be applied to a particular law without construction and interpretation. What do they mean in such a situation? Are they to be interpreted according to their etymological signification; or in conformity with the meaning which they had in the minds of the men who put them into the Constitution; or in accord with the meaning which has been attached to them by judicial usage? All three of these standards have been used by the courts, but none of them to the exclusion of the other two. The second has been rejected in many decisions, including the Dartmouth College case, where the word "contract" was construed to include a college charter.[7] Judicial usage in the construction of any constitutional provision is disclosed in the decisions that are cited by the Court as precedents. Undoubtedly, this standard has had more weight in judicial reasoning than either of the other two.

Writing before the invalidation of N.I.R.A., Edward S. Corwin, professor of jurisprudence at Princeton University, and one of our highest authorities on the Constitution, declared that the Supreme Court had then before it a group of precedents which would justify it in sustaining the principal enactments of the New Deal, and another group of prece-

[7] "Confusion of Property With Privilege: Dartmouth College Case," Jesse F. Orton of the New York Bar. Reprinted from the *Independent*, August 19 and 26, 1909, in *The Relation of Property to Government and Industry*, Samuel F. Orth, pp. 7–42.

dents which would warrant it in holding all these laws un-constitutional.[8] When the first New Deal measures came before it, the Court was evidently guided by the unfavorable precedents. Through his reorganization plan, President Roosevelt hoped to establish the supremacy of the favorable precedents in future decisions by the Court on the constitutionality of his reform laws. He maintained that the Supreme Court could honestly and reasonably uphold as constitutional all the economic legislation that is needed by the country. What the Constitution requires is not amendment but more liberal interpretations. The principal clauses which, under a more liberal interpretation, would uphold the necessary laws are those dealing with due process of law, with interstate commerce, and with the general welfare.

The fairest and most realistic way of looking at the President's plan is to compare it with a proposal for new legislation by Congress. Courts do and must act as legislators. Every judicial decision, particularly one coming from the Supreme Court, which applies a law to a new situation, virtually creates a new law, or a new rule which has all the practical force of a statute. Before the decision in the District of Columbia case, the law required employers to pay minimum wages to women workers; for fourteen years afterward, employers were not so obligated; when the decision was reversed in the Washington State case (1937), the District of Columbia law came to life again and bound such employers. The interpretations which the President sought from a reorganized Court would have been in effect new judicial legislation to take the place of old judicial legislation; for neither the old nor the new judicial interpretations are explicitly or implicitly commanded by the Constitution. They are clarifications or additions or virtual amendments.

[8] *The Twilight of the Supreme Court*. Yale University Press, 1934, p. 182.

The amending function of the Court has been neatly described by William H. Hessler:[9]

> In truth, we have two national constitutions in America. One is the familiar document appended to school-books and dutifully reprinted every year in the World Almanac. The other is the immensely longer, unfamiliar mass of verbiage emitted by the Supreme Court in a century and a half. The one is our national fetish and the source of our political institutions. The other, called constitutional law, is the array of rules and precedents by which we are governed. This heterogeneous accumulation of judicial opinions may be regarded properly as a great bundle of amendments to the original charter.

Through the changes which he desired to make in its personnel the President expected that the Court would select from this second "constitution" a set of "rules and precedents" different from those which had been utilized to nullify the A.A.A. and the Guffey Coal Act. Specifically he sought more liberal interpretation of the due process, interstate commerce, and general welfare clauses. In passing, it should be noted that the precedents underlying the unfavorable decisions of the Court in the cases mentioned above had been accumulated in a period of less than fifty years, mainly since 1895, when the Sugar Trust case was decided,[10] whereas a liberal interpretation could trace its authority back to the year 1824, when Chief Justice Marshall wrote the decision of the Court in *Gibbons v. Ogden*. The end which the President aimed at, namely, more liberal interpretations, was not only laudable but in full harmony with authoritative traditions of the Court.

Although the method or means by which Mr. Roosevelt pursued this end was rejected by the Senate (July 22, 1937) the end itself was attained. As the President said afterwards, "We lost the battle but won the war." While the bill was yet under acrimonious discussion in Congress and through-

[9] *Our Ineffective State*. Henry Holt and Company, New York, 1937, p. 185.
[10] *U. S. v. E. C. Knight Co.*

out the country, the Court by a majority of five to four upheld the National Labor Relations Act, construing the interstate commerce clause in a manner directly contrary to that
adopted by the Court when, by a vote of six to three, it had
invalidated the Guffey Coal Act. This contradiction was
vigorously asserted in the opinion of the four dissenting
justices.[11] Less than a year's time separated these two decisions. And the interval had witnessed no change in the personnel of the Court. What did happen in that short period
was that two of the justices adopted a different interpretation
of the interstate commerce clause in the N.L.R.A. case from
that which they had upheld in the Guffey case. When their
votes were added to those of the three who had dissented in
the latter case, they made a majority in favor of the constitutionality of N.L.R.A. The same shift in the attitude of these
two justices is seen in their votes for the constitutionality of
the Social Security Act, as compared with their votes against
the constitutionality of the A.A.A., while one of them reversed his position on the legal minimum wage.[12] In these
instances the mutually contradictory decisions were separated in time by a little more and a little less than one year,
respectively.

Why did these two justices "change their minds?" The
answer is intimated if not explicitly stated in the following
excerpt from an article by Dean Alfange of the New York
Bar:

It was under the tense agitation stirred by the President that the
Court made its recent path-blazing interpretations of the "due process," "commerce," and "general welfare" clauses. The Court has

[11] Cf. Corwin, *The Constitution and What it Means Today*, sixth edition. Princeton
University Press, 1937, pp. 39-40.

[12] In *West Coast Hotel Co. v. Parrish*, 1937. The decision in this case not only con-
tradicted those rendered in the *Tipaldo* (N. Y.) and *Adkins* (D. C.) cases but explicitly
reversed the latter. Speaking for the Court, Chief Justice Hughes said: "Our conclusion is that the case of *Adkins v. Children's Hospital*, *supra*, should be, and it is, overruled."

undone in a month its handiwork of a quarter of a century; witness the frank reversal of the minimum wage cases, the reversal of the Guffey Coal case by the Wagner Labor Act decisions, and the enlargement of the ambit of "general welfare" in the momentous Social Security cases which, in effect, reversed the Court's position in the Hoosac Mills decision that wrecked the A.A.A. No one can honestly contend that these reversals and new interpretations were unrelated to the President's determination to reorganize the Judiciary.[13]

This is what the President meant when he said, "We lost the battle but won the war." Had he not made his fight for "liberalizing" the Court, the three acts just mentioned would today be unconstitutional, and the enormous benefits conferred by them upon wage earners and the aged would be non-existent, for it must be kept in mind that these decisions were rendered before the President had appointed any new member of the Court. It is true that since his appointment of five members he has six who are favorable to New Deal legislation in addition to the two justices who changed their attitudes in the spring of 1937; however, they would have found great practical obstacles in the way of granting a rehearing on the three acts in question and of reversing the earlier decisions, if these had been unfavorable. These facts and considerations are too often forgotten or ignored by persons who denounce without qualification Mr. Roosevelt's attempt to "pack the Supreme Court." That attempt failed technically but it triumphed practically.

In the early spring of 1937, I prepared a pamphlet on "The Constitution and Catholic Industrial Teaching," in which I contended that a large part of the legislation needed to apply Catholic social teaching would be constitutional under more generous interpretations of the general welfare, due process, and interstate commerce clauses. Before the process of printing was completed, I was able to get into the pamphlet a statement of the fact that the three decisions which we have

[13] *United States Law Review*, September, 1937.

been considering had been rendered, thus substantiating my view of the Constitution. These decisions gave me great personal satisfaction; for they vindicated opinions about the Court that I had been publicly defending ever since the nullification of the District of Columbia minimum-wage statute. In particular, the decision in the Washington State minimum-wage case proved that I had been right on every point in my controversy with the San Francisco lawyer mentioned in Chapter XIV. Taken together, the three decisions furnished a crushing refutation of a virulent editorial in a prominent weekly journal. The writer was particularly severe in his treatment of a paragraph of my Manchester speech in which I contended that more liberal interpretations of the Constitution would not do violence to its wording, but would merely take the place of previous interpretations, and be at least equally faithful to the language of the Constitution. This statement of mine, said the editor, implied that, "the framers of the Constitution were blockheads or fools who simply put down words which have been misunderstood for one hundred and fifty years, and which are only being understood now by the bright men of the day who are supporting President Roosevelt's packing project."

This exquisite sentence betrays profound ignorance and misconception of the problem; yet it expresses substantially the notion entertained by probably the majority of Americans. The problem is not one of understanding or misunderstanding the words of the Constitution. It is a question of interpretation. Some clauses of the document have been variously, and even contradictorily, interpreted by equally honest and competent judges. The main reason for these variations, in construing, for example, the interstate commerce, due process, and general welfare clauses, is neither varying degrees of skill in the understanding of words nor varying equipments of legal knowledge on the part of the judges. It is the differences in their ethical, economic, social, and political principles; also in their education and associations. Such authorities on the Constitution as Pound, Corwin, Cushman, Haines, and a host of others have over and over again called attention to these facts.[14] This explanation will not be questioned by any intelligent person who takes the trouble to read carefully both the majority and the minority opinions in the minimum wage and the other cases discussed in the foregoing paragraphs. If the relevant clauses of the Constitution were as clear as they are naively assumed to be in the sentence quoted above, none of those decisions would have been accompanied by a dissenting opinion. Unfortunately the process of interpreting the Constitution is not quite so simple as an exercise in geometry.

The latest important social reform enacted under the Roosevelt Administration was the "Fair Labor Standards Act of 1938." Its wage provisions require the payment of a minimum rate of 30 cents an hour during the six years following October 24, 1939, and 40 cents an hour thereafter. It covers all employees engaged in interstate commerce or in the production of goods therefor. Unlike the great majority of state minimum-wage laws, this federal statute applies to men as well as to women. While it does not attempt to define or to establish living wages, it avows as one of its aims the elimination as rapidly as practicable of labor conditions detrimental to the maintenance of "the minimum standard of living necessary for health, efficiency, and general well being of workers." This language expresses quite as high a standard as that set forth in any of the state statutes. To be sure, even the maximum rate which will come into effect in 1945, is not a living wage for the head of a family in more than a few parts of the United States. The maximum hours fixed by the Act being 40 per week, the maximum wage for that period

[14] Cf. Haines, *op. cit.*, pp. 500-510.

cannot exceed $16. This is the equivalent of not more than $800 a year. However, as soon as improvement becomes politically feasible the wage rates can be raised by Congress.

When I began to advocate the establishment by law of a family living wage, I did not dare to hope that so near an approach to it would be made by the federal government less than three and one half decades later. Although the Act has not yet been tested for its constitutionality, we have good grounds for hoping and believing that if and when the judicial test is made, the verdict will be favorable. So much seems clearly indicated by the recent decisions and by the present complexion of the Supreme Court.[15] This outcome will become even more probable if the question does not come before the Court until President Roosevelt has had the opportunity to fill one or two vacancies in its membership.

This chapter was begun a few days before and is being finished a few days after, the presidential election of 1940. All intelligent and sympathetic students of social progress and social justice should rejoice in the outcome; for they must realize that the reforms established under the present national administration have been safeguarded and the prospects for more legislation of the same character have been greatly improved by the re-election of Franklin D. Roosevelt. These were the most important issues of the campaign. To be sure, the attitude of our government toward participation in the current European war and aid to Great Britain would have been of greater urgency if the presidential candidates had differed on these matters: since they were in substantial agreement on both points, the social and economic issues became dominant. Nevertheless, millions of fairly intelligent

[15] The decision in the *Darby* case, referred to in Chapter XIV, above, has vindicated this forecast, for it upheld the constitutionality of the minimum-wage provisions of the Fair Labor Standards Act. Again I repeat, "time moves on." It is now thirty-six years since I began to advocate legal minimum wages for both men and women throughout the United States. The last obstacle is now overcome. See *A Living Wage*, pp. 301–318.

voters missed or ignored this fact. They made their choice between the candidates on the basis of racial or religious animosities and prejudices, sentimental or personal antipathies and suspicions, pseudo-political or constitutional issues, and many other irrelevant and trivial considerations.

At stake in the recent campaign was not merely the formal continuation of the reforms noted in previous paragraphs of this chapter but their protection against insidious mutilation. This statement applies particularly to the National Labor Relations Act, which is probably the most just, beneficent, and far-reaching piece of labor legislation ever enacted in the United States. Of even greater importance, however, was the problem of abolishing unemployment and providing genuine economic welfare for all the people. Here the candidates took diametrically opposite positions. Mr. Willkie asserted again and again that he favored a program of practically unlimited production. While he never described the specific methods or measures by which an enormously increased volume of products could be sold, he seemed to expect that they would find purchasers automatically. Let the government "encourage" business and investors, thus inflating them with "confidence," and the problem of providing adequate buying power for the masses would be automatically solved. He refused to admit that his proposal was substantially identical with the method and theory which had dominated business in the 1920s and was directly responsible for the great depression.

Mr. Roosevelt has accepted and acted upon the opposite theory, the mass-purchasing-power theory to which I have already made frequent reference. He believes that governmental policy and legislation should strive to bring about a better distribution of the product, so that those who would like to buy more goods will have more income, while those who are unwilling to buy more will have less to contribute to the country's volume of excess saving; that when the purchasing power of the masses is vastly increased the demand for products, the volume of industrial operations, and the amount of required new investments, will correspondingly expand. President Roosevelt would put the horse before the cart. Mr. Willkie would reverse that order.

The great and difficult problem before the President and his administration is to find and apply specific measures to bring these industrial processes into operation. In my opinion, the required measures are all outlined in the last paragraph of the immediately preceding chapter. A part of the task will be accomplished in carrying out the program for national defense. When that has been completed and when the war is ended, the problem of continuing the work to a successful conclusion will no doubt become more acute and more difficult; but the economic and political policies required to meet the problem will remain essentially the same as they are today and have been for the last two decades.

Chapter XVII

ECCLESIASTICAL PROMOTION: MISCELLANEOUS ITEMS

ON AUGUST 12, 1937, His Eminence, Eugenio Cardinal Pacelli, then Papal Secretary of State, now Sovereign Pontiff, announced that His Holiness, Pope Pius XI, had conferred upon me the honor of Domestic Prelate in the Papal Household, with the title of Right Reverend Monsignor. Naturally, I was gratified with the distinction and grateful to the Holy Father. In this generous act, I saw not only gracious recognition of my services to the Church but authoritative testimony to the soundness of my social teaching. This implication of the honor was stressed by many of the Bishops, monsignors, priests, nuns, and lay persons who sent me messages of congratulation. It was also mentioned by more than one of the newspapers that took note of the occasion. Following is a paragraph of the letter sent me under date of September 9, 1933, by His Excellency, Amleto Giovanni Cicognani, the Apostolic Delegate:

Please accept my cordial congratulations and best wishes. The honor, conferred on you by His Holiness is a well-deserved recognition of your services to the Catholic University and in the fields of Economics and Social Action. May God bless and preserve you *ad multos annos*.

On December 8, I was formally "invested" by Archbishop Curley, Archbishop of Baltimore and chancellor of the University, with the robes appropriate to my new dignity. The ceremony took place in the National Shrine of the Immaculate Conception at the University. An eloquent sermon was preached by Archbishop Murray, of St. Paul, Minnesota. That evening a testimonial dinner was held at the Willard Hotel, with Most Rev. James H. Ryan, then rector of the University, now Bishop of Omaha, presiding, and the Right Rev. David T. O'Dwyer acting as toastmaster. The other speakers were: Rev. Doctors Patrick J. Healy, William J. Kerby, and Francis J. Haas; Miss Frances Perkins, Secretary of Labor; Honorable George W. Norris, United States Senator from Nebraska; Honorable Henrik Shipstead, Senator from Minnesota; and Honorable Edward Keating, editor of *Labor*. The total number of guests was about three hundred.

Dr. Healy emphasized the derivation of my social thought and action from the Gospel of Christ and the traditions of Christianity. Dr. Kerby pointed out the specific and practical character of my teaching, as contradistinguished from theory and speculation, and declared that I had brought ethical and spiritual ideals into economic discussion.[1] Dr. Haas, who had been a pupil of mine, credited me with an "unaffected passion for truth, searching for the major difficulty and meeting it, fairness to adversaries, intolerance only with sham and make-believe, and, throughout, the humility of the scholar." He also said that in advocating the economic wisdom of high wages more than thirty years previously, I had been far in advance of my time. Recalling the social and labor reforms of which I had been an early advocate, Secretary Perkins pointed out that I had lived to see many of the underlying conceptions generally accepted and some of the reform proposals adopted by industry and government. Senator Norris gave to my book, *A Living Wage,* some of the credit for beneficial labor legislation. In the name of the people of Minnesota, Senator Shipstead thanked me for the services I

---

[1] Shortly after the date of this dinner, Dr. Healy and Dr. Kerby received from the Holy Father the same honor that they helped me to celebrate. Both have since died.

had "rendered to the people of America, as a voice crying in the wilderness telling of the problems of the workers." Speaking for the workers of America, Mr. Keating summarized my efforts on their behalf and declared that if he were an instructor of youth, he "would be disposed to burn the ancient textbooks dealing with economics . . . and substitute therefor half a dozen pamphlets which have come from the pen of the gentleman who is our guest of honor tonight."

Responding to these addresses, I acknowledged my great indebtedness to the Catholic University of America both for my social training and for "ample freedom of expression both within and without the academic walls." Referring to the surprise not infrequently expressed by non-Catholics that one so active in the field of economics should occupy the chair of moral theology at the University, I pointed out that this science governs all human conduct, including economic transactions, and that the ethical aspect of economic actions—their rightness or their wrongness—had always been my chief interest in economic problems.

MISCELLANEOUS ITEMS

1. *The Declining Birth Rate.*—At a meeting of the American Association of Social Workers in Toledo in March, 1933, I gave an address on "The Social Menace of Our Declining Birth Rate." After noting the very rapid fall since 1922 and estimating that its continuation would mean a stationary population some time between 1945 and 1960, I summarized its evil effects upon our economic, social, and ethical life. On the question of causality, I said: "All students of the subject are agreed that by far the most effective cause of the falling birth rate in the United States is the deliberate limitation of families through artificial devices of contraception." As causes of this predominant cause, I noted: low family

incomes; life in apartment houses; addiction to ease and pleasure and aversion to hardship; "social" striving and inability to withstand "social" disapproval; and, most fundamental of all, "the decline in old-fashioned religion and morality and the adoption of the ethics of hedonism." As regards remedies, I rejected the fatuous assumption that when deaths come to equal births the factors which brought about that condition would suddenly cease to operate, and the groundless hope that any substantial proportion of birth-control practitioners would be induced to have more children either by the restoration of economic prosperity or by appeals to patriotism.

My own remedy was offered in the following sentences:

The only assurance against a continuous decline of our birth rate and against a declining population in the near future lies in a revival of genuine religion. By genuine religion I mean at least a clear and firm belief in God, acceptance of the moral law as the commandment of God, and belief that birth control practices are not only bad for society but evil in themselves. The Catholic position, which formerly was also the Protestant position, is that the morality of some acts can be determined without reference to their economic or social consequences. It declares the practices which produce certain effects to be wrong in themselves and therefore forbidden. This intuitive and metaphysical judgment is confirmed by the consequences. The voice of nature and reason concerning the intrinsic wrong is in harmony with the voice of nature speaking through experience. In other words, an adequate perception of the moral law enables one to pronounce birth control wrong without waiting for its disastrous effects upon individuals and society.

The propositions in the foregoing quotation I have set forth and expanded during the last thirty-five years in many articles and addresses, including several statements before committees of the United States Senate and the House of Representatives. For example, at a session of a joint subcommittee of the Judiciary Committees of the Senate and

House, held on April 8, 1924, I pointed out that the Catholic Church held artificial birth control to be "immoral—everlastingly, essentially, fundamentally immoral . . . more so than even adultery, because adultery does not commit an outrage upon nature nor pervert nature's functions."

Only recently have American students of the social sciences become notably concerned about our declining birth rate and its effects and implications. In his book, *Mankind at the Crossroads,* published in 1923, Professor E. M. East declared that America was moving toward a condition of overpopulation. In 1927, Professor E. A. Ross repeated the warning in his volume *Standing Room Only?* Probably neither of these writers would so express himself today. At the "Conference on Tomorrow's Children," held at Harvard Summer School, August, 1940, Dr. Clyde V. Kiser, of the Milbank Memorial Fund pointed out that the number of persons under twenty in the United States is two million less than ten years ago; and that the decline in the birth rate is now more rapid in the rural areas than in the cities. Another speaker, Professor Carl C. Zimmerman, declared that the reduced family size is becoming serious in native-born and self-supporting working-class groups. Dr. Warren S. Thompson, one of the most competent American students of population, estimates that the number of elementary school pupils (between six and fourteen years of age) was 1,500,000 smaller in 1940 than in 1930 and that by 1950 the decline will amount to 2,700,000.[2] In the public schools of New York City the yearly enrollment has dropped steadily since 1935, particularly in the elementary grades. In Pittsburgh, four hundred and forty-six teachers have lost their positions since 1930 on account of the reduced number of pupils. These facts and trends seem to be pretty general throughout, at least, our northern and western areas.

[2] *Annals of the American Academy of Political and Social Science*, November, 1940, p. 22.

A similar, if not so pronounced tendency is evident in the Catholic parochial schools. The grade schools show a decrease of about 190,000 pupils between 1930 and 1940. Only eleven dioceses present increases for the school year, 1939–1940.[3] While the birth rate among Catholics seems to be somewhat higher than that of non-Catholics, the degree of excess does not justify an attitude of complacency.

Some fifteen years ago, I concluded an article against birth control with the following paragraph:

More than seventeen centuries ago the great Christian writer, Tertullian, addressed the superior classes of his day, the rulers of the Roman Empire, in these words of triumph: "We are but of yesterday, yet we fill your cities, islands, forts, towns, councils, camps, tribes, decuries, the palace, the senate, the forum; we have left you only the temples." Paraphrasing the statement, those who reject birth control might thus challenge the superior classes of today: "We, too, are of yesterday, but tomorrow we shall be the majority. We shall occupy and dominate every sphere of activity; the farm, the factory, the countinghouse, the schools, the professions, the press, the legislature. We shall dominate because we shall have the numbers and the intelligence, and above all, the moral strength to struggle, to endure and to persevere. To you we shall leave the gods and goddesses which you have made to your own image and likeness, the divinities of ease and enjoyment and mediocrity. We shall leave to you the comforts of decadence and the sentence of extinction."[4]

Today, I find no sufficient reason for hoping that this optimistic forecast will be verified within a period of time that is of interest or concern to our generation.

2. *At the University of Wisconsin.*—In 1934, I carried on two courses of lectures at the summer session of the University of Wisconsin. So far as I know, I am one of the very few Catholic priests who have been invited to fill a teaching engagement at that institution. At the suggestion of Mr.

---

[3] Rev. Edgar Schmiedeler, O. S. B., in *The Sacred Bond*. P. J. Kenedy & Sons, New York, 1940, p. 39.
[4] *Questions of the Day*, p. 273.

Ordway Tead, Editor of Economic Books of Harper & Brothers, I revised for publication the lectures given in one of these courses. They were published by that firm in the spring of 1935, under the title, *A Better Economic Order*. The main topics discussed were: the 1929 depression, and its causes; methods of recovery, and the national recovery legislation of 1933 and 1934; methods, acceptable and unacceptable, of economic reconstruction. More comprehensively than any other publication this little volume sets forth my views on unemployment, depressions, and the reconstruction of economic society. On the whole, the reviewers treated it adequately and favorably. The following paragraph concludes a fairly long notice in the *New York Herald Tribune,* written by Professor H. A. Overstreet:

At the present moment, most of our economic and social thinking is of the either-or type. The battle is on between the individualists and the collectivists. While that battle continues, a discriminating and integrating mind like that of Dr. Ryan will fare badly. But one may venture the guess that the day is rapidly approaching when we shall change from the either-or stage and begin to make a more intelligent estimate of both the good and the bad in the present system. If that day is not too long delayed, Dr. Ryan may be accepted as one of its prophets.

Although the summer of 1934 was exceedingly hot, and I was kept pretty busy preparing two sets of lectures and delivering additional addresses outside the classroom, I keenly enjoyed those six weeks in Madison. My relations with the students who enrolled for my courses and with those members of the faculty whom I met, were pleasant and stimulating. One of the most precious mementos of that academic engagement is the following letter written me by Dr. S. H. Goodnight, director of the summer session:

Before you take your departure I want to express to you my very deep appreciation of your splendid service to the Summer Session of the University of Wisconsin this year. The large registration in your courses, the good attendance at the public lectures which you have given, and the enthusiasm of all your students are a testimonial to the quality of your academic work. Further than that, you have given unsparingly of your time in lecturing in the community outside the University. Your colleagues are all enthusiastic about their association with you this summer, and I am writing to acknowledge a sense of indebtedness to you, which I am sure we all feel. We are grateful to you for having come, for your unstinting service while here, and for the pleasure of our personal association with you. Our best wishes go with you as you leave us.

3. *Two Benedictions.*—At the request of the Honorable Frances Perkins, Secretary of Labor, I delivered the following invocation, February 25, 1935, at the dedication of the new Department of Labor Building:

Almighty God, Creator of heaven and earth, Creator of men, bless, we beseech Thee, this glorious edifice. We recall today the words of the Psalmist: "The heaven of heavens is the Lord's, but the earth He hath given to the children of men." We know that Thou hast made the earth for *all* Thy children. But we may not forget the primordial sentence: "In the sweat of thy face shalt thou eat thy bread, till thou return to the earth out of which thou wast taken." We recall, too, the injunctions of Thy great Apostle: "If a man will not work neither shall he eat;" and, "every man shall receive his own reward according to his own labor."

We trust, O Lord, that we are not presumptuous when we invoke these great pronouncements of Holy Writ in support of the following principles: our land and our resources are destined for *all* our people; private owners are merely stewards of this divine inheritance; faithful stewardship would permit and enable every willing laborer to live as a human person, as a creature made in the image and likeness of God and redeemed by the blood of Christ; and the public authorities are under solemn obligation to enforce these righteous principles.

We believe, O Lord, that all these principles are implicit in the spirit and purposes of the Department of Labor. We beg Thee, O Lord, to inspire and guide all Thy public servants who are charged with the responsibilities of this Department. Infuse them with light and courage to apply and effectuate these great truths, even more faithfully in the future than in the past. Graciously extend Thy all-powerful help to the Honorable Secretary and all her co-workers, to our beloved Chief Magistrate and to the Congress. May they all, working loyally to-gether, cause Thy justice and Thy charity to dominate and permeate all the relations of industry and labor. Through Christ, Our Lord. Amen.

At the close of the exercises accompanying the inaugura-tion of President Roosevelt, January 20, 1937, I pronounced the Benediction. So far as I can ascertain, this was the first time that a priest had participated in the ceremonies of a presidential inauguration. Moreover, it was the first occasion of this nature which included a Benediction as well as an Invocation. The latter is always the first act in the exercises and it is usually performed by the chaplain of the Senate. Some of my critics saw in the unusual introduc-tion of a Benediction the purpose of the President to recog-nize my radio speech on his behalf.[5] Perhaps they were right. If so, I have no reason to be ashamed nor is the honor thereby diminished. At any rate, here is the text of the Benediction:

Almighty God, Ruler of nations, we beseech Thee to bless the people of the United States. Keep them at peace among themselves and in con-cord with all other peoples. Cause justice and charity to flourish among them, that they may all be enabled to live as persons created in Thine own image and likeness.

Do Thou bless abundantly our Chief Magistrate. Inspire his leader-ship. Grant him, O God of infinite wisdom and power, the light and the strength to carry through the great work that he has so well begun, and to pursue untiringly his magnificent vision of social peace and social justice. Through Christ, our Lord. Amen.

4. *Mr. Justice Brandeis.*—On November 14, 1938, I de-livered one of the two addresses at the unveiling of a portrait of Justice Brandeis in the law school of Harvard University. The other speaker was C. C. Burlingham, a prominent at-

[5] See my book *Seven Troubled Years*, pp. 295–301; also the daily papers of October 9, 1936.

torney of New York City. He spoke for the legal profession, while I had been asked to represent the "laity" (in the usage of the lawyers). My address was entitled, "Louis D. Brandeis: Lover of Social Justice." His judicial opinions, both for the Court and in dissent, I placed first among his services to the people, because in the exercise of the jurist's legislative function they vindicated the principles of social justice. I had in mind particularly his long and consistent opposition to those strained interpretations of the Constitution which inflicted injury upon the weak and the lowly. (For example, in the minimum wage and other cases discussed in Chapters VII and XIV.) I concluded my address with this statement: "Justice Brandeis is one of the two or three genuinely great Americans of our time."

I first met Louis D. Brandeis just after he had finished a speech on "Monopoly," at Minneapolis, in 1912. As I left the hall, I said to a friend: "That speech is like a breath of fresh air blowing through the foggy and stifling talk about 'good' and 'bad' trusts." The next time that I had occasion to consider Brandeis was when the Judiciary Committee of the Senate was discussing his nomination to the position of associate justice of the Supreme Court. The hearings of the Committee, some of which I attended, lasted from the latter part of January, 1916, until the end of the following May. The four months' delay in confirming him was due to powerful, bitter, even vicious, opposition. Members of the bar, politicians, and representatives of a variety of other groups, protested to the Committee that Mr. Brandeis was unfitted for membership on the Supreme Bench. He was denounced as "radical," "a theorist," "a self-advertiser," a man with "socialistic tendencies" who lacked the "judicial temperament." The climax of reckless accusation was reached in the minority report of the Committee, signed by five senators, three of whom were prominent and distinguished. Among other notes of condemnation, these five characterized Mr. Brandeis as: "One whose reputation for honesty and integrity amongst his associates has proved to be bad, which reputation has been justified by his own conduct."

When Justice Brandeis resigned from the Court, more than twenty-two years later, the two signers of the minority report who were still living (only one survives today) must have felt thoroughly ashamed of that performance. Seldom in our history has a retiring justice received such general acclaim and praise for his services on the Supreme Bench. The testimony of the *Christian Century,* February 22, 1939, was entirely warranted: "Today, Justice Brandeis is regarded by Americans of all political and social stripes as the great exemplar of what a judge should be."

Why, then, to quote the words of the same journal, were "the furies loosed," when President Wilson nominated him to the Court, less than a quarter of a century before? Undoubtedly part of the answer, a relatively small part, is "professional jealousy" of his exceptional attainments and achievements; but the major part of the explanation is to be found in the fact that, despite his conspicuous legal triumphs and the large emoluments which he derived therefrom, Mr. Brandeis had for many years fought the battles of the common man with a large measure of success, and shown himself a consistent and resourceful foe of plutocracy. In other words, he had been an effective champion of social justice. Happily, he has lived long enough to let his deeds refute and discredit his traducers and establish his integrity upon a basis that will permanently endure.

Justice Brandeis has one of the keenest intellects that I have ever known. No man of my acquaintance possesses a finer sense of honor, honesty, and decency. In his conception of life values, his tastes, and his manner of living, he approaches the standards of an ascetic. His wide human sympathies, his faith in the capacities of ordinary men and women, are deep, and his eagerness to advise and assist those who seek his counsel is universally recognized. From personal association, as well as from his writings and his judicial opinions, I have derived not only stimulating knowledge but genuine inspiration.

5. *Mr. Justice Black.*—In September, 1937, I was interviewed by the "Indiana Catholic" on the then recent appointment of Senator Hugo L. Black to the United States Supreme Court. Concerning his former membership in the Ku Klux Klan, I said that it ought to be forgotten and forgiven if he would now repudiate the Klan and its principles. This he did soon afterward. Moreover, I pointed to some extenuating circumstances: Justice Black had joined the Klan early in his political career, apparently for about the same reasons that have moved other politicians to become affiliated with the Elks or the Knights of Columbus; he had never participated in the un-American performances of the Klan nor, indeed, been an active member in any other respect; his subsequent career in the Senate had shown him to be a genuine liberal, a champion of social justice and a vigilant defender of the Negroes. I also called attention to the fact that Louis D. Brandeis had been violently assailed and vilified when his name was under consideration by the Senate for confirmation as a Supreme Court justice in 1916, and expressed the opinion that the main, even though undisclosed, motive behind the opposition was the same in both cases, namely, dislike of Brandeis' and Black's championship of the economically weak against the economically strong.

This interview provoked some strong criticism from a few Catholic papers. As I observed afterward, the critics seemed to take the position that joining the Klan was an unforgivable sin which could not be expiated by any amount of subsequent good deeds.

My confidence that Justice Black's youthful indiscretion in joining the Klan would not prejudice his course of action on the Supreme Bench, has already been abundantly confirmed. Writing in the *New Republic,* June 8, 1938, on "Mr. Justice Black's First Year," Dr. Walton Hamilton showed that the new Justice had in that short period made for himself a distinguished and commendable record, particularly in three notable dissenting opinions. The doctrine of one of the dissents was substantially adopted by the Court, itself, in a decision rendered a few weeks later.

On February 12, 1940, the Supreme Court unanimously reversed a decision by the highest court of Florida which had upheld the conviction of and sentence of death passed upon four impoverished Negroes. The reversal was based upon the fact that the condemned men had been coerced into confessing at the trial and therefore that they had been deprived of that "due process of law," which is guaranteed by the Fourteenth Amendment to the Constitution. The opinion of the Court was written by Mr. Justice Black. A prominent metropolitan newspaper, which had, less than three years earlier, severely criticized Black's appointment, now declared that the opinion in this case was "far and away the most direct, sweeping and brilliantly written application of the Fourteenth Amendment to human rights that has come from our highest Court." Yet it was composed by a man who, according to the "logic" of his erstwhile critics, was incapable of such liberality. April, 1940, I published an article in the *Catholic World,* describing this case and decision, and claiming vindication of my defense of Justice Black in 1937.

6. *Anti-Semitism.*—In the *Commonweal,* December 30, 1938, I published an article entitled "Anti-Semitism in the Air;" it was reprinted in *Current History,* February, 1939, under the heading, "Catholics and Anti-Semitism." Following is the second last paragraph:

It would seem that the enormous cruelties inflicted upon the Jewish people of Germany, no matter what offenses might have been committed by a small minority of Jewish individuals, ought to move every Christian heart to pity, ought to prevent any Christian from doing and saying anything which would mock their sufferings, outrages and sensibilities, and make their lot harder to bear. This involves Jews everywhere, even those Jews who are our fellow citizens in the United States. In this situation all Catholics and all Christians might well follow the example of the Holy Father. More than once he has denounced Hitler's persecution of the Jews and condemned anti-Semitism.

Under the auspices of the "American Committee to Combat Fascism and Communism," I delivered two radio addresses in March, 1939. The first was entitled, "Americanism;" the second discussed "Communism and Democracy." They have been combined by the Paulist Press of New York, in a pamphlet, bearing the title, "American Democracy vs. Racism, Communism."

In the first speech, I showed the incompatibility not only of American democracy but of Catholic principles with the doctrines of totalitarianism as professed by Fascist Italy, Communist Russia, and Nazi Germany, and particularly with the Nazi doctrines and practices of racism and anti-Semitism. The second address opened with the question: "Can a Believer in Democracy be a Communist?" After presenting the essentials of both democracy and Communism, I answered with an unqualified negative. I concluded the address with the following paragraph on the practical implications of the Communist movement in the United States:

The universal and unchanging fact is that the Communists are a grave liability to any organization in which they exercise any degree of influence. Should they ever obtain political control in the United States, they would prove as deceitful, as dictatorial and as cruel as their "comrades" in Russia. For they have the same philosophy, the same selfishness, the same training, the same tactics, and the same purposes. They are an unlovely and impossible sect. In fact, they are a total loss.

CHAPTER XVIII

SEVENTIETH BIRTHDAY ANNIVERSARY: RETIREMENT FROM THE UNIVERSITY: EPILOGUE

IN EARLY April, 1939, I informed Father McGowan, assistant director of the Department of Social Action of the National Catholic Welfare Conference, that my seventieth year of life would be completed May 25, and I suggested that a few of us might enjoy a little dinner together by way of celebration. Father McGowan promptly accepted the suggestion and conveyed it to several other friends. Presently they had expanded the project beyond all resemblance to the restricted proportions which it had held in my thoughts. A committee of twenty-five, with Rev. Dr. Maurice S. Sheehy as chairman, was formed to arrange an elaborate public celebration. So comprehensively did the committee carry out the enlarged plan that on the evening of my birthday anniversary more than six hundred guests sat down to dinner at the Willard Hotel.

It was one of the most distinguished banquets ever held in Washington. At the speakers' table were seated: Justices Black, Douglas, and Frankfurter, of the Supreme Court; Bishop Ireton, of Richmond, Monsignors Corrigan, rector of the Catholic University, and Ready, general secretary of the National Catholic Welfare Conference; Secretaries Perkins and Morgenthau of President Roosevelt's Cabinet; Rev. Arthur O'Leary, S. J., president of Georgetown University; Senator James M. Mead, of New York; and my two brothers from Minnesota, the Rev. Lawrence F.

and Maurice. The assemblage included a large number of labor union officials; some thirty-five or forty members of the Senate and House of Representatives; many other public officials; editors, journalists, physicians, lawyers, university and college professors, clergymen, businessmen, students, and representatives of other callings and occupations. The one hundred sponsors of the dinner were equally varied and representative, including one Associate Justice of the Supreme Court, other judges and, to my great satisfaction, several well-known industrialists and bankers: Henry Ford, M. B. Folsom, Robert B. Fleming, O. H. P. Johnson, John J. Pelley, Bernard J. Rothwell, Gerard Swope, and Richard Tobin.

Monsignor Ready, who acted as toastmaster, pointed out that "the Church and Churchmen have very often been labeled reactionary and unprogressive," whereas what they had been opposing was "the doctrine of *laissez-faire* taught in the system of nineteenth century liberalism." Justice Frankfurter declared that my distinction was to have applied "dogmas avowedly conservative to the solution of problems affecting the welfare of the masses in ways that have gained for him general recognition as a foremost liberal." He concluded his remarks with the following paragraph:

We confidently wish that Monsignor Ryan will carry on, unmindful of the clock, for many years, and that on the troubled and uncharted seas which the world now sails, his wisdom may point out stars for the course and his kindness may bring comfort to the weary mariners. And may the tribute of this dinner be remembered by him as testimony of our gratitude and as proof of a life greatly lived.

Here is the concluding paragraph of the address given by Senator Mead:

Dr. Ryan is a pioneer today in the field of liberalism just as he was a pioneer in liberalism thirty or more years ago. But it is not to his books nor to his professorships at the highest institutions of learning, great and scholarly as they are, but to his innate progressiveness and his ceaseless struggle for the betterment of mankind that I pay tribute. He may yield to none in the mastery of clear thinking, conscientious service, indomitable will, and long-ranged vision. He inspires the nation's leaders of liberal thought; he advances the well-being of the common man; with exemplary dignity and Christlike humility, he has given his intellectual talents and his physical strength to the service of his Church and his country.

Secretary Perkins reviewed my early advocacy of social reforms that have since been realized and then added:

We have still not caught up with Father Ryan's thinking, thirty-three years later, but we are coming closer to it. Only lately has business begun to realize that economic policies are subject to ethics, and that a moral obligation to pay a good wage falls on the employer of labor as a consequence of his position of power over the fruits of the earth. Only recently has the world recognized the wage earner's status of human dignity on the statute books and in practice. . . .

To the field of labor problems, Father Ryan's contribution and influence have been broad and deep and practical. There is no greater tribute I can give his persistent influence on American thought and action than to quote his own words. "Never before in our history," he says, "have Government policies been so deliberately and consciously based on the conception of moral right and social justice."

The Right Rev. Joseph M. Corrigan, rector of the Catholic University of America, ended his short address thus:

When it has come to anyone, as it has come to Monsignor Ryan, to find he has sown blessed seed in the fertile soil of the hearts of a people, then we can understand why the glory of his years of service must be to him tonight a matter both of proper pride and of happy consolation. We can rejoice with him that through it all he has kept the simple heart of a priest; that he has never been swayed out of the balance required to keep him constantly in the footsteps of his Master, conscious that, like his Master, his steps were taking him among the beloved of the Master—the poor.

. . . It would be difficult indeed to vision the Catholic University in the past quarter of a century without the pioneering work and untiring ability of Father John Ryan. That his own peace and happiness be the best measure of his success in the many years we hope are before him, is the wish of his colleagues at the Catholic University of America.

Responding to these tributes, I recounted briefly the origins of my interest in social questions; the most important factors in my early social education, particularly the encyclical "On the Condition of Labor," issued by Pope Leo XIII in 1891; the comparative neglect of that great message for many years, and the meager amount of labor legislation during that period; the greatly increased Catholic appreciation of the encyclical since the publication of *Quadragesimo Anno* in 1931; and the "immense progress" made in social and labor legislation since 1932. I concluded the first part of my remarks with the following sentences:

Yes, there has been progress toward social justice in my lifetime. Those of us who have been active in the movement know that the struggle has been well worthwhile. It has been interesting, zestful, stimulating, soothing to the conscience, and sufficiently fruitful to assure us that our labors and efforts have not been in vain.

Turning to the future, I said that before us were two economic problems "more perplexing than any of those that have been solved." The first was that of unemployment; the second, "the reconstruction of the social order, the reorganization of our industrial system." Concerning the first, I offered the program which I have defended more than once in this volume, namely, "a better distribution of purchasing power." As to the second, I declared that, while the private ownership and private profit must be continued, "historical capitalism cannot and ought not to survive." We must strive for, I continued, "the adoption and adaptation of the Guild System as outlined by Pope Pius XI in his recommendation concerning occupational groups. This program offers the only escape from the twin extremes of Fascism and Communism." My final paragraph was this:

The shock of realizing that I am now definitely among those who have been overtaken by old age, is considerably cushioned by your touching manifestations of esteem and affection. "My way of life" may be, like that of Macbeth, "fallen into the sere, the yellow leaf," but, unlike Macbeth, I have "that which should accompany old age, as, honor, love, obedience, troops of friends."

Worthy of inclusion here are a few of the messages of congratulation read at the banquet:

The White House
Washington, May 10, 1939

Rt. Rev. Msgr. John A. Ryan, D.D.,
    The Catholic University of America
        Washington, D. C.

My dear Monsignor Ryan:

Because of your perennially youthful spirit and your zest for service in behalf of your fellow men—particularly the underprivileged—it is difficult to realize that you have attained the scriptural age of three score and ten.

But your birthday gives your friends a welcome opportunity to break through the reserve which your modesty has built up and to tell you of their appreciation of the good works which you have wrought through all the years of your active career. With voice and pen, you have pleaded the cause of social justice and the right of the individual to happiness through economic security, a living wage, and an opportunity to share in the things that enrich and ennoble human life.

Happily, at seventy you are unwearied in your labors. In extending congratulations, may I express the hope that for long years to come you may continue to labor for those causes of which you have been such an earnest advocate and unselfish champion.

Very sincerely yours,

Franklin D. Roosevelt

Detroit, Michigan
May 25, 1939

Rt. Rev. Msgr. John A. Ryan, D. D.,
  Catholic University
    Washington, D. C.

With keen regret that I am unable to attend your seventieth anniversary dinner tonight, I send, in the name of the Administrative Board
of Bishops, heartiest felicitations and the fervent prayer for continued
devoted service in the Church and nation.

Edward Mooney
Archbishop of Detroit
Chairman, Administrative Board of Bishops
National Catholic Welfare Conference

St. Paul, Minnesota
May 25, 1939

Rt. Rev. Msgr. John A. Ryan, D.D.,
  Catholic University
    Washington, D. C.

Heartiest felicitations on your distinguished observance of your
seventieth birthday, with best wishes for health and happiness. Con-
secration of St. Mary's Church keeps me here.

John G. Murray[1]

Apostolic Delegation, United States of America
Washington, D. C., May 22, 1939

Rt. Rev. Msgr. John A. Ryan, S.T.D.,
  Catholic University of America
    Brookland, Washington, D. C.

Right Reverend and Dear Monsignor:
  With pleasure have I learned of the testimonial dinner that is being
offered in your honor on the occasion of your seventieth birthday, and
it is my desire to extend heartfelt felicitations and sincere wishes to you
who have labored so many years for the betterment of general social
conditions.

[1] My ecclesiastical superior, the Archbishop of St. Paul.

With this anniversary you also mark twenty-five years of teaching in The Catholic University of America, whence you have brought thousands to a realization and better understanding of the problems that confront society. Permit me, therefore, my dear Monsignor, to congratulate you most sincerely, and to voice my ardent wishes that the Lord may grant you many more years in His service.

With sentiments of deep esteem, and most cordial regards, I beg to remain

Sincerely yours in Christ,

A. G. Cicognani
Archbishop of Laodicea, Apostolic Delegate

Finally, I include some extracts from the "Testimonial" which was presented to me at the dinner and printed on all the menu cards:

More than thirty years ago you began your pioneering labors. Through the tangled forests of economic greed and selfishness you slashed the trail for men to follow, hewing with the axe of the moral law.

At the turn of the century, following in the footsteps of Leo XIII, you formulated for America the doctrine that the toiler has a right in justice to an income at least sufficient to support himself and his family in comfort. You went further than mere assertion. You flung out the challenge that the law may not be indifferent but must enforce this right. . . .

You have done all this, but you do even more.

When the threat looms that man's liberties will be crushed by despotic states you write, speak and live for human freedom.

When the right of labor unions to exist and the duty of government to protect them is at stake you speak, write and work—as you have worked for more than two decades—for that right.

When the economic and governmental organization of America for the common good is proposed you advise, not vaguely, but practically how to proceed.

When world cooperation for world justice and world peace is the issue you stand at the crossroad of decision, showing the way to the peace promised to men of good will.

When the supremacy of religion is in question you hold high the beacon of your Faith.

When, in God's time, social and economic life shall rest on generous thought for others you, the soul of the charity which Christ taught from the Cross, shall have your name set in letters of gold upon the cornerstone of that new social order.

So truly has justice been your watchword that, as we think of you, there comes to our minds the song of the Psalmist: "Thou has loved justice and hated iniquity." Knowing you, we understand the better the jubilant triumph of his conclusion: "Therefore God, thy God, hath anointed thee with the oil of gladness above thy fellows."

May the God Whom you have served so well grant you many more years of the same fruitful service you have always given Him in the cause of justice, freedom and brotherhood.

In conformity with the rule for compulsory retirement of instructors at seventy, I was obliged to discontinue my connection with the University a few days after the birthday celebration. Likewise I was required to give up my residence on the campus, in Caldwell Hall. Both changes caused me keen regret. In my twenty-four years of teaching, I had always enjoyed the most pleasant relations with my students and my colleagues. Of those who were on the faculty of theology in 1915, only two remained in June, 1939. Those who have departed I hold in affectionate memory; those who remain are still my very good friends.

One of my students, the Rt. Rev. Monsignor F. J. Haas, is now dean of the School of Social Science of the University; he is one of the most competent authorities on labor conditions in the United States and one of the most valued advisers to government officials in that field. Another former student, Rev. Dr. John F. Cronin, has been for several years professor of economics at St. Mary's Seminary, Baltimore, and has done much effective work as author and lecturer. A third is Rev. Raymond A. McGowan, who has been for more than twenty years my assistant in directing the activities of the Department of Social Action of the National Catholic Welfare Conference. Without his intelligent and unceasing activity, the achievements of the department would have been considerably less in quantity and poorer in quality.

Since the latter part of September, 1939, I have resided at the National Catholic School of Social Service. My living quarters are ample and attractive and my fellow residents, Rev. Lucian Lauerman, the director of the School, and Rev. R. A. McGowan, are congenial and companionable. I am still on the faculty of the School, teaching social ethics, the assignment which I accepted when the institution opened, in September, 1921. Likewise, I am still on the faculty of Trinity College. Beginning in 1915, I conducted a course in economics there for two years; since that period, my subject has been political science. And I am still the director of the Department of Social Action of the National Catholic Welfare Conference.

Epilogue

The most encouraging recent publications dealing with Catholic social doctrine and social action are: "The Twentieth Anniversary Edition of the Bishops' Program of Social Reconstruction" (April, 1939); the Papal encyclicals, *Summi Pontificatus* (October, 1939) and *Sertum Laetitiae* (Nov. 1, 1939); and the statement of the Archbishops and Bishops of the Administrative Board of the National Catholic Welfare Conference, entitled, "The Church and Social Order" (February, 1940). The first of these publications, carrying an Introduction by Archbishop Mooney, the chairman of the Administrative Board of the N.C.W.C., was clear testimony to the fact that a pronouncement which twenty years before had been deplored by reactionaries as "radical" was still orthodox in the eyes of the American Hierarchy. The two encyclicals presented abundant evidence that the present Holy Father is as keenly interested in social justice as were his predecessors, Pius XI and Leo XIII. The fourth publication mentioned above shows a forthright recognition of present economic evils and advocates a comprehensive group of specific remedies and reforms.[2]

In the last ten years, the number of men who have become intelligently active in advocating Catholic social doctrine and exemplifying Catholic social action has undergone a considerable increase. Twenty or twenty-five years ago, I could name only a few participants in the work. Frederick P. Kenkel, of the Catholic Central Verein, Dr. James E. Hagerty, of Ohio State University, Dr. David A. McCabe, of Princeton, Rev. J. Elliot Ross and Rev. Peter Dietz, all of whom are living, deserve special mention; as also do Monsignor Kerby, Rev. Frederic Siedenburg, S. J., Rev. Joseph Reiner, S. J., and Rev. John W. Maguire, C. S. V., who have passed away. Among the larger and later group the most notable are: Bishops Lucey and O'Hara (a former student of mine at the St. Paul Seminary), Monsignor Haas and Rev. Wilfrid Parsons, S. J., of the Catholic University, Revs. R. A. McGowan and John M. Hayes, of the Department of Social Action of the National Catholic Welfare Conference, Revs. John F.

[2] Forty years ago, a distinguished Catholic Englishman, Wilfrid Ward, editor of the *Dublin Review* wrote a paper on "The Conservative Genius of the Catholic Church." Two or three extracts from it may not be inappropriate here:

"True conservatism involves constructive activity as well as resistance to destructive activity. Periodical reform and reconstruction belong to its very essence. . . .

". . . There are two classes of enemies to the true conservatism which would preserve for present use an ancient building—those who would pull it down, and those who would leave it untouched, without repairs, without the conditions which render it habitable in the present, superstitiously fearing that to alter it *in any respect* is to violate what is venerable and sacred. . . .

". . . Had the Church been content with a false conservatism—the conservatism of mere resistance to innovation—and then remained passive, having escaped the dangers of aggression, she would have succumbed to the danger of decay. She alternated instead, not between resistance and passivity, but between resistance and the most active process of adaptation and assimilation. . . .

"The difference between the two processes is, as Cardinal Newman has pointed out, that the first process, of resistance, is the work of authority, of Rome itself; the second, of assimilation, is the work of individuals, authority only tolerating and not necessarily helping it, until it is so far tested that authority can more or less ratify what individuals have initiated."

Cronin, of St. Mary's Seminary, William A. Bolger, C. S. C., of Notre Dame, and John P. Monaghan, of New York. Many other names are not yet so well known but they will receive increasing recognition as the years go on.

Has it all been worthwhile? Decidedly, yes. In Chapter III I described the motives and the hopes which had influenced me in the beginning. Now I can testify that those hopes have been as nearly fulfilled as anyone could have expected in this uncertain world. I have seen the misconceptions of the Catholic position on social reforms almost completely dissipated and the social doctrine of the Church come to be received with universal respect, if not with complete approval. I have seen a great and fundamental advance in the recognition by Catholics, including priests and Bishops, of the relation between Catholic principles and economic life. I have seen the feeling of the laboring class about the Catholic Church become much more understanding and friendly. I have seen a great improvement in the attitude of the average legislator toward the needs of the masses.

As I recall some of the earnest and sincere non-Catholic men and women with whom I was associated in the campaign for social justice, I am still uncertain about their effective motivation. Those who professed some form of Christianity or of orthodox Judaism could no doubt appeal to motives of religion. They could say: "I am helping my brothers because they are made in the image and likeness of God and because such is the command of God." Even those without religious faith could, if they were able to grasp metaphysical conceptions, and if they believed in a spiritual and indestructible soul, hold that in making sacrifices for their fellow men they were acknowledging the highest values in existence; that they were observing a rational proportion in their comparative valuations; that they were subordinating the lower to the higher things of life, that they

were loving the best that it is possible to love. But those who
did not believe that man possesses a soul essentially higher
than the animating principle of the brute; those who held
that man is merely a more highly organized animal, not a
being of intrinsic worth and sacredness: how could they
logically and rationally consider human welfare or social
reform worth fighting for?

Probably they were moved by one or both of two factors:
natural human sympathy and the traditional Christian
principle concerning the worth of the human being; this
principle had permeated their education and environment,
even though it was not accepted by them as a reasoned
postulate. Such persons could persevere as reformers, despite
disappointments, failures, and lack of appreciation by their
fellows; but they were necessarily the few, the elite of the
non-believers.

The social philosophy of the Christian believer is definite,
fundamental, and comprehensive: man is not only possessed
of a spiritual and immortal soul; he is not only made in the
image and likeness of God; he has been called to a supernatural status which makes him an adopted child of God;
hence his worth is measured not only by his natural endow-
ments but by his supernatural and filial relation to God. Thus
considered, man is worthy of an infinitely higher love than
when considered merely as a rational animal. The material,
intellectual, and other goods which the Christian reformer
strives to bring within the reach of the masses, are necessary
to enable them to develop personality and pursue perfection
as adopted children of God. Thus, the object and justification of social reform are lifted to the highest conceivable
plane, and they provide the loftiest motives for the practice
of social charity and social justice.

Moreover, and this is of great practical importance, the
conviction that earthly life is only a temporary interlude

between birth and eternity, enables the Christian believer to contemplate in its proper perspective the appalling amount of poverty and suffering which are the lot of countless fellow beings. It is good, noble, and Christlike to battle for social conditions which will permit an ever-increasing host of persons to live in a manner worthy of adopted children of God. But the Christian believer realizes all the time that the masses who fail to obtain these goods need not fail utterly; they can all aspire to a blessed existence in their everlasting home, where "God shall wipe away all tears from their eyes." Many times, since the awful slaughter and cruel mal-treatment of innocent multitudes began in the fall of 1939, this reflection has given me comfort and consolation. The same reflection and the same faith frequently sustained me during my writing and working for the betterment of social conditions here in America. The number of human beings into whose lives reformers can bring more sunshine is relatively small; the number that they cannot reach is legion; but these can still cherish the supreme hope of life everlasting. Nevertheless, God wishes all His children to have the means to live worthy human lives, even to reach "that higher level of prosperity and culture which provided it be used with prudence, is not only no hindrance but is of singular help to virtue."[3]

Let no Christian excuse his indifference to the enforced poverty of his fellows with the lazy and selfish reflection that all their troubles will be solved in the life beyond the grave. For this attitude there is no authorization in the teaching of Christianity nor in the practice of its Divine Founder, Who "went about doing good," Who miraculously fed the multi-tude in the desert because He "had compassion on them" and Who promised everlasting blessedness to those who "fed the hungry, gave drink to the thirsty and clothed the naked."

[3] *Quadragesimo Anno*, p. 25, N.C.W.C. edition.

The address given by Mr. Justice Felix Frankfurter at my anniversary banquet included this sentence: "Perhaps it will be permitted one outside his faith to suggest that the practical pursuit of Monsignor Ryan's convictions has been strengthened by the thought that in promoting his conception of social justice, he was faithfully carrying out the commission his Church gave him to preach." My good friend of more than a quarter of a century was right. In fact, he could have made his statement stronger; for my efforts on behalf of social justice have not only been "strengthened" but fundamentally motivated by the command to preach and expound the Gospel of Christ. In striving to fulfill this commission, to comply with this command, I have, indeed, concentrated upon that part of the Gospel which applies to social and economic relations. My natural inclination thus to specialize was strongly reinforced by my realization that the number of priests who were laboring in this portion of the Lord's Vineyard was pitiably small. For whatever I have accomplished in this field, I humbly thank Almighty God, Who inspired me with the desire to preach His social gospel and Who has sustained and guided me through all the years of my life.

INDEX

Agricultural Adjustment Act, 255, 256, 257; declared unconstitutional, 250, 251

Alfange, Dean, on success of Court reorganization, 256, 257

Allied Powers, 207

Altgeld, Governor, 31–32, 54–56

America, articles in, 197, 200–202, 204

America and the Balance Sheet of Europe, 207, 208, 209

American Catholics, and nationalism, 211; and social movements, 124 (footnote)

American Civil Liberties Union, the, 173–176; author's resignation from, 175–176

American Ecclesiastical Review, the, 152; article on prohibition laws, 179; article on *Quadragesimo Anno*, 242

Anti-alien Bills, 172

Anti-injunction law, Norris-Walsh-La Guardia Act, 228

Anti-saloon League, 232

Anti-Semitism, 275, 276

Ashley, Sir William, 64

Associated Charities of St. Paul, vice-president of, 94

Atheistic Communism, encyclical on, 82

Atlantic Monthly, the, 231

Baker, Hon. Newton D., 225

Baldwin, Roger N., 175

Barry, Canon William Francis, 33–38; influence upon author, 37, 38; on destitution and Christianity, 35–37; on London slums, 34, 35; opinion of *A Living Wage*, 38; social aims of, 35

Benedict XV, Pope, peace proposals of, 137, 139, 211

Benedictions: at dedication of Dept. of Labor Building, 270–271; at President Roosevelt's second inauguration, 271

Better Economic Order, A, 269

Birth Control, 3, 4, 80

Birth Rate, declining, author's discussion of, 265–268

Bishop's Program of Social Reconstruction, 228, 285

Black, Mr. Justice Hugo L., 277; author's defense of, 274–275

"Black and Tans," 191, 194, 195, 196

Blaine-Cleveland, presidential campaign, 9, 11

Boland, Harry, 193, 194

Bolger, Rev. William A., C.S.C., 287

Borah, Hon. William E., 210

Bouquillon, Rev. Dr. Thomas J., 63

Boycotts, author on, 111

Brandeis, Mr. Justice Louis D., 220, 221, 222; author's appreciation of, 271–274

Bridges, Harry, 172, 173

Brookings Institution, vols. of: on income and economic progress, 238, 240; on reparations and war debts, 207

Bryan, William Jennings, 56, 57

Buell, C. F., 127

Burlingham, C. C., 271

Burton, Hon. Theodore, debate with, 209, 210

Caesar's Column, 16

Canadian Conference of Social Work, address before, 103

Capitalism, characteristics of, 245

Capper-Johnson Bill, author's opposition to, 212

Cardozo, Mr. Justice Benjamin N., 222

Catholic Association for International Peace, 155; objects, purposes and publications of, 213, 214

Catholic Charities Review, 159–161; editor of, 96; editorials; on disfranchising socialists, 165, 166; on "International Obligations of Charity," 141; on national prohibition, 181, 182

Catholic Conference on Industrial Problems, 155, 156, 237

Catholic Encyclopedia, 90, 110

Catholic losses, numbers, 129, 130

Catholic University of America, 62–77; author's retirement from, 284; author's